Applied Informetrics for Information Retrieval Research

Recent Titles in
New Directions in Information Management

Automating Literacy: A Challenge for Libraries
Linda Main and Char Whitaker

Cataloging: The Professional Development Cycle
Sheila S. Itner and Janet Swan Hill, editors

Information and Information Managment
Michael Buckland

Vocabulary Control and Search Strategies in Online Searching
Alice Yanosko Chamis

Planning in the University Library
Stanton F. Biddle

The Information World of Retired Women
Elfreda A Chatman

Insider s Guide to Library Automation: Essays of Practical Experience
John W. Head and Gerard B. McCabe, editors

Hypertext and the Technology of Conversation: Orderly Situational Choice
Susan H. Gray

Academic Libraries: The Dimensions of Their Effectiveness
Joseph A McDonald and Lynda Basney Micikas

Recruiting, Educating, and Training Librarians for Collection Development
Peggy Johnson and Sheila S. Itner, editors

Information Seeking and Subject Representation: An Activity-Theoretical Approach to Information Science
Birger Hiøland

Cllosing an Era: Historical Perspectives on Modern Archives and Records Management
Richard J. Cox

Applied Informetrics for Information Retrieval Research

Dietmar Wolfram
University of Wisconsin-Milwaukee

New Directions in Information Management,
Number 36

LIBRARIES UNLIMITED
A Member of the Greenwood Publishing Group
Westport, Connecticut London

British Library Cataloguing in Publication Data is available.

ISBN: 0-313-31970-7
ISSN: 0887 3844

First published in 2003

Libraries Unlimited, Inc., 88 Post Road West, Westport, CT 06881
A Member of the Greenwood Publishing Group, Inc.
www.lu.com

Printed in the United States of America

The paper used in this book complies with the
Permanent Paper Standard issued by the National |
Information Standards Organization (Z39.48-1984).

10 9 8 7 6 5 4 3 2 1

For Emmi

Contents

List of Illustrations

Table

Figures

Preface

Like many monographs, the content of this work grew out of years of discovery, accumulation, and reflection. As an undergraduate student in the history of science I first encountered quantitative studies of recorded discourse, the study of which I didn't even know had a name at the time. In classic works by Derek de Solla Price, I was introduced to ideas of scientific growth as measured by the production of research literature over time. The ability to better understand the nature of scientific culture through the quantitative study of its products of intellectual discourse was a novel, fascinating idea. At about the same time, having also been a student in computer science, I had been introduced to computer modeling and simulation. I found the idea that one could summarize many physical processes through mathematical functions to be equally fascinating. With an understanding of the observed process, one could develop computer simulations to study outcomes under different circumstances. At the time I made no connection between these two seemingly disparate areas of study, one firmly based in the social sciences and the other in the applied sciences.

It was as a graduate student in library and information science that common threads between these two distinct areas of study began to emerge for me. After having been introduced to concepts of bibliometrics ("informetrics" was just starting to gain recognition at the time), I saw how observed regularities in recorded discourse could serve as more than just intellectual grist for the class assignment mill, and actually had utility. In doctoral courses on bibliometrics and modeling of information systems taught by the late Jean Tague-Sutcliffe at the University of Western Ontario, ideas I had first encountered in the history of science were now being presented in the context of information system contents and their use. I gained a deeper appreciation for the inherent regularities in information production and use, not only for their functional forms but also for how these regularities could be applied. These encounters with informetrics and information retrieval (IR) system studies helped to shape my initial research interests in empirical regularities in information retrieval system content and use, which I have continued to explore from different perspectives.

Research into an earlier review paper on the topics covered in this work (Wolfram, 2000a) convinced me there was a sufficient foundation of research literature and growing research interest to merit monographic treatment. Currently there is no monographic source that focuses on the intersection of IR and informetrics, although a number of researchers such as

Bookstein (1974) and Egghe and Rousseau (1990) have long recognized connections between informetrics and IR theory. Many books on information retrieval have been written over the past four decades, but the majority of these works have focused on the mechanics of the information storage and retrieval process, the models used to implement IR systems, or more recently, user-centered approaches to IR research. Within these works there has been some recognition of the importance of observed regularities in how IR system contents are stored or used, but the treatment of these topics has been at best cursory. With the growing popularity of IR systems to store and access documentary content in many settings, there continues to be strong interest in the efficient and effective design of IR systems as well as their evaluation. The topics covered in this book provide often-overlooked perspectives on meeting these goals.

Another motivation for developing this work stems from my observation that researchers may be aware of one these areas of investigation but are unaware of their relationship to each other. As IR becomes an area of research interest by investigators outside of its traditional home of computer and information science, recognition of the connections between IR and informetrics can be lost. Researchers who have been introduced to IR outside of its traditional context are largely unaware of the existence of informetrics research, other than perhaps Zipf's law, as an area that can contribute valuable tools and methods for IR study. As an example, in the past several years studies involving Internet search engines have appeared in the research and professional literature from investigators in a range of disciplines. Observations of inverse power laws applying to World Wide Web content and use are viewed as novel findings. However, these regularities have long been known by informetricians to apply to print-based and electronic literatures. Yet these research efforts remain largely uncited by investigators outside of the information sciences. The lower profile of informetrics in contrast to IR makes it less likely that investigators outside of information science (and sometimes even within information science) are aware of the contributions of informetrics research.

From another perspective, this work may also introduce novel areas of investigation to researchers in informetrics who presently rely on IR systems for the access they provide to bibliographic citations as the data sources for study but may not appreciate that the IR systems themselves can also serve as sources of investigation. It is hoped that this work will bridge a gap by making contributions in both areas more readily apparent. In a time when the wealth of scholarly research produced makes it impossible for investigators to be aware of all potentially relevant contributions in academically distant or even allied disciplines, despite today's sophisticated IR systems indexing millions of bibliographic resources, the need for works that bridge disciplinary distances is as important as ever.

Finally, I believe the time is right for a book on this topic. The growth in the number of researchers and the maturation of informetrics and IR research have resulted in a sufficient body of research in each area so that a monographic treatment of such a specialized area is warranted. Over the past several decades there has been sporadic treatment of the intersection of these two topics in the computer and information science literature. Research findings combining these two areas are currently scattered across many journals or are mentioned in passing within monographic sources. The amount of literature that has been produced has grown to the point where a consolidation of the findings is needed. This work sets out to synthesize what has been studied over the years, in addition to presenting techniques for informetric study of IR systems.

It is unfortunate that informetrics/bibliometrics is often viewed by students in library and information science as a dry, theoretical subject area. For master's degree students preparing for careers in the information professions, this topic is usually covered briefly in a foundations or information science course. The ideas introduced are then quickly forgotten after completion of the course, to make way for more practical knowledge. Years later, students' only recollection of the topic is that it had something to do with counting citations.

Very few courses focusing on informetrics are currently offered in information science programs in North America. Most are geared toward advanced graduate students, with usually only a few takers. Part of the problem may be the perception that degrees in mathematics and statistics are needed to understand the concepts or to contribute to them. Although some understanding of mathematical and statistical concepts is certainly needed, a look at the attendees of conferences with a focus on informetrics and allied areas reveals that researchers represent a range of backgrounds from the social and physical sciences to the humanities. Some exposure to quantitative methods is most certainly needed, and most of the best theorists in the field possess advanced degrees in these areas, but other disciplinary perspectives are also valued and contribute to the diverse nature of the field.

It is my hope that this work will provide a useful perspective on observed regularities associated with IR system content and interaction that will be informative for both IR system designers or evaluators and researchers involved in informetrics.

Acknowledgments

I am indebted to a number of individuals for the feedback they have provided over the course of the development of this work and for discussions held over the years. Their comments and perspectives have provided valuable input. I would like to thank my colleague Jin Zhang for many stimulating discussions on information retrieval and for providing the point of view of an IR system developer. I would also like to thank Isola Ajiferuke for his insights into quantitative methodologies and informetrics from the vantage point of a statistician. Thanks also go to Michael J. Nelson who, along with Jean Tague-Sutcliffe, has defined research in the informetric modeling of information retrieval systems. I would also like to acknowledge Don Kraft, whose multidisciplinary perspectives encompassing computer science, operations research, and informetrics provided insightful comments made throughout this work. Terrence Brooks provided valuable comments on an earlier draft of this work.

Informetrics and IR research cannot take place without the availability of data sets for study. I would like to acknowledge Excite@home for making available query logs of Excite search sessions over the past several years. These data sets have been invaluable in collaborative and personal projects on search engine query studies. The data have provided a rare snapshot of typical user search behaviors in a time when end-user searching is rapidly evolving. I must also thank Sally Drew of the Wisconsin Department of Public Instruction Reference and Loan Library for making available database usage logs for Wisconsin's BadgerLink service. The BadgerLink data sets provide a different perspective on Web-based searching of more traditional bibliographic databases of print-based resources and offer contrasting experiences to the systems that index publicly available content on the Web. I would also like to thank the National Technical Information Service (NTIS) for the use of data from the NTIS database that were used in several earlier research projects into database content regularities, some of which are reported here.

Finally, I wish to express my appreciation to my family for their ongoing support of my academic ventures.

1

Introduction

The book [of nature] is written in mathematical language and its characters are triangles, circles, and other geometric figures.

—Galileo Galilei, 1623

1.1 Overview

From the earliest days of codified thought, there has been a need to organize information for timely access. Over the centuries many technological innovations have facilitated the long-term storage of information, but fundamental innovations in the way we access information have been rare. During this time the mechanisms developed for effective access have been primarily intellectual as opposed to technological. This is still largely the case, although timely access to information resources has greatly improved. The study of issues surrounding information representation, storage, and retrieval has laid the foundations for the emergence of the field of information science. Information science can be summarized as the study of the production, representation, organization, storage, retrieval, dissemination, and use of information (Borko, 1968). As a discipline, it has been recognized since the 1950s, having coalesced from several allied fields, including documentation, library science, and computer science.

This book deals with the intersection of two key subareas within the discipline of information science: informetrics and information retrieval. Subspecialties within information science focus on one or more of the processes enacted upon containers of information (e.g., documents such as journal articles, monographs, or bibliographic citations) and their use. Each of these subareas has a notable history of its own, with antecedents dating back to before the recognized emergence of information science itself.

Information retrieval (IR) focuses on the study of processes involved in the storage of, access to, and representation of information containers, along with the systems that implement IR concepts. More recently IR investigations have expanded to include user perspectives, examining user information needs, information seeking behaviors, and user interactions with IR systems. Information retrieval has attracted a growing number of investigators as efficient storage and effective access to increasing amounts of information must be managed in many types of environments. The study of information retrieval is not tied to a single technology. In fact, most IR concepts are independent of the technologies used to implement IR systems. However, when one thinks of modern information retrieval, the implementations of IR systems are invariably computer-based. The widespread use of IR systems today, whether as Internet search engines for public or organizational document-based information resources, text search systems in application software help routines or electronic encyclopedias, or bibliographic citation databases, has made information retrieval functionality available to broader audiences. In fact, many users may not be aware that they are engaged in information retrieval interactions when using these systems. Information retrieval systems have simply become another tool used in many people's daily lives.

In a nutshell, informetrics is the study of quantifiable regularities in recorded discourse. Older related terms, such as *bibliometrics* and *scientometrics,* are also still used to describe similar areas of investigation. Informetricians, or those who study informetrics, are interested in discovering and understanding patterns in how information is produced and used. As a subdiscipline within information science, informetrics has had a lower profile than IR, although the two areas share important conceptual foundations. Because the outcomes of informetric studies often do not directly result in the development of a tangible product, familiarity with informetrics and participation in its research areas remains largely limited to specialists with an interest in quantitative aspects of recorded discourse; however, this is changing. Studies examining the most popular search topics on Internet search services, which have become a topic of popular interest, or the usage patterns of books within libraries, of interest to library managers, are examples of research topics within the scope of informetrics. As society becomes more accustomed to reports involving statistics of social import, recognition of informetric studies also increases. Just as has IR, informetrics has benefited from developments in computer technology. Informetric investigations are still undertaken without the use of computers, but with many of today's information resources now available in electronic form, access to electronic data on information content and use is more convenient. At the heart of informetrics research is an interest in understanding the operations of information systems, whether these systems are scholarly communication networks through which scholars share ideas, libraries through which books and magazines are circulated, or the IR systems that provide access to documentary sources.

Computer-based IR systems make it possible to collect large quantities of system content data related to searchable words within the system, document characteristics, and content growth patterns over time. It is also possible to automatically analyze that content. With greater interest in system usage, many IR systems now monitor resource utilization and log user interactions in the form of query logs, which may serve as raw data for analysis. All of these sources present valuable data for informetric analysis. Researchers in IR and informetrics have known for decades that regularities exist in the way information is stored within IR systems and in how these system contents are used. However, to date informetrics and information retrieval have been largely treated as separate areas of investigation, with occasional research forays into specific informetric aspects of IR. With an understanding of the patterns that exist within IR systems, knowledge of these regularities in IR system content and their use can be quite useful in the physical design of IR systems and in modeling overall searcher behavior.

1.2 Intended Audience

This work has been developed with several audiences in mind. In recent years I have noticed growing interest in empirical regularities of IR system content and use, particularly among researchers in computer science and information science. This book may be used as a text in an advanced undergraduate or graduate course in applied information retrieval or informetrics, whether from the perspectives of computer science or information science. It could also serve as a reference for researchers and practitioners investigating either area.

Although Chapters 2 and 3 introduce basic concepts fundamental to information retrieval and informetrics, respectively, readers would benefit most by having some familiarity with at least one of these areas. The reader who is unfamiliar with both areas should seek additional in-depth sources on IR and informetrics. Each of these topics alone can easily fill a monograph.

The quantitative aspects of this work require familiarity with basic probability theory and inferential statistics, but no more than one would encounter in social science statistical methods classes at the advanced undergraduate or graduate level. A substantial background in higher mathematics is not assumed. Familiarity with computer programming is desirable to implement some of the ideas presented, but it is not a requirement. The emphasis of this work is on applications as opposed to theory development. However, sources providing theoretical underpinnings are included for consultation by readers interested in detailed coverage of theoretical foundations.

1.3 Distinctions from Related Areas

The study of metrics of human processes is not unique to informetrics. Many social sciences have quantitative subspecialties. Of note are econometrics within the field of economics, which focuses on the development of models to describe economic processes, and sociometrics within sociology, which models societal processes. Commonalities between the observed regularities developed for different social phenomena are apparent. For example, several classic "laws" found in informetrics bear a striking resemblance to Pareto's law of the distribution of wealth within a community (Pareto, 1897) (see Chapter 3, Section 3.2). Informetrics does not hesitate to adopt mathematical models found to hold true in other social contexts. What distinguishes informetrics from other quantitative studies of social processes is its focus on the creation, storage, dissemination, and use of the products of recorded human discourse, regardless of the medium in which the products are stored. As we continue to evolve into an information and knowledge-based society in which national economies are driven by the production and use of information, interest in the units of study in informetrics will undoubtedly increase in other social science disciplines.

At first glance, informetric studies of electronic resources may appear similar to the research area known as data mining, which attempts to automatically detect meaningful patterns within databases (Berson, Smith, & Thearling, 2000; Mena, 1999). It is most frequently used for business applications, where pattern detection methods may be used to identify trends or characteristics inherent within the data sets from which predictive models may be developed. Data mining relies on an arsenal of techniques to analyze database content, including database querying, statistical analysis, clustering methods, neural networks, deviation detection, and other forms of network and link analysis (Yoon, 2000). It goes beyond more traditional online analytical processing (OLAP) tools for multidimensional data analysis that rely on user-generated queries. Data mining has applications for customer identification and service as well as marketing and can be applied to a data warehouse containing large quantities of retrospective and current data from which patterns may be revealed. There are some common interests between data mining and informetrics, but they have arisen from different traditions, with different emphases. Both attempt to discover patterns, but in the case of informetrics these patterns are not usually automatically extracted.

In recent years researchers interested in data mining have expanded their areas of exploration to encompass areas that overlap directly with informetrics. This is most evident in the emerging area of text mining (Trybula, 1999). Data mining is usually applied to numeric content, whereas text mining attempts to detect patterns based on unstructured textual content. Patterns extracted from textual corpora may reveal knowledge connections that were not obvious due to the large quantities of textual documents. The complementary characteristics of data mining and informetrics have recently begun to be explored. For example, Kostoff, del Río, Humenik, Garcia, and Ramírez (2001) provide a rare synthesis of both areas of study by examining how citation analysis techniques, commonly used in informetric analysis, may be combined with text mining techniques to analyze the impact of one area of research upon another.

1.4 Summary of Chapter Contents

This introductory chapter provides an overview of topics to come. Because this work integrates aspects of much larger subdisciplines within information science, chapters devoted to fundamental concepts in information retrieval and informetrics as separate entities are included. After introducing the reader to these foundations, subsequent chapters deal with informetrics as it relates to IR systems, culminating with a treatment on applications.

Chapter 2, "Information Retrieval," focuses on key concepts related to information retrieval and the systems that implement information storage and retrieval mechanisms. Information retrieval itself is quite broad, with many monographs already having been devoted to various aspects of the field. It is impossible to provide any depth on any one topic within the confines of a single chapter. The chapter is organized to familiarize readers with the key terminology and concepts of IR, which are central to the content of subsequent chapters. Readers should realize from the chapter that IR does not just involve system processes but also, and more important, user processes. Although traditionally studied by a small group of computer scientists and researchers in library and information science, IR research has grown tremendously in the past decade with the wider availability of vendor bibliographic and full-text databases, multilingual and multimedia resources, and particularly publicly available search tools now accessible via the Internet.

Chapter 3, "Informetrics," introduces the reader to this subdiscipline. Readers will gain an appreciation for the wealth of informetric studies, which extend much farther back in time than the name of the field itself. Although much of informetric study has concerned itself with empirical regularities in print-based documentary sources, the concepts associated with information production processes are medium-independent and translate readily to machine-readable environments, which is the focus of the present work. It should also be noted that the newer electronic environments permit the study of processes that may not exist or are much more difficult to study in the print-based environment.

With an understanding of IR and informetric concepts in place, the remaining chapters focus on informetric characteristics of IR systems and their use and resulting applications. In Chapter 4, "Data Collection and Model Development Techniques," methods for data collection and analysis are introduced. As with any empirical social study, the quality of data collected will affect the ability to model system and user behaviors. Data can be extracted from a range of systems with different levels of detail for both user and system-based data. Due to the wealth of data now available, it may be more practical to sample from large data sets. The selection of appropriate models to characterize the distributions studied, which are vital to the accurate representation of observed phenomena, is presented. A number of potential theoretical distributions, with different applications in modeling observed data characteristics, are possible. Depending on the observed distribution being modeled, different techniques may be used to fit observed data to theoretical distributions. Methods such as moment estimators, linear and nonlinear least squares, minimum chi-square, and maximum likelihood estimation have their own advantages and disadvantages. Once data sets have been modeled, they may be applied for different purposes.

Informetric aspects of IR systems may be conveniently divided into two broad categories: system-based characteristics that arise from the documentary content of IR systems and how they are indexed, and usage-based characteristics that arise from how users interact with system content and the system interfaces that provide access to the content. Chapter 5, "Informetrics and IR System Content," introduces the range of system content attributes for which empirical regularities have been or can be observed. Characteristics of these regularities, research findings, and candidate distributions for modeling observed behavior are discussed. Examples of system content regularities include the frequency distribution of terms indexed within the system, the level of term assignment (indexing exhaustivity) within documents, the co-occurrence of terms within documents, document connections based on hypertext linkages or citations suggesting interdocument relationships, document content characteristics, database and index growth, and domain-level analysis in distributed environments.

Chapter 6, "Informetrics and IR System Use," introduces empirical regularities in how different types of IR systems are used. Some of the same attributes studied in system content-based studies have analogs on the user side; others are unique to system usage. Frequency of usage of system content terms provides a sense of search vocabulary usage. Similarly, query term frequency distributions provide comparable insights but do not have to limit themselves to system-indexed terms. The distribution of terms used per query provides an indication of user effort in query construction and varies greatly with user audience and the type of IR system used. Query term co-occurrence reveals how users relate search terms. Unlike system content studies, usage studies may also be extended to include query frequency distributions across users to determine frequent topic searches. Regularities in user browsing and searching will help system developers better understand how systems are being used, both correctly and incorrectly. Finally, patterns in electronic resources usage, whether World Wide Web documents or bibliographic records, reveal general user search interests.

Applications of informetrics for system modeling, design, and use are presented in Chapter 7, "Applications." Potential applications have been demonstrated in a range of studies, but many more await investigation. Applications include the modeling and simulation of IR systems to better understand system processes and provide the researcher with the ability to test hypothetical system conditions without having to resort to subjecting an operational system to these tests. Simulations may be used to aid in the study of file design and for space planning purposes when combined with informetric models of system content. Observed regularities in system content and usage can inform system design and evaluation research. System content characteristics can provide insights into interface design and automatic indexing policies, while usage regularities may inform system performance and usage evaluation. From a marketing perspective, system usage patterns and subject searching commonalities can provide valuable insights into the targeting of products and services.

Finally, Chapter 8, "Future Directions," looks at emerging and future areas of research in informetric applications for IR research. Current high-profile areas of research in IR may benefit from informetric study, such as information visualization, where normally intangible relationships among system contents are made visible to users. As we move toward multimedia-based IR systems that incorporate graphic and audio content and informetric analysis of nontextual segments of system content, a better understanding of the regularities inherent in these components provides similar application opportunities. Finally, with the increased availability of user-based data incorporating larger audiences, areas for further study are suggested.

1.5 Cautionary Note

Quantification and measurement are fundamental to science. As the quote from Galileo at the beginning of this chapter (along with many similar often-quoted words from the history of science such as those of Lord Kelvin) suggests, there has been a longstanding belief in science that nature can be understood through mathematics and quantification. However, it must be kept in mind that the ability to express observed regularities quantitatively alone cannot always explain why the observed patterns exist. Numeric representation can nevertheless provide a basis for comparison and evidence for the building of theory. Although many of the quantifiable ideas presented in this work relate to IR systems, a physical and seemingly nonhuman-related entity, these characteristics still ultimately are the products of social phenomena, whether related to the use of human language, the production of information in documentary form, or the use of these documents. Ultimately, any theory development of IR system design and usage must recognize the influence of the individual in shaping an understanding of social phenomena in theory development and, unlike the physical sciences, these theories must take into account variability inherent in social processes, aptly described by Bookstein (1997) as "the ubiquity of uncertainty." Although the focus of the present work is on quantitative aspects of information retrieval system contents and their use, the reader should keep in mind that the social influences that underlie the observed regularities and their characteristics still ultimately dictate the patterns observed.

2

Information Retrieval

There is no practical obstacle whatever now to the creation of an efficient index to all human knowledge, ideas and achievements, to the creation, that is, of a complete planetary memory for all mankind. And not simply an index; the direct reproduction of the thing itself can be summoned to any properly prepared spot.

—H. G. Wells, 1937

2.1 Introduction

In this chapter fundamental concepts related to information retrieval are introduced. To date, many monographs have been written on the design, development, and evaluation of IR systems. The breadth of IR does not permit a detailed treatment of information retrieval research within the confines of a single book chapter. Instead, the intent of this chapter is to present a primer on IR concepts important to the main focus of this work. The content will be useful for readers who are unfamiliar with IR or may serve as a review for those who already have some knowledge of information retrieval. The reader is encouraged to consult sources discussed throughout this chapter for a more detailed treatment of the topics outlined.

2.1.1 Information Retrieval Basics

What is information retrieval? When defining IR, one must first deal with the nebulous concept of information. Information can mean different things in different environments, from philosophy to telecommunications. A classic information theoretic conception of information often used in signal processing defines it as a reduction of uncertainty (Shannon & Weaver,

1959). The concept of information is frequently, and perhaps mistakenly, used interchangeably with related terms such as *data* and *knowledge*. A datum on its own, such as a numeric value, does not inform because it lacks context. Knowledge, on the other hand, can be considered to be the purposeful application of information. Buckland (1991) identified information by its context of use as a process, a thing, or knowledge. Most relevant to this work is Buckland's definition of information-as-thing, represented by something tangible such as a document or a text that may impart information.

Definitions of information retrieval abound. Since Mooers' first use of the term (Mooers, 1951), authors have taken different views of the central issues related to IR and the systems used to implement IR principles. It should be noted that information retrieval deals with the process of how information is represented, stored, accessed, and presented. Information retrieval systems represent implementations of these processes. As can any form of information system, an IR system may exist independent of the technology that is used to implement it. However, it is the technology implementation that we see as the tangible representation of IR. Gerard Salton (1989), a pioneer of information retrieval research, states that IR systems "process files of records and requests for information, and identify and retrieve from the files certain records in response to the information requests" (p. 229). More recently, Kowalski (1997) has defined an IR system as "a system that is capable of storage, retrieval, and maintenance of information" (p. 2). Grossman and Frieder (1998) point out that IR is a selective process "devoted to finding 'relevant' documents, not just finding simple matches to patterns" (p. 1). Finally, Meadow, Boyce, and Kraft (2000, p. 2) emphasize IR as a communication process. Although the term *information retrieval* makes no reference to information storage and representation, these ideas are implicit in any comprehensive definition of IR. Also implicit in today's IR systems is the idea of interaction. Users are able to interact with IR systems to modify search parameters and to provide feedback on the IR process. To date, most IR systems have focused on the storage, representation, and retrieval of text-based content because of the ease with which textual symbols may be represented and manipulated within computers. But in recent years IR systems for other media formats have also emerged (see Section 2.5.2).

Information retrieval systems need not be computer-based, but as with many information processing tasks, particularly for large quantities of information, computers are extremely useful in speeding up the process. The earliest IR systems existed prior to the advent of modern electronic computers. Library card catalogs, which have existed for well over 100 years, represent one of the earliest forms of manual IR system. Each card encapsulates the essential content needed to identify a book or other form of published work. During the mid-twentieth century, as electronic digital computers were first being developed, other manual systems that relied on punched or notched cards to represent documents were developed. These pioneering systems were among the earliest to use Boolean logic for the retrieval of information (Meadow, Boyce, & Kraft, 2000). Today, IR systems have evolved and taken on many forms. Applications of IR research over the past half-century have resulted in new ways to store, represent, and retrieve information.

Many approaches have been developed for the design of IR systems. However, several concepts are integral to all IR systems. For example, each IR system provides access to a document set. A *document* represents an object that is retrieved by an IR system. It may consist of the complete content of the information requested, in which case it is considered a *full-text document*, for example a Web page or journal article. Within bibliographic retrieval systems, often the full text of the document is not available, so a summary, called a *document surrogate,* which encapsulates identifying content such as bibliographic citation information and abstracts to help identify the document, is stored instead. The word "document" is used throughout this book, although the item retrieved may be a document surrogate. Documents may range in length from short passages of text to complete monographic works, or may consist of other media formats such as images, videos, or sound clips.

Documents accessible by an IR system are retrieved as the result of processed user queries. A *query* is the representation of the user information need entered into the IR system. A query consists of one or more terms and possible operators that define the scope of the documents to be retrieved. A *term* is an unbroken string of alphanumeric characters in text-based IR systems that serve as the basic unit for searching. Terms can be associated with indexes for documents or queries. During query processing, query terms are matched to index terms, also called *keywords*, which define the searchable terms within the database. Queries can take many forms. Boolean queries combine terms with operators that define the context of the terms. Natural language queries rely on linguistic structure and positioning of words to identify context. Some systems permit strings of terms to be entered, with the proximity of terms to one another determining their relationships. With natural language queries, users need not be familiar with artificial query languages that define valid query operations. Information retrieval systems may implement free text searching or may rely on a controlled vocabulary. A *free text* search does not limit the searchable terms available to a set of predefined terms. A *controlled vocabulary*, usually implemented as document subject headings or *descriptors,* limits searches to a set of recognized terms that have been indexed. Controlled vocabularies rely on developed thesauri or subject heading lists (e.g., ERIC descriptors used in education databases, or Medical Subject Headings (MeSH) used in medical databases) to ensure standardized usage of vocabularies.

2.1.2 Examples of IR Systems

Information retrieval systems may be classified by their content or by the models used to represent and extract content. Information retrieval system models are dealt with in Section 2.2. Traditionally, IR systems have been used to store document surrogates. Historically, text-based surrogates have been the primary document representation. This was due to the high cost associated with storing information electronically and the low capacities of storage technologies. In more recent years, with dramatic increases in storage capacities and reductions in costs, there has been a shift toward complete document representation and storage, including nontextual components such as graphics.

Early applications of IR systems that continue to be important include bibliographic database systems and online public access catalogs (OPACs). Library OPACs provide access to document surrogates of indexed holdings within the library. Record contents will often contain additional document descriptions used in cataloging items that are not usually found in other bibliographic databases. Many bibliographic databases, accessible online or in CD-ROM format, are made available through database vendors such as DIALOG and OVID and may provide access to document surrogates or, increasingly, full-text content of documents.

Information retrieval functionality has recently been incorporated into other applications. For example, electronic encyclopedias available in CD-ROM format will permit searching of keywords. Many online help systems associated with software applications will also permit simple searches to be conducted on help content. Undoubtedly the main reason for the growth of IR technology since the early 1990s has been the growth of the Internet. Resource discovery tools such as search engines have become an essential fixture of the Internet. Search engines are, in fact, IR systems used to index the distributed contents of the Web and other parts of the Internet, or they may be used to index local content only. These search services provide access to huge quantities of full-text documents in a user-friendly search environment. At present search features of these systems tend to be more limited than more established bibliographic database services and cater to broader audiences with different information needs and levels of search expertise. This has introduced additional challenges for the design of user-friendly IR systems (see Section 2.3).

Unless one is a system developer, one's interaction with an IR system will be limited to searching. Therefore for most users IR systems are treated as "read-only" systems, where users simply search for content provided by a vendor or organization. In the past, custom-built systems were developed in-house, or expensive IR system software was purchased for the development of organization-specific applications. A range of software is now available for different computer platforms to allow organizations to create their own databases with IR system search functionality. Inmagic's DBTextWorks for the microcomputer environment permits the creation of custom-designed textbases with flexible indexing and search features. InQuery, developed at the Center for Intelligent Information Research at the University of Massachusetts at Amherst, permits system-savvy developers to select indexing and search features. Many other examples too numerous to mention are now available. The growth of organizational intranets and digital libraries has made the use of search engine software a necessity for accessing documents internal to these systems.

2.1.3 The General Process of Information Retrieval

The process of information retrieval involves a dialogue between the user and the IR system. Terminology related to computerized IR has been intentionally kept to a minimum in this section so that IR concepts may be presented at a general level. Further details of computerized IR are covered in Section 2.2. Key features of the information storage and retrieval process are summarized in Figure 2.1.

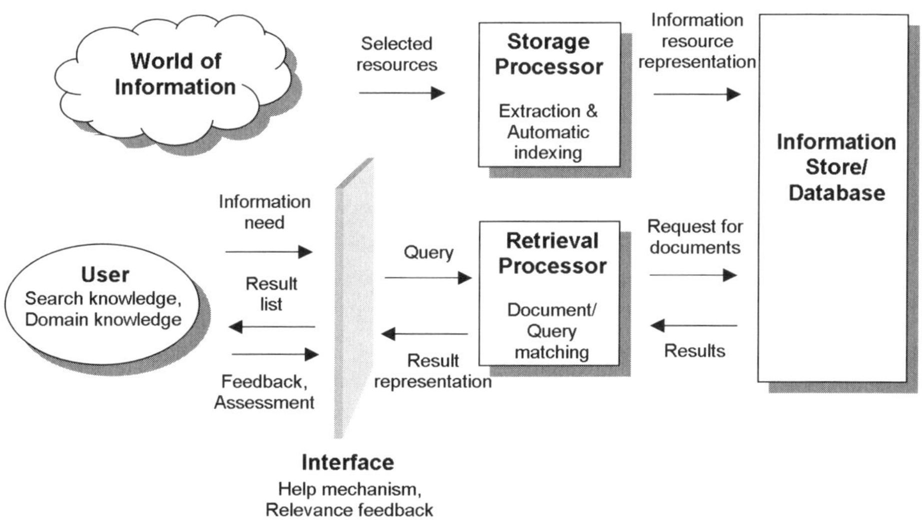

Figure 2.1. Representation of the IR Process

The use of an IR system is prompted by a user information need. The user recognizes that the database/information store to which the IR system provides access may contain resources to fill this need. Based on the user's understanding of the subject domain of the information need and search knowledge of the IR system to be used, the user formulates an initial query that is submitted to the IR system. The query represents the topicality of the information need. Interaction with the IR system is facilitated by a user interface. Prior to the wider use of computerized IR systems, this interface between the user and the system was often a person, a search intermediary with search expertise and understanding of the IR system and its contents. This role is still played by reference librarians, who help the user (library patron) to first define his or her information need, then assist the user in identifying and locating resources within the information store (library collection) that best address this need. Contents from the store that match the query parameters are retrieved for the user to examine. Based on the perusal of candidate items, the user may then further refine his or her information need and queries to the system; this is called *relevance feedback*. This process is repeated until the information need has been satisfactorily addressed, or the user concludes that the IR system cannot fill this need, at which point the search process ends.

The storage tasks performed within the IR system are invisible to the user but are equally important in ultimately determining how well the system is able to meet the user's information needs. Even today's most comprehensive IR systems are not able to include all the information resources in the world. Therefore the system uses a process of selective inclusion, whereby resources of greatest importance to the purpose of the IR system are included in the database/information store. The system must find a way to effectively represent the information content. In the past, due to storage space restrictions or incompatible formats between the resource and the system, only summarizations of an information resource encapsulating key attributes could be stored. Even with the ability to include complete resource content, the way the resource is represented in the system remains an issue.

2.1.4 Distinctions Between IR Systems and Database Management Systems

The question may arise how IR is different from other related computerized systems such as database management systems (DBMSs). On the surface, off-the-shelf IR software, particularly for microcomputers, may resemble a DBMS, but there are important physical and philosophical differences that distinguish these two environments. These distinctions arise from the different purposes for which each system was created and reflect the features that are most important in each environment.

Database management systems are primarily used for the storage, retrieval, and presentation of discrete data facts such as names, addresses, and identification numbers, and contain similar design and querying features. For commercially available software, a "layout" or "structure" defining data contents (fields) and data types is developed for both systems prior to the entry of records. In general, IR systems are more flexible in handling variable length entries because no field widths are required, as they are in most DBMSs. Repeating field entries, useful for fields such as multiple authors, or to allow subfields, are also easily handled. In addition, IR system content may be less structured, particularly in the full-text environment.

A key advantage of a DBMS is the way in which content is stored. Data models have been developed for DBMSs to represent complex relationships between different types of data and to reduce problems associated with data integrity and security. The relational DBMS model has been the most widely implemented since the 1970s, although the object-oriented model may be a successor in the future (see, e.g., McFadden, Hoffer, & Prescott, 1999). In most IR environments, record contents are stored as simple flat-file databases. These simplify record storage requirements but make data redundancy and integrity potentially problematic. Also, from a conceptual level DBMSs can distinguish a broader range of attributes, whereas IR systems focus on search operations based on terms, although field searching is often possible.

The greatest distinctions between the two environments can be found in the way search results are evaluated. Each permits querying, but at different levels of detail. Database management systems in almost all cases will only index down to the field level, making searches for words within fields awkward. Information retrieval systems will usually index down to the individual word level within fields. This requires additional search features such as proximity searching and relevance ranking, which are not found in Structured Query Language (SQL), the standardized language used for searching and other database functions in relational DBMSs. The concept of *relevance* is central to IR (Saracevic, 1975) but plays no role in DBMSs. When queries are constructed for DBMSs, all items retrieved are equally relevant to the query. In IR systems, items retrieved may or may not be relevant, although they meet the criteria for retrieval. Due to the imprecision of language, not all items retrieved will be equally relevant to the user's need.

The need for flexible data models found within DBMSs and powerful search features of IR systems has made the integration of the two environments desirable. It is possible to incorporate the structure and contents of an IR system within a relational DBMS with extensive programming (see, e.g., Grossman & Frieder, 1998, ch. 5). Whether one views an IR system as an implementation of a DBMS (Grossman & Frieder, 1998) or as a separate class of information system (Frakes & Baeza-Yates, 1992; Kowalski, 1997; Salton, 1989) may become moot in the future. Features once unique to one type of software increasingly become available in others. Commercial software that combines the strengths of both approaches has been available for a number of years. FileMaker Pro® for the microcomputer environment, for example, combines indexing and search features common in IR systems with the data organization strengths of a relational DBMS.

2.2 IR System Models

Just as for DBMSs, different approaches have been developed to designing IR systems. The mathematical models on which systems are based define how the retrieval process will take place and how system relevance judgments are made. Baeza-Yates & Ribeiro-Neto (1999) present a useful taxonomy of different IR models and discuss the relationships between each. Grossman & Frieder (1998) also present a detailed treatment of different models. Summaries of the most significant classical IR models in use and their more recent variants are presented here. Other models exist but are not covered in this work.

2.2.1 Boolean and Related Set Theoretic Models

Among the earliest and still most widely used, the Boolean model is the most familiar to IR system users. The classic Boolean model is based on set theory and Boolean logic, where users construct queries consisting of search terms and Boolean operations (e.g., AND, OR, NOT). Other search constructs such as proximity operations may be used to specify how close two terms must be to one another in a search field. Phrase searching takes this one step further, where terms must be beside each other in the specified order. To effectively use a Boolean-based system, the user must be familiar with Boolean operations and query construction. Simplified user interfaces not requiring a familiarity with Boolean logic may be implemented, but usually there is a trade-off in the sophistication of queries that are possible.

Exact matching is applied so that all document surrogates meeting the query criteria are retrieved. The retrieved list of items is then presented to the user for perusal. The simplicity of the Boolean model has made the implementation of systems based on it straightforward. However, the model has drawbacks that have become particularly apparent in recent years. A strict Boolean-based implementation assumes binary relevance judgments based on the existence or absence of search terms within a document. Either the document is relevant (i.e., it matches all of the query terms according to the Boolean operations used) or it is not (i.e., it does not match all of the terms according to the operations), and no distinction is made in the retrieved list as to which documents are most relevant. If ranking of retrieval sets is used, it is based on frequency counts of terms within documents, not semantic relationships that define the relatedness of documents and queries.

The extended Boolean model (Salton, Fox, & Wu, 1983) permits more flexible searching and relevance judgments to be made. Weights may be assigned to document terms to permit fine-grained relevance judgments. Weights range from 0 to 1, with 1 representing the highest level of relevance. Document relevance calculations against a query may be as simple as cumulating weights assigned to each of the document terms matching the query terms, although more sophisticated calculations are frequently used (see Salton, 1989, pp. 238-239; Baeza-Yates & Ribeiro-Neto, 1999, pp. 38-41). Only those documents with calculated relevance values exceeding a minimum threshold value are retrieved. Weights may also be assigned to query terms to specify the importance of each term for the information need. Fuzzy set theory (Zadeh, 1965) has also been applied to IR environments, where boundaries between Boolean sets are not sharply defined. Combinations of subsets of the query terms may also be processed in a quorum-level search (Cleverdon, 1984), resulting in a coarse-grained assessment of document relevance. Documents containing all query terms are most relevant, those with n-1 query terms are less relevant, those containing fewer terms are even less relevant, and so forth. This method is not widely available on IR systems but is employed in some Web search engines.

2.2.2 The Vector Space Model

The vector space model developed by Salton (1989) represents both queries and documents as vectors in an *n*-dimensional space. Relevance judgments are based on the calculated similarity between queries and documents. A term document matrix *V* for a document set consisting of *m* documents and *n* terms will take the form

$$V = \begin{bmatrix} t_{11} & t_{12} & \dots & t_{1n} \\ t_{21} & t_{22} & \dots & t_{2n} \\ \dots & \dots & \dots & \dots \\ t_{m1} & t_{m2} & \dots & t_{mn} \end{bmatrix} \qquad (2.1)$$

where t_{ij} represents the *i*th term in the *j*th document in a high-dimensional document space. If term *i* exists in document *j*, its value is set to 1 or an appropriate weighted value for its significance; otherwise it is set to 0. Because of the potentially large numbers of documents and the large numbers of terms, most document vector elements will be 0. Queries (*Q*) are also represented as vectors, where $Q = \{t_1, t_2, \dots t_n\}$. One or more similarity measures are then used to compare the query-document or document-document vectors based on angular differences between two vectors or distance differences in the document space. The cosine similarity measure has been used most frequently, but other measures including the inner product, Dice coefficient, and Jaccard coefficient are also used.

The spatial representation of documents and queries makes the vector space model amenable to visualization (see Section 2.5.1) for graphical representation of documents (Zhang & Korfhage, 1999). It is also well suited for cluster-based retrieval by grouping documents with high similarity. Documents within a cluster may be summarized using a cluster centroid, representing the average document vector within the cluster. Searching may then take place using cluster centroids instead of individual documents, thereby reducing some of the computational overhead. Retrieval of clusters is based on the assumption of the cluster hypothesis, which states that documents with high document-document similarity are related to one another (van Rijsbergen, 1979).

The vector space model has attracted considerable research attention over the past forty years. The use of term weighting for relevance ranking and approximate matching makes it more flexible than the Boolean model. However, it has been criticized for being computationally expensive. Each time a new document or term is added, the document space is changed, requiring the recalculation of centroids. Also, its assumption of term vector orthogonality, where terms are assumed to occur independently of one another, can be problematic (see the discussion of term dependence in Chapter 5, Section 5.4.2). Despite these drawbacks, the vector space model continues to be very popular with IR researchers as a model for representing sophisticated information retrieval processes (Baeza-Yates & Ribeiro-Neto, 1999). Features of the Boolean and vector space models have been combined in hybrid models, most notably the generalized vector space model and the extended Boolean model.

Unlike the classic vector space model, latent semantic indexing (Deerwester, Dumais, Furnas, Landauer, & Harshman, 1990) adopts the principle that the relevance of a document is not necessarily determined by the presence or absence of query terms within the document. Because different terms could be used to describe the same concept, retrieval is based on concept similarity instead of term similarity. A term-document matrix is initially adopted, as in the vector space model. Through a process of singular value decomposition, the dimensionality of the term-document space is reduced to form a concept-document space. Queries are processed as pseudo-documents within the concept space to determine query-document similarities within the new space.

2.2.3 Probabilistic Models

As do other models, the probabilistic model uses a similarity coefficient between a query and a document. Similarity is based on the assumption that a document will be relevant to the query. Using probability theory, the presence or absence of query terms within documents may be used to determine the likelihood that a document is relevant. Term weights may be aggregated so that documents exceeding a threshold value are retrieved. The effectiveness of the model ultimately relies on training data from which initial probability assessments are made.

The probabilistic model also has the advantage of providing a ranked list of documents, but it has been criticized for some of its initial assumptions. Most applications of the model assume that terms occur independently of one another (e.g., if the term "chocolate" exists in a document, it is just as likely to occur with the term "automobile" as with the term "cake") . The handling of Boolean operations may also be problematic. Further details of probabilistic approaches to IR are discussed in Fuhr (1992).

Other models based on probabilistic approaches have shown promise in IR. Systems that incorporate inference networks, such as the InQuery system (Broglio, Callan, & Croft, 1994), rely on evidential reasoning to estimate the likelihood that a document will be relevant to a query. Known relationships between documents and terms may be used to infer additional relationships.

2.2.4 Models Based on Browsing

Searching and browsing are considered two different strategies for information seeking (Marchionini, 1995). Information systems may adopt either or both to provide access to documents. Browsing models permit users to engage in more informal and opportunistic information seeking. A system based on a subject hierarchy, for example, allows users to navigate the hierarchy by selecting initially broad topics that lead to more specialized subject areas. At the lowest layers of the hierarchy are documents that may fill the user information need.

Many subject hierarchies are structured examples of hypertext systems. Unlike standard text structures that encourage sequential access to content, a hypertext permits nonlinear access to textual content, called *nodes*, through directed connections between the nodes, called *links*. The size and composition of a node may vary. It may be a short textual passage, it could be part of a larger monographic work, or it could also lead to a media file (sound, image, moving image), in which case the system would be classified as hypermedia. Links between nodes usually indicate some semantic relationship and are visually represented as clickable buttons, highlighted text or hotwords, or clickable areas within images, called image maps. Clicking on the link will take the user from the originating node to the destination node. The concept of hypertext extends back at least to the 1940s (Bush, 1945), with the formal model's mathematical roots lying in graph theory. The Web is often considered to be the world's largest hypertext system. Although it does make use of hypertext linkages, it would be more accurate to say that the Web is a conglomeration of separate hypertexts, with no standardized adoption of design principles for content and access.

The primary advantage of the hypertext model is its facilitation of browsing. Users with vague or ill-defined information needs and lack of familiarity with potential search terms with which to formulate queries may use a hypertext system to explore possible options. Once found, a node with relevant content may contain links to additional nodes also with relevant content. The exploration of nodes may then help users to better define their information needs or to modify their needs in a direction they may not have considered. Unlike the previously discussed models, in which searching is based on the exclusion of the majority of the document set, hypertext is based on inclusion, in which additional nodes (documents) are made available to the user as links without having to reformulate queries.

The purely hypertext environment has several drawbacks. In the course of navigation from one node to the next, users may become disoriented. System maps that show users where they have been in the system are helpful in reducing this side effect. As the number of nodes in a hypertext system increases, effective linking between documents may become difficult. In turn, too many links from a single node may overwhelm the user, while too few will not bring to light important relationships between nodes. Also, as the system becomes larger, perusal of large numbers of nodes for potentially relevant content becomes tedious; hence the need for keyword search tools for the Web. Although some systems permit users to develop their own links within a system, links are mostly established by developers or automated routines. As hypertext features become more integrated into large IR systems, automatic generation of hypertext linkages continues to be an important area of research.

2.3 IR System Storage and Retrieval Operations

Thus far the topics covered have examined IR at a high, descriptive level without delving into the details of the actual retrieval process. The physical process of search and retrieval can present a significant computational burden depending on the IR model implemented. As a result, efficient storage and retrieval of documents and the associated mechanisms continue to generate research interest. Different models will use different techniques for the storage and retrieval processes. Processes discussed in this section relate to Boolean-based systems using inverted files. The inverted file approach, discussed in more detail below, has been the primary method used by most commercial systems.

2.3.1 Document Storage and Indexing

Documents or their surrogates stored in an IR system must first be processed to provide sufficient access points to facilitate retrieval. In an *inverted file* environment, terms are used as the basis for finding documents matching the query parameters. Searchable terms within a system are listed in a term or index file, which includes a count of the number of documents within the indexed document set containing the term. The term entry will link to a location in a postings file. A *posting* is simply an indexed instance of a term within a document. Once a document has been identified as containing a term, it may be retrieved. The relationships among terms, postings, and documents are represented in Figure 2.2. The inverted file format has been criticized for its storage inefficiencies because it can re-create a large percentage of the document file within the indexes themselves unless compression methods are used. For a more detailed treatment of inverted files, consult Frakes & Baeza-Yates (1992, ch. 3).

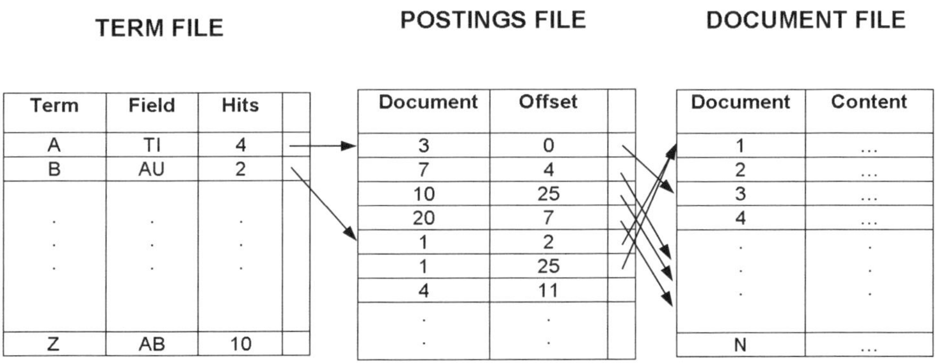

Figure 2.2. IR System File Representation

When integrating new documents into an IR system, the document contents must first be parsed to identify searchable terms. The parsing process will identify what constitutes a term through valid delimiter characters. For example, valid terms may be required to begin with an alphanumeric character and will be delimited by nonalphanumeric characters. Identified candidate terms are first compared to a *stopword* list that identifies words that will not be indexed. Stopwords include frequently occurring words such as articles (e.g., "the," "to," "for," and "a") that provide little substance for searching, or frequently used words in a given subject area common to all documents. *Stemming* algorithms may also be applied to identify morphological variants of index terms. The variants may then be condensed to a common root. Exclusion of stopwords from the term index can help to reduce the size of the postings file, while stemming can help to reduce the size of the term file. The candidate term is next searched in the term file. If it does not yet exist in the file, a new record is created, the number of *hits* or occurrences is set to 1, and a new record is added to the postings file linking the term to the document in the document file. If the term already exists in the term file, the number of hits is simply incremented and a new entry is added to the postings file. Where field searching is permitted, a field identifier may be added to the term file. If the term occurs in more than one field, additional entries may be added for the same term, representing each unique field occurrence. In addition, if proximity searching is supported, multiple locations of a given term within a field must also be represented. In this case, multiple posting entries for each occurrence of the term will be added. An *offset* value from the beginning of the field will identify where within a field the term occurs, so a term at the beginning of a field would have an offset of "0," the second word will have an offset of "1," etc. This could greatly increase the size of the postings file in systems indexing fields with lengthy text strings. Term frequencies within a field or document may be used as the basis for calculating a term weight providing an indication of its importance within a document.

The indexing policy of a system may be as simple as including all possible terms, which are easily identified during the initial document processing. To provide added value and additional search opportunities, commercial IR service providers will rely on human indexers to identify appropriate subject headings or descriptors for searching. Since this is a time and labor-intensive task, IR system designers have developed automatic indexing routines to identify appropriate terms. Kowalski (1997, pp. 55-56) points out that automatic indexing algorithms result in more predictable outcomes due to the variations that arise in human indexer judgments.

2.3.2 Query Operations and Processing

Many of the techniques used in document indexing may also be applied during searching. Queries initially entered by users are first parsed to identify terms and operators such as Boolean operations and search limiters. New search interfaces may rely on natural language processing to identify key query attributes. In a simple Boolean-based system postings associated with a query term are compared based on the Boolean operation indicated. So, the "AND" operation between two query terms will result in a returned list that consists of postings common to both terms. The "OR" operation would merge the two postings lists and eliminate duplicate identifiers. The final postings list is then presented to users, with summaries of document contents. Users may then elect to retrieve one or more of the documents on the list.

In more sophisticated systems weights may be assigned to each query term, indicating its significance in the query. Stemming algorithms may also be applied. Whereas stemming attempts to reduce searching to common root terms, query expansion techniques may be used to cast a broader net for searching. Using *query expansion*, additional search terms are included through the use of a constructed thesaurus that identifies related terms, or through query reformulation. Query reformulation strategies could also be implemented through relevance feedback, whereby users supply input on the relevance of retrieved items. The system may then modify the query accordingly by assigning different weights to query terms or may introduce additional terms based on the content of the items identified as relevant or nonrelevant.

Returned sets of documents or their surrogates may be presented to users in different ways. The order of presentation could be based on the document's age, alphabetical arrangement by author or title, or, increasingly, by the system's calculated relevance. Many algorithms are in use for determining relevance. In commercial Internet search engines, how relevance assessments are calculated is often kept secret to maintain the search engine's competitive edge. Generally, relevance assessments will be based on the frequency of search terms' appearances in a document, factoring in the document's length, the terms' locations in the document (in the title or subject headings, or close to the beginning of the document), and their proximity to one another in the document.

2.3.3 File and Data Structures

Information retrieval systems require efficient access methods to quickly locate term and record contents. This is especially true for today's systems, which may index terabytes of content, resulting in hundreds of thousands of identifiable terms and billions of postings. Different structures are used in various IR models to permit search and retrieval of system content. Each method has its own time and space trade-offs. Processing speed is also affected by whether contents are already stored in main memory or must be retrieved from secondary storage. If retrieval is necessary from secondary storage, the number of data blocks (retrieval units of data) to be retrieved or number of disk accesses should be minimized.

Inverted files may be implemented in several ways. Processing costs associated with searching and structure maintenance must be factored in. Sequential access files, which require a sequential search of each record within the file from beginning to end, are possible but are impractical given the number of searchable terms in large systems, even if all contents are stored in main memory. Sorted term lists stored in a dynamically accessible list structure, called an array, can be more efficient if a binary search is used, reducing the search time to approximately $\log_2 n$ accesses for n terms. Efficient access to terms can be achieved through the use of a tree structure consisting of a hierarchical organization of nodes and pointers that connect to nodes the next level down. Computational search burden is greatly reduced by dividing up the index among the nodes such that the worst-case search becomes equivalent to the maximum number of levels in the tree. B-trees, an example of a dynamic tree structure widely used in computing, can greatly reduce the computation necessary for searching. A B-tree of order m contains up to m pointers per node and $m - 1$ keys, or terms in this case (Knuth, 1973, p. 473). With sufficiently large m, even trees containing hundreds of thousands of keys can be reduced to three or four levels. Other tree structures such as the trie and its descendent the PAT tree rely on digital decomposition of character strings. These structures can be quite useful for search features such as substring identification (Frakes & Baeza-Yates, 1992, ch. 5). Hashing may also be used to quickly locate terms. A hashing function is used to assign a term to one of n "buckets." In a perfect hashing scheme, m terms are randomly and (assumed to be) evenly distributed across all buckets with m/n terms per bucket. If n is large enough, bucket contents may be achieved in a single disk access. In practice, hashing is not usually so uniform but still results in efficient access to bucket contents. Once a term is located, its associated postings must be accessed, retrieved, and compared, introducing a new set of processing efficiency issues.

Other methods that do not rely on inverted files may also be used for storing terms and processing queries. *Signature files* are used to quickly identify potentially relevant documents by creating lengthy bit strings of documents, called signatures, which, in theory, can distinguish documents from one another by differences in the bit strings. Indexable terms for a given document are first converted to word signatures, with selected bits in the string converted to "1," and are then superimposed with a logical "OR" operation over all word signatures. Documents are retrieved based on bit matching against a query that has also been converted to a signature. Lengthy signatures of several hundred bits, depending on the number of terms per document, ensure that document signatures are not overwhelmed with "1s," which would cause many documents to have the same signature, resulting in the retrieval of potentially many nonrelevant documents. By itself the search process of signatures may be sequential, but with compression and partitioning of signatures using a tree structure, search time can be significantly reduced (Faloutsos & Christodoulakis, 1987; Faloutsos, 1990).

Storage and retrieval methods used in vector space and probabilistic model-based systems can be similar to the previous methods, with more matrix processing structures needed. Applications of informetrics for file structure design and usage are discussed in Chapter 7, Section 7.3.

2.4 Evaluation of IR Systems

2.4.1 Types of Evaluation Measures

Performance evaluation is important in helping to gauge IR system effectiveness and efficiency. Evaluation measures may be categorized in different ways. They may be system-centered or user-centered. They also may relate to the retrieval process itself or to system outcomes. System-centered measures evaluate the efficiency and effectiveness of an IR system's retrieval performance for different retrieval tasks. The effectiveness of an IR system, or how well it works, depends not only on its ability to retrieve relevant documents but also on its ability to exclude nonrelevant documents (van Rijsbergen, 1981). As discussed in Section 2.4.2, these are not simply two sides of the same coin. Systems may be quite effective in retrieving relevant documents, but in doing so, additional nonrelevant documents may be retrieved and must be filtered out by the user. This can be compared to the process of harvesting on a farm, where the equipment used may be quite effective in collecting all available crops (relevant documents). However, additional extraneous material may also be collected during the process (nonrelevant documents), which must then be sifted out. Efficiency measures, on the other hand, evaluate how much effort or system resources must be expended in identifying and retrieving relevant documents. The ideal IR system should only retrieve those items deemed relevant, with a minimum of overhead. Often there is a trade-off, where effectiveness takes priority over efficiency.

Early IR system evaluation efforts largely relied on system-centered measures focused on retrieval performance, with user considerations being secondary or nonexistent. Today, user-centered measures for IR system design and evaluation have become important considerations, particularly due to the broad audiences with varying levels of IR experience and understanding who now use IR systems. Any benefits of a system's effectiveness are lost if the system is not usable by its intended audience. User-centered IR evaluation measures include quantitative assessment of system usability as well as user affective response to a system.

Many evaluation measures ultimately rely on the concept of relevance. This is complicated by the fact that relevance itself may be measured in different ways. For instance, relevance may be assessed based on the user information need or the query submitted (Korfhage, 1997, p. 192). The user may make document relevance judgments, or these may ultimately be made by the system evaluators for given information tasks. Often relevance is treated as a binary assessment; either a document is considered to be relevant or it is not. Documents may also be judged as having varying degrees of relevance. The degree of relevance may change if one considers the possibility of changing information needs as the users peruse documents. Therefore, relevance may be situational under some circumstances (Wilson, 1973). Concepts related to relevance may also be applied to the evaluation. *Pertinence* measures how well a document matches an information need. Nontopical factors such as *usefulness* relate to how well a document may serve a different information need, or the novelty that information within a document provides. Hence, relevant documents whose contents are already known may not be considered useful (Korfhage, 1997). These are more user-centered measures and are discussed in Section 2.4.4.

2.4.2 System Effectiveness Measures

Two of the earliest and still most widely used effectiveness measures based on document relevance are *recall* and *precision*. They are single value measures calculated as

$$Recall = \frac{\text{Number of relevant documents retrieved}}{\text{Total number of relevant documents in the collection}} \quad (2.2)$$

$$Precision = \frac{\text{Number of relevant documents retrieved}}{\text{Total number of documents retrieved}} \quad (2.3)$$

It is useful to provide an indication of both measures, for the reasons stated in Section 2.4.1. High recall can be achieved at the expense of precision and vice versa. Ideally, an IR system should provide both high recall and precision, although in practice studies have found an inverse relationship between the two.

Precision may also be considered an efficiency measure. With high precision, fewer nonrelevant documents are retrieved, thereby requiring less user effort to sort through the list of retrieved items for relevant documents. In large-scale evaluation studies, values for each measure are often averaged, providing a general sense of performance, although plots of recall versus precision for different retrieval tasks are more informative.

Variations of recall and precision have been used in IR evaluation studies. With today's very large databases or indexed resources such as the Web, recall calculation is not feasible because the total number of relevant items in such a large collection is not known. In this case, search experts will perform specified retrieval tasks to identify as many relevant documents as possible. These judgments then serve as the baseline from which recall and precision for user tasks are calculated.

Recall and precision or their variants continue to serve as the benchmark measures for IR system retrieval performance. There has been increasing criticism of the use of recall and precision because of the ambiguities associated with the concept of relevance, which is the foundation on which these measures are constructed (Saracevic, 1995). With effective relevance ranking procedures now part of many IR systems, precision may also lose its importance as a result of the availability of relevant documents near the top of a retrieval list, which makes the number of documents in the list less important. Ultimately, users are more interested in quality than quantity (Su, 1992).

Many researchers also have proposed single system effective measures (see, e.g., Meadow, Boyce, & Kraft, 2000, sect. 16.3.4). The classic *E* measure (Swets, 1969) measures the ability of a system to separate relevant documents from those that are not relevant. A variation of the *E* measure proposed by van Rijsbergen (1979) that combines recall (*R*) and precision (*P*) is

$$E = 1 - \frac{1}{\alpha(1/P) + (1-\alpha)(1/R)} \tag{2.4}$$

where $0 < \alpha < 1$ is the weighted importance assigned to precision. Another single measure is the average search length, defined as the expected position of a relevant document in a ranked list (Losee, 1998, pp. 89-92). In practical terms, it measures how many documents must be examined to reach a 50 percent recall level. Additional single value effectiveness measures are presented in Boyce, Meadow, and Kraft (1994, pp. 196-198).

2.4.3 System Efficiency Measures

Efficiency measures relate to the effort required or resources expended to perform different processing tasks. Often these measures are of primary interest to system designers who seek more efficient ways to process queries. Because IR systems now potentially index billions of documents, even with faster processing technologies today, the use of algorithms for efficient processing of retrieval requests continues to be important.

Response time is the most frequently used metric for gauging efficiency. Response time is relative because the type of computer hardware used or the amount of the computer's internal resources devoted to the process plays a major role in determining response time. The time-independent measure of the number of block or disk accesses required to retrieve a document set may also be used (Wolfram, 1992b).

2.4.4 Usage and User-Centered Measures of System Performance

System evaluation measures need not involve users, but increasingly users are recognized as essential to the evaluation and ultimate usefulness of an IR system. User-centered measures may be based on time, commands used to complete a search task, or the number of records retrieved (Boyce, Meadow, & Kraft, 1994, ch. 14). These measures are useful in assessing how users interact with the IR system.

User-based assessments of output relevance are also becoming more common, where ultimately it is the end user who decides the relevance of retrieved items. Keen (1971) proposed the use of coverage and novelty ratios. The coverage ratio is the fraction of relevant documents known to the user that have been retrieved, whereas the novelty ratio is the fraction of relevant documents retrieved that are unknown to the user. Of particular note, Tague-Sutcliffe (1995) derives a general measure of informativeness based on user-record interactions to aid in the evaluation of information services.

User response to an IR system can also be indicative of its performance. Measures of satisfaction with the outcome of a search or frustration with the system can provide system designers with valuable feedback on user responsiveness as a whole or subsets of the user population (Korfhage, 1997). Finally, process measures of system usage may be used to understand how users interact with IR systems. Regularities in these measures are discussed in detail in Chapter 6.

Evaluation measures may be extended to the system interfaces to determine ease of learning and use. Display design and content presentation, color combinations used, and interface features such as menus and windows can greatly affect the usability, and hence the value, of the system to a user population. Many works are now available on user interface design. Among these, Shneiderman (1998) specifically addresses issues related to information searching.

2.5 Current Issues in IR Research

Even with the many developments in IR research that have taken place over the past fifty years, there are many areas that merit further research attention. Other areas are just now being investigated that move beyond traditional views of IR in the textual, stand-alone system environment. The importance of the user in shaping IR system design and evaluation is receiving more attention, as is the need for standardization as IR technology becomes more ubiquitous.

2.5.1 Visualization

The application of visualization techniques to IR environments presents a new way for users to interact with the system itself and with its contents. Instead of relying on symbolic representation of content, visualization uses geometric representations (McCormick, DeFanti, & Brown, 1987). In most IR systems, documents are presented to users as lists of textual summaries, with no indication of how one document relates to another or to the information need, other than perhaps as a ranked list of retrieved items. Until recently, IR systems have not explored the visual paradigm as a tool for allowing users to assess system interactions and results. Visualization frees the user from the constraints inherent in a primarily textual interface by presenting visual summaries of queries, documents, or their relationships. As computer users have become accustomed to graphical user interfaces, their expectations of software, including IR systems, have increased.

Information visualization uses many approaches. Through the use of properties such as color, texture, shape, location, and proximity, document attributes or relationships among documents may be presented to the user. The user can then quickly understand the visual summary of content. As a two-dimensional medium, the computer screen can be used to map relationships among documents. Three-dimensional simulations in the two-dimensional environment are also possible. Many prototype systems incorporating visualization techniques have been developed. Shneiderman (1998) and Marchionini (1995) summarize a number of examples of information systems that have incorporated visualization.

A primary goal of visualization is to reduce the complexity inherent in the relationships among documents. By hiding details and allowing users to focus on subsets, cognitive overload can be minimized. For example, the VIBE system (Olsen, Korfhage, Sochats, Spring, & Williams, 1993) relies on similarity ratios of documents to two or more specified reference points represented in a two-dimensional display. Reference points provide a basis from which document locations may be projected onto the display. Zhang and Korfhage (1999) developed the Distance Angle Retrieval Environment (DARE) system, which uses visualization to reduce the complexity of an n-dimensional document vector space down to two dimensions. Figure 2.3 displays the results of a sample query in DARE. Documents are distributed in the two-dimensional space based on their distance and angle from a query vector. Threshold levels may be set by the user to eliminate documents that are beyond a certain distance or angle threshold from the document space origin.

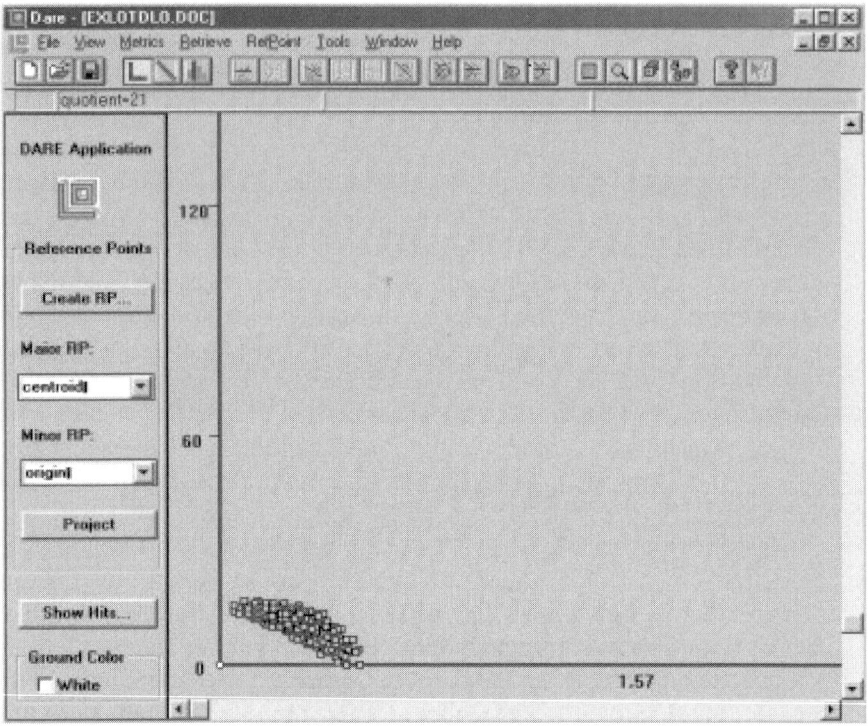

Figure 2.3. Sample Screen from the DARE Visual Retrieval Environment

Information visualization continues to grow as an area of IR investigation. In addition to visualization, aural interfaces that rely on properties of sound (pitch, volume, duration, timbre) are being investigated for information retrieval purposes (Kramer, 1994).

2.5.2 Multimedia IR

Information retrieval systems have traditionally been used to store and retrieve textual content. This is due to the attributes of text that make it easy to represent and store electronically. The documents themselves are textual in nature, and queries are formed as strings of text that are easily translated into symbolic representations to be processed. Information retrieval concepts may now also be applied to other media formats. With efficient digital storage devices to house collections of sound/music files, images, and video files, multimedia IR has become feasible. Research in this fast growing area has focused on issues of document representation, querying techniques, and efficient access.

Two approaches are currently used to support image retrieval. Concept-based retrieval relies on textual representations of image contents (themes, colors, objects found within the image, proximities of objects) and attributes (creator, size, creation date, technique/format) as image surrogates. The retrieval process takes place in much the same way as text-based retrieval. Users formulate textual queries based on content and attribute parameters. Unlike text-based document retrieval systems, which may rely on automatic indexing of keywords within documents, considerable human effort is needed to supply the textual representations of the image. Content-based retrieval relies on pattern recognition of the image properties themselves as the basis for the retrieval. Queries may consist of sample images to serve as the template for a similarity search, where stored images are retrieved based on shapes, textures, or colors. Content-based image retrieval is still relatively new but is evolving quickly. Concept- and content-based methods may also be applied to moving image retrieval, with the added dimension of a temporal component with which to contend. Several commercial examples of image IR systems are now available, including Virage's VIR Engine and Image Read/Write Toolkit, Attrasoft's ImageFinder, and IBM's QBIC (Query By Image Content).

Sound retrieval presents similar challenges, with similar solutions being applied. In addition to general sound retrieval, systems may focus more specifically on music retrieval and voice retrieval. Music information retrieval has been studied for decades, but as with other media formats it is gaining popularity. In addition to concept-based retrieval using attributes associated with musical pieces (titles, composer/writer, lyrics, musicians, instruments, recording date), retrieval based on notes has also been investigated. Queries may be based on note representations. Downie and Nelson (2000) demonstrate that music retrieval based on note representation as strings can follow similar characteristics as observed with text (see Chapter 8, Section 8.3). Examples of music information retrieval projects include Themefinder (http://www.themefinder.org) and the New Zealand Digital Library's Meldex (http://www.nzdl.org/cgi-bin/library).

2.5.3 Distributed IR

Networked environments have permitted the creation of distributed IR systems, in which the content indexed may reside on computers elsewhere on the network. Processing can take two forms. First, the indexing mechanism may search for remote resources and index them locally to create a single index of searchable documents. Many search engines on the Web, such as Google and AltaVista, use this approach. Conversely, the local search interface may act for clients by making requests to remote servers containing their own indexes of resources. In this sense, all IR processing takes place remotely. Items returned can be filtered for duplication before presentation to the user. "Meta" search services such as Ixquick, Profusion, and Dogpile rely on this approach. Wide area information servers (WAIS), which gained some popularity in the early 1990s and may still be found used on the Web, and IR systems that comply with the Z39.50 standard (see Section 2.5.8), also permit distributed querying of remote sources.

The widely dispersed geographic distribution of indexable content creates several challenges for system developers. The first challenge is that of resource discovery. If not all indexable sites are known, then the index component of the IR system must be able to discover new locations. On the Internet, this entails becoming aware of new Internet Protocol (IP) addresses for Web servers. Second, once locations have been identified and indexed, they must be revisited and re-indexed regularly to reflect changes in content. For bibliographic database systems and OPACs, content is less volatile, where documents may be added to the system but are rarely changed. On the Web, content can be highly volatile, with many changes made to documents on a regular basis. Third, the lack of consistent structure in the distributed environment makes it difficult to identify common document attributes such as titles, authors, or subject headings. Although markup languages such as the Hypertext Markup Language (HTML) and particularly the eXtensible Markup Language (XML) permit the identification of document attributes, document developers do not use them consistently. Fourth, redundancy of content, or the availability of different versions of a document, can be problematic. Systems should be able to decide which version is intended.

Additional challenges for the user and the retrieval system are discussed by Baeza-Yates and Ribeiro-Neto (1999, pp. 368-369). Grossman and Frieder (1998) also discuss processing issues in the distributed environment.

2.5.4 Cross-Language IR

The world corpus of information resources extends well beyond those stored in any single human language. Access to documents in other languages continues to generate considerable research interest, particularly now with the availability of Internet resources in many languages. Cross-language information retrieval (CLIR) supports the ability to retrieve documents in one language using queries entered in another language. Special requirements exist for different steps in the CLIR process, beginning with query formulation, document matching, selection, examination, and delivery (Oard & Diekema, 1998). A key problem is that of language identification within documents. Without specific identifiers to indicate a document language, the system must be able to determine which language has been used. Once identified, rules used in word construction must be known. Translation methods vary. Systems may rely on ontologies such as multilingual thesauri; bilingual dictionaries; machine translation lexicons; or corpora of translation sets based on the document, sentence, or term level. Most CLIR research has focused on the use of controlled vocabularies within designated languages, but in the past decade free text methods have been explored. To find out more about recent developments in CLIR, consult the Cross-Language Evaluation Forum (CLEF) at http://clef.iei.pi.cnr.it/, which sponsors an annual research program, or consult recent proceedings of the forum (Peters, 2000).

2.5.5 User versus System-Centered Research

Historically IR system research has focused on system-centered perspectives in the design and evaluation of systems. This approach has emphasized efficient and effective design of algorithms and evaluation based on system processes without the interaction of users. This has been the more common approach taken by IR researchers coming from computer science. In recent decades, a user-centered perspective has emerged, emphasizing the cognitive, situational, and interactive aspects of IR. Researchers in the information and cognitive sciences have primarily been developing this approach. Recent monographs such as those by Allen (1996) and Marchionini (1995) emphasize user information seeking behavior in the design and evaluation of information systems. Saracevic (1997) contends that a significant divide exists between the two approaches. There has been little interaction or cross-fertilization between both camps to the mutual benefit of each other, as is evident from IR research appearing in the proceedings of the Association for Computing Machinery (ACM) Special Interest Group on Information Retrieval (SIGIR) and recent conferences dealing with digital libraries.

2.5.6 "Real World" and "Experimental" IR

Another distinction in IR research that has emerged in recent years is largely due to the availability of transaction log data from different IR system environments, such as OPACs and Web search services. Most user-based IR studies have relied on limited samples of user populations in controlled circumstances. Users may be assigned a series of information tasks requiring that they formulate a search strategy and then search one or more systems to locate documents relevant to the information need. Search activities are then monitored and recorded. Participants may also undergo pre- and post-interviews to gather additional data on the user search processes. This is the experimental approach to IR system study. It has been widely employed among user-centered IR researchers and provides several advantages. The close contact with system users allows researchers the opportunity to gather detailed data on many aspects of the IR process. The ability to focus on identifiable subjects allows the researchers to understand individual differences in how the system is perceived and used. It also permits the researchers to test hypothesizes in a controlled environment, where the impact of external influences on the retrieval process may be reduced.

However, this approach has limitations. Often the sample drawn from a population is quite small due to the time and effort needed for each subject in a study. Also, the controlled environment is not "natural" because constraints may be placed on the participants, who are well aware that they are being observed.

With the wider availability of IR systems in public environments such as the Internet, a new research environment that casts a broader net is now available. Unobtrusive studies of how end users make use of the Web, for example, are possible through the analysis of transaction logs of user sessions (Jansen, Spink, & Saracevic, 2000; Spink, Wolfram, Jansen, & Saracevic, 2001). With transaction logs, researchers may analyze data on user queries entered, query modification, resources requested, and time taken. With heavily used services, the data sets can be quite large, consisting of many thousands of users. With transaction logs, factual accounts of searching can be easily collected, but follow-ups with users are not possible unless they are specifically identifiable. More important, transaction logs on their own cannot provide an indication of user motivation for different search behaviors. Even with accompanying survey instruments, respondents are a self-selected group that may or may not represent the user population at large.

Regardless of the methodology used, researchers must still contend with the influence of database content, search features, and purpose of use in the study of different IR systems. With different contexts having emerged for IR, researchers are discovering differences in how IR systems are searched. Jansen & Pooch (2001), for example, found that there were differences in user search behavior among Web-based transaction log studies, OPAC studies, and traditional bibliographic database studies.

2.5.7 IR Standardization

Standardization plays a key role in technology acceptance and interoperability. Several organizations are responsible for the development of standards that affect information systems. In the United States, the American National Standards Institute (ANSI) is responsible for the development of standards in many areas. It has accredited the National Information Standards Organization (NISO) to approve and maintain information standards (Kowalski, 1997). Globally, the International Standards Organization (ISO) is responsible for the development of international standards in many areas. In addition to the development of standards, ISO may adopt or modify regional standards for an international audience.

Unlike DBMSs, for which standardized data models (e.g., relational and CODASYL) and querying approaches (e.g., SQL for the relational model) have been developed, IR systems in general have not been developed within a standardized framework. A few examples of standards for the IR environment do exist. The ISO 2709 standard specifies the requirements for bibliographic record content interchange, but it is system-independent. The standard outlines the representation of variable length field records and how fields and documents are delimited but does not define the nature or content of the fields. Unicode, a two-byte character code for the major character sets of the world, is increasingly being used to universally represent document content without having to convert document contents from one single-byte code to another for compatibility.

Distributed information retrieval has at least brought IR query standardization to the forefront. But for the most part, search commands and operators still vary from one system to another. The ANSI/NISO Z39.50 standard for database searching and document retrieval has been under development since the late 1980s. The standard does not define the IR system itself but rather a common method for client-server searching and document retrieval. Searches are initiated on a local client in the client's native search language. The client then translates the query into a Z39.50-compliant format. The translated request is sent to one or more servers for processing. Once received by the server, the request is translated back into the server's native search language for processing. Resulting hits are converted to a standardized format and are sent back to the local client, where it is converted into the local native equivalent format. A strength of the standard is that the client may also integrate the results from several servers. The current version, Z39.50-1995, has been adopted internationally. At the time of the writing of this book, a newer version was still under development.

From a user perspective, Z39.50 creates a single, seamless IR environment. Users need only be familiar with their local search interface but are able to request resources from different locations with a single search. Developers of OPACs were among the first to adopt the standard to permit searching among many catalogs. Examples of Z39.50 implementations may be found on the Web (see for example the Library of Congress Z39.50 Gateway at http://lcweb.loc.gov/z3950/gateway.html). Earlier versions of the standard emphasized bibliographic record contents. The 1995 standard expanded to include full-text document and image handling. Specific details on the standard and its development may be found at the Library of Congress Z39.50 Maintenance Agency Page (http://www.loc.gov/z3950/agency).

Markup languages to represent document content, such as SGML (Standardized General Markup Language) and more recently HTML, used in documents accessible through the Web, provide a method for tagging document parts for formatting, structure, and retrieval purposes. The more recently developed XML, which provides more flexible markup features than HTML, may succeed HTML as the standard markup language for network-accessible documents (Luk et al., 2002). Along with the more powerful structural and content tagging options to aid in the retrieval process are emerging proposals for standardized document representation, relationships, and query languages to be used on XML-tagged document sets.

2.6 Summary and Additional Readings

Over the past fifty years IR systems have evolved from specialized technologies used predominantly by information professionals into ubiquitous tools to store and provide access to large quantities of information. Multiple approaches to the development of IR systems have led to a variety of technologies for query-document matching. This chapter has highlighted the key concepts of IR and current areas of research. The reader is encouraged to consult sources providing a more detailed treatment of the breadth of IR. Sources will take different approaches, emphasizing models, design algorithms, and/or evaluation.

For a comprehensive, technical treatment of IR concepts from a computer science perspective, including IR models used, consult Baeza-Yates and Ribeiro-Neto (1999) or Grossman and Frieder (1998). Kowalski (1997), Korfhage (1997), and Meadow, Boyce, and Kraft (2000) also provide readable overviews of design and evaluation for broader audiences. The content of van Rijsbergen's classic monograph (van Rijsbergen, 1979) is now available on the Web at (http://www.dcs.gla.ac.uk/Keith/Preface.html). Sparck Jones and Willett (1997) have compiled a collection of classic papers on IR that spans forty years. Papers included address not only conceptual but also system implementation issues. For coverage of specific IR models such as the vector space model, sources such as Salton (1989) or Salton and McGill (1983) should be consulted. Fuhr's (1992) treatment of probabilistic models will be of interest to readers with a technical background. Few sources provide detailed treatment of algorithms and file structures for IR tasks. In addition to Salton (1989), Kowalski (1997), and Baeza-Yates and Ribeiro-Neto (1999), Frakes and Baeza-Yates (1992) devote several chapters to different structures that permit efficient access to text-based documents.

Detailed treatment of system performance is often lacking in IR literature. Boyce, Meadow, and Kraft (1994) devote several chapters to measurements used in IR systems and their application to system evaluation. Many factors may influence the outcomes of any IR experiment. These will depend on the databases and queries used, the operationalization of variables, and how the resulting data are analyzed (Tague-Sutcliffe, 1992). Losee (1998) provides a detailed treatment of the theoretical performance of IR systems for the retrieval of natural language text. In addition to Allen (1996) and Marchionini (1995), who take a user-centered approach to IR system and service development, Shneiderman (1998) provides a more general treatment of human-computer interaction, with some emphasis on IR examples.

Current research in IR may be found in a number of periodicals and conference proceedings. The ACM's SIGIR publishes a newsletter and annual conference proceedings on the latest developments in IR research. Proceedings of the annual Text Retrieval Conference (TREC) also provide cutting-edge research in IR. The TREC proceedings also have the advantage of containing research in different IR research tracks. Within each track, the retrieval tasks carried out by participants are predetermined, thereby permitting comparisons among the approaches used. Publications of the ACM Special Interest Group for Computer-Human Interaction (SIGCHI) increasingly include human-centered IR research. The conference proceedings on digital libraries sponsored by the ACM and Institute of Electrical and Electronics Engineers (IEEE) also contain IR-related publications. With the growth in interest in IR, conferences dealing with the Web increasingly deal with IR topics as well. Periodicals in the computing and information sciences that frequently publish IR-related research include *Information Retrieval*, *Journal of the American Society for Information Science and Technology*, *Information Processing & Management*, *ACM Transactions on Information Systems,* and *Journal of Documentation*.

3

Informetrics

Any human action will be a manifestation of the Principle of Least Effort in operation, if this Principle holds true.

—George K. Zipf, 1949

3.1 Introduction

The word *informetrics*, although relatively recent in origin, identifies what is, in fact, one of the older areas of research within information science. Informetric phenomena had already been studied for decades by the time the discipline of information science coalesced in the late 1950s. Unlike other areas of information science such as information retrieval, it has not attracted the same high profile and level of research interest, although it has a devoted core of researchers that is growing as interest increases in informetric applications. The literature base of informetrics is less consolidated than that of IR, with fewer monographs and articles on the scope of the field having been written to date. The goal of the present chapter is to present an overview of the fundamental concepts related to informetrics and its subdomains.

3.1.1 What Is Informetrics?

Informetrics was first used in the late 1970s (Nacke, 1979) to describe the area of information science "dealing with the measurement of information phenomena and the application of mathematical methods to the discipline's problems" (Wilson, 1999, p. 111). This quantitative study of recorded discourse may relate to any medium, although until recent decades print media have dominated informetric research. With the wider availability of documentary resources and records of discourse in electronic formats, particularly through machine-readable databases and more recently the Internet, informetric research based on electronic data sets has become commonplace. The older and still more widely used related terms *bibliometrics* and *scientometrics* are sometimes used synonymously with informetrics or are subsumed by informetrics (Brookes, 1988). The use of the term *informetrics* has been growing since the early 1990s. It has been recognized by international organizations such as the Federation Internationale de la Documentation (FID) and has been adopted by the International Society for Scientometrics and Informetrics (ISSI). *Informetrics* is used in this book, as opposed to related terms, due to its broader, nonformat- and nondiscipline-specific definition of information related phenomena. The term is also assumed to subsume cognate areas of investigation such as citation analysis and other areas of scholarly communication, which are sometimes treated as distinct from informetrics (Garfield, 1998).

Informetric research is undertaken by scholars from many disciplines, including library and information science, history of science, computer science, communications, sociology, and linguistics. The different disciplinary perspectives have shaped researcher motivations for undertaking informetric studies and the processes studied. Objects studied include the documents themselves, the creators of documents (authors), document dissemination (publication) and utilization, and document content attributes. These objects are studied within contexts defined by time frames, geography, and the disciplines in which the objects are used. In library and information science and computer science, applications of informetrics extend to information services and system analysis and design. In the history and sociology of science informetrics may be used to study the development and interactions of disciplines and subspecializations. Within the sciences, applications may extend to the measurement of scientific indicators and ultimately to the development of national science policies. From a linguistic perspective, analysis of word pattern usage is helpful in understanding document content and differences between documents. Finally, communication and sociology researchers use informetrics to perform social network analysis through the study of citations and co-citations.

On a very high level, informetric phenomena may be thought of as *information production processes* or IPPs (Egghe, 1990), where measurable *sources* produce *items*. For example, an author (source) produces articles (items), a text produces words, and a user produces queries. Each of these processes may be studied and measured. Egghe's terminology—IPPs, sources, and items—is used in subsequent chapters when they present general concepts as they relate to informetric methodologies. Strict tallies of an informetric process such as the growth in the total number of documents in a collection over time may be thought of as a one-dimensional IPP. Two-dimensional IPPs involve classic source and item relationships as one-to-many relationships (e.g., the number of authors who produce *x* documents). It is also possible to have three-dimensional IPPs, where multiple sources and item relationships exist. From a data modeling perspective, these can be thought of as many-to-many relationships, which, for simplicity, may be decomposed to two one-to-many relationships. Data storage models to support informetric data sets are discussed in Chapter 4, Section 4.3.4.

3.1.2 Bibliometrics, Scientometrics, and Other -metrics

The historical antecedents of informetrics can be traced back to at least the early twentieth century when the term *statistical bibliography* was used to describe quantitative studies of disciplinary literatures. However, quantitative analysis of the contents of documents may have originated as early as the Middle Ages (Paisley, 1990). Pioneers of this developing field of study have included Lotka (1926), Bradford (1934), Zipf (1935, 1949), and Price (1963), who have examined regularities in authorship, journal publications, word usage, and scientific literature growth, respectively.

With the growing recognition of the emerging study of empirical regularities in recorded discourse, Pritchard (1969) proposed the use of the term *bibliometrics* to match terminology used for quantitative studies of other subject areas such as econometrics and psychometrics. The term was quickly adopted and is still widely used, particularly in North America. Wilson (1999) reports that the average number of publications appearing annually using the term *bibliometrics* still outnumbers related terms but has been in decline since the mid-1990s, with the term *informetrics* increasing in use during this time.

At approximately the same time that the term *bibliometrics* was coined, the term *scientometrics* (*naukometriya*) was proposed by Nalimov and Mul'chenko (1969) in the former Soviet Union to describe research on the quantitative study of scientific activities. The term *scientometrics* has been more widely used in Europe and the former Soviet Union. Clearly it has considerable overlap with bibliometrics, but it limits itself to quantitative study of scientific disciplines and associated activities related to scientific research and development. The journal *Scientometrics* has been publishing both scientometric and bibliometric research since the late 1970s, and other journals in the information sciences also have been publishing bibliometric/scientometric research for many decades (see Section 3.9).

Many other terms related to more specific subareas of informetrics have been proposed over the past thirty years, but none has yet gained widespread support. Two relatively new terms whose origins are too recent to gauge their long-term impact relate specifically to Internet/World Wide Web-related studies. *Webometics* has been proposed (Almind & Ingwersen, 1997; Björneborn & Ingwersen, 2001) to identify informetric studies of Web phenomena. The term *cybermetrics* has also been proposed for these studies, but broadens its definition to go beyond the Web to include all aspects of electronic resources. The latter has received some recognition, particularly as a result of the publication of the electronic journal *Cybermetrics*. The increased interest in quantitative studies of the Internet is evident in the recent publication of studies on the growth of the Internet/Web, search engine index coverage, and Web resource usage in high profile scientific journals such as *Science* and *Nature* (Huberman, Pirolli, Pitkow, & Lukose, 1998; Lawrence & Giles 1998a; Huberman & Adamic, 1999).

3.1.3 Informetric Models

Informetric models attempt to generalize the patterns of information production processes. Raw data, or items, collected from an information production process are usually tallied to form observed distributions (e.g., how many sources contribute one item, two items, etc). Based on observed regularities in the distribution, mathematical models that re-create the observed behavior are developed to describe and ultimately help to explain the observed patterns. To determine the appropriateness of a potential model, it is fit to the observed data distribution (see Chapter 4, Section 4.5). Numerous theoretical distributions have been developed and applied to the range of informetric phenomena. Many, in fact, are found to be similar to one another, or represent special cases of more general distributions (see Section 3.8) and have applications beyond the area of study for which they were initially developed. Most informetric phenomena are characterized by well-defined inverse relationships, with most sources contributing only one item, and follow a "reverse J-shape" with long tails, also called Large Number of Rare Events (LNRE) distributions (Baayen, 2001). Figure 3.1 is an example of an inverse distribution for author productivity (see Section 3.2.1), where the majority of authors contribute few publications and only a few authors contribute many publications. Other informetric distributions may follow a unimodal pattern, with modes occurring at higher item values than the lowest possible value of (usually) "1" or (sometimes) "0." Figure 3.2 illustrates a hypothetical distribution for the number of terms assigned per document with a mode of seven terms per document.

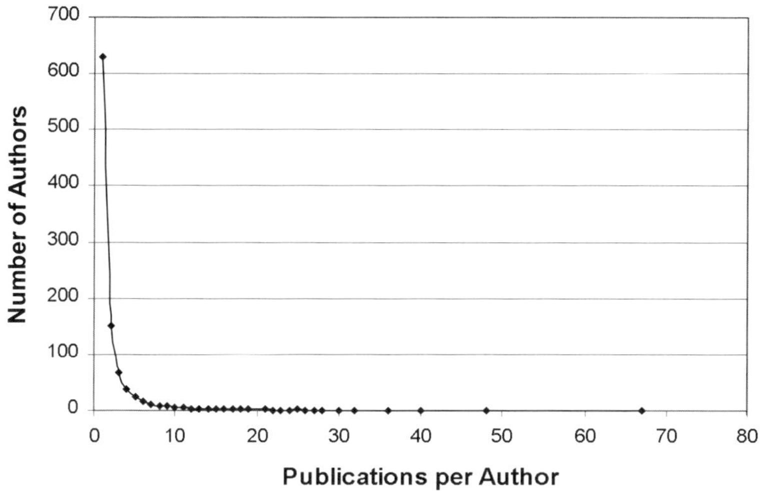

Figure 3.1. Hypothetical Author Productivity Distribution

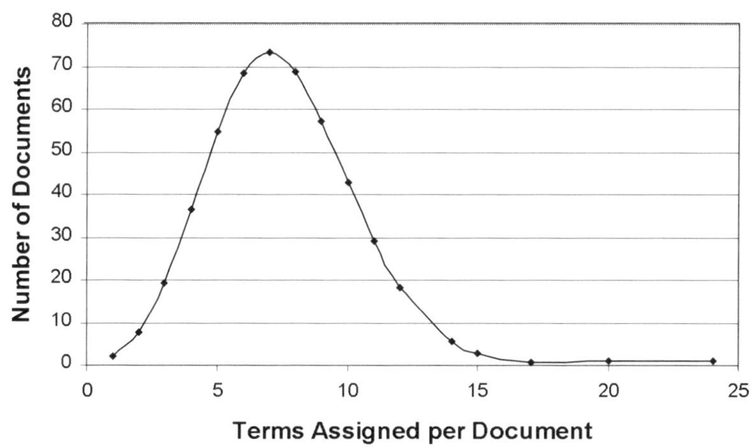

Figure 3.2. Hypothetical Distribution of Terms Assigned per Document (Mode = 7 Terms per Document)

Several approaches may be used to represent the distributions of sources and items. In *size-frequency* representation, the number of items contributed by a source represents the size of the source. The tally of the number of sources that contribute a given number of items represents the frequency associated with a given size. In graphic form, size is plotted on the x-axis (abscissa), with frequency plotted on the y-axis (mantissa). Author productivity studies (see Section 3.2.1), for example, traditionally use this approach. *Rank-frequency* representation orders sources in decreasing order of productivity (i.e., the number of items contributed by a given source). Rank is plotted on the x-axis, with frequency of items plotted on the y-axis, in effect the reverse of the size-frequency approach. In rank-frequency form, many tied ranks are encountered at the tail end of the distribution (see Figure 3.3), which may be handled in several ways (see Chapter 4, Section 4.4.1). Cumulative forms of both size-frequency and rank-frequency distributions may also be used, for example, in literature growth and journal productivity studies, respectively (Wilson, 1999).

Author	Articles
A	5
B	3
C	2
D	2
E	1
F	1
G	1
H	1

Initial Data

Size	Frequency
1	4
2	2
3	1
5	1

Size-Frequency Form

Rank*	Frequency
1	5
2	3
3	2
4	2
5	1
6	1
7	1
8	1

Rank-Frequency Form

* *Note:* There are at least five ways to rank data to deal with ties in frequency. See Chapter 4, Section 4.4.1.

Figure 3.3. Two Data Representations for Authorship Productivity

The plotting of data sets to visually convey distribution characteristics often requires transformation of the plot axes. Large data sets containing high frequencies and sizes/ranks will result in data points that hug the axes. In these situations it is useful to apply a logarithmic transformation on one or both axes to provide a better sense of the data distribution. Another option is to truncate the high value data to reduce the range of values plotted. Logarithmic transformations are also useful in converting exponentially and negative exponentially distributed data into a linear form, which can simplify the fitting of observed data to theoretical models. Note that informetric distributions are technically discrete, although continuous approximations are also occasionally used. Regardless, most data plots will use continuous curves to represent the discrete data.

3.2 Classic Informetric "Laws"

Regularities in recorded discourse observed by early researchers in informetrics are often referred to as "laws." These should not be confused with more immutable laws found in the physical sciences. The term "law" is used by informetricians in its loosest sense, describing what in reality amounts to a mathematical generalization of an observed regularity in information production and use. Over time, researchers have found that more sophisticated mathematical distributions may be needed to satisfactorily model large data sets, but the general distribution of data described by the early models largely holds true for smaller data sets.

3.2.1 Lotka's Law of Author Productivity

A. J. Lotka (1926) studied authorship patterns in the fields of chemistry and physics. He observed that when one tallies the number of publications a given author contributes to a discipline over time, most contribute a small number; very few are prolific contributors. Although not initially presented in the following form, Lotka's law for author productivity may be summarized as

$$f(x) = \frac{k}{x^b}, \quad x = 1, 2, \ldots, x_{\max} \tag{3.1}$$

where $f(x)$ denotes the proportion of authors contributing x publications, and k and b represent constants or parameters defining the distribution characteristics of a given discipline. The parameter x_{max} indicates the largest value of x and may be calculated or assigned an *a priori* value. Lotka found that for his physics data set, $k = 0.6709$ and $b = 2.02$, whereas for chemistry $k = 0.5669$ and $b = 1.88$. Note that k also represents the proportion of authors contributing a single paper. By multiplying the resulting $f(x)$ value by the total number of authors within a data set, one can determine the number of authors for each x.

The validity of Lotka's law has been studied by a number of researchers who have applied the model to data sets in many subject areas. Most notable are the contributions of Nicholls (1986, 1989) and Pao (1985, 1986), who found that the Lotka model fitted the majority of the data sets studied.

Publications with multiple authors can present a dilemma in productivity studies because there are several ways for authors to receive credit for publications they have co-authored, including the following:

- **Complete count:** Each occurrence of an author is recognized and receives equal treatment, regardless of the number of authors associated with a given article. Therefore, an author receives equal credit, whether he or she is the only author of a publication or one of many.

- **Straight count**: Only the first author is counted, based on the assumption that the first author is the primary contributor to a publication. This counting method can be somewhat arbitrary, particularly when author orderings are alphabetical and are not based on level of contribution.

- **Adjusted count:** Authors receive fractional credit for publications with multiple authors (e.g., 0.5 for a publication with two authors, 0.2 for five authors). The credit received also may be weighted based on the author order, so that preceding authors receive more credit than subsequent authors.

Studies of authorship extend beyond productivity investigations. The distribution of authorships within publications has also been studied. Different disciplines have different traditions of research collaboration, with the humanities traditionally showing the lowest levels of co-authorship, whereas the sciences show the highest. Ajiferuke (1991) investigated authorship distributions for data sets from engineering sciences, medical sciences, physical sciences, mathematical sciences, social sciences, and the humanities over six time periods. Based on initial assumptions about the research process, a shifted Waring distribution to model the data was proposed, but the data sets were also fitted to fifteen other distributions. Ajiferuke concluded that a shifted inverse Gaussian-Poisson distribution was most generally appropriate to model patterns of co-authorship (see Chapter 4, Section 4.4.3).

Related to author productivity, Price (1963) concluded that the number of prolific authors in a subject area (i.e., producing about half of the publications in the field) was approximately equal to the square root of the total number of authors in the field. This has since become known as Price's law. The law was derived from earlier ideas espoused by social theorists Galton and Rousseau (Diodato, 1994, p. 131). The validity of Price's law has been challenged more recently by Nicholls (1988).

3.2.2 Bradford's Law of Scatter

S. C. Bradford (1934, 1948) studied the inverse relationship between the number of articles published in a subject area and the number of journals in which the articles appear, referred to as journal productivity. He undertook his investigation having expressed concern that abstracting and indexing services for periodical literature were missing as much as two-thirds of total literature on a given subject. Analysis of journal productivity has also been used as a tool for collection management in libraries by identifying core journals in subject areas, thereby providing evidence for journal subscription decision making.

In a well-defined subject area, a small number of journals account for a sizeable portion of the total publications in that area, whereas increasing numbers of journals publish fewer and fewer articles in the area. Numerous formulations for Bradford's law have been proposed. Qiu (1990) studied twenty-two models proposed for Bradford analysis. The common model used in rank form can be represented as

$$G(r) = a + b \log r \tag{3.2}$$

where $G(r)$ represents the total proportion of articles contributed by the r ranked most productive journals, and a and b represent parameters. Again, the total number of articles represented by $G(r)$ may be calculated by multiplying $G(r)$ by the total number of journals in the data set.

Bradford presented his findings in graphical form, observing that the ranked journals could be grouped into categories, called Bradford zones, each containing roughly the same number of articles and increasing numbers of journals in each subsequent zone. The first zone, called the core zone, contains the small number of highly productive journals. The ratio between the number of journals in subsequent zones was observed to be approximately $1:n:n^2:\ldots$, where n is referred to as the Bradford multiplier.

Investigators of Bradford's law have observed that for some data sets in cumulative form, there is a visible "droop" in the tail end of the distribution, resulting in an S-shaped curve, instead of the concavely increasing curve expected. This phenomenon was first outlined by Groos (1967) and is referred to as the Groos droop. The droop indicates that fewer articles than anticipated are being contributed by the least productive journals. The Groos droop has been attributed to incomplete data sets, particularly for the many low productivity journals. Qiu and Tague (1990) demonstrated through generated data sets using computer simulation that this was not the case. More recently, Heine (1998) has contended that the observed droop is a result of an excess of low productivity journals, which contain a lower than expected number of articles.

Alternative models derived for productivity analysis have also resulted in other "law" appellations, most notably Leimkuhler's derivation (Diodato, 1994, pp. 100-101):

$$G(r) = a \ln(1 + b\,r) \tag{3.3}$$

where $G(r)$ is the cumulative number of articles contributed by journals ranked 1 through r, and a and b are parameters. Similarly, Brookes derivation (Diodato, 1994, pp. 28-29) for journal productivity takes the form

$$G(r) = a \ln(b\,r) \tag{3.4}$$

3.2.3 Zipf's Law of Word Frequencies

Zipf's law is perhaps the most widely quoted and applied empirical regularity in recorded discourse, having applications in social science disciplines such as linguistics. Philologist G. K. Zipf (1935, 1949) studied the frequency of words within a document, finding that the relationship between the frequency of a word and its rank can be represented as

$$r \times f = C \tag{3.5}$$

where r is the rank of a given word, f its frequency, and C is a constant. More generally, the law has been represented in a form more closely resembling that of Lotka, but in rank form (Egghe & Rousseau, 1990):

$$f(r) = \frac{A}{r^b} \tag{3.6}$$

where $f(r)$ is the frequency of the rth ranking word, with A and b representing parameters. Distinct words may be referred to as different *types*, with a single occurrence of a word referred to as a *token*, so that the above equation may be restated as $f(r)$ representing the number of tokens associated with the rth ranked type.

This two-parameter form of the model was further generalized by Mandelbrot (1953, 1954), sometimes called Mandelbrot's law, to include a third parameter (h) that shifts the outcome along the x-axis:

$$f(r) = \frac{A}{(1+hr)^b} \tag{3.7}$$

A variation of this distribution has the denominator as $(r + h)^b$.

Zipf equations have traditionally used a rank-frequency approach; however, size-frequency forms have also been used (Nicholls & Tague, 1987; Nelson, 1989; Ajiferuke, 1991; Wolfram 1992a) such that $f(x) = A / x^b$, where $f(x)$ represents the number of types containing x tokens. A third shift parameter can also be used in the denominator, such that

$$f(x) = \frac{A}{(x+c)^b} \tag{3.8}$$

The size-frequency form reverses the treatment of the data so that the low end of the distribution represents the many singly contributing sources, whereas in rank-frequency form, the low end of the distribution represents the most productive sources presented in rank order. This will affect the values of the parameters defining the distribution. For large data sets, the number of tokens contributed by the most productive sources generally will not be as high as the number of tokens contributed by all singly occurring sources. Therefore, the proportional contribution of the source with a rank of one will be lower than for sources of size one, thus affecting the values of the A and c parameters.

Studies of word frequency may also report a type-token ratio (i.e., the number of different words compared to the total number of words).

Other forms of word analysis are discussed in Section 3.4.

3.2.4 Other Notable Regularities

Key informetric laws appear to be quite similar to those developed in other social sciences, so it is not surprising that informetrics researchers have borrowed models from these other disciplines. Two examples merit mention.

Pareto's law, named for economist V. Pareto (1897), deals with the distribution of wealth within a community, and is formulated as

$$r = \frac{A}{y^a} \tag{3.9}$$

where r is the number of members of a community who earn more than y dollars annually, with A and a being parameters. Bookstein (1990a) has pointed out that this is a variant of Zipf's law, where y is treated as continuous instead of discrete.

The 80/20 rule, long used as a rule of thumb in commercial applications, states that 80 percent of transactions involve 20 percent of resources. This could apply, for example, to library book transactions (Trueswell, 1969). Knuth (1973) suggests that the 80/20 rule can serve as a realistic representation of the behavior of record transactions for online databases. He also notes that the rule extends to subsets of the resources, so that the top 4 percent of resources see 64 percent of the use, and so on. Other aspects of resource utilization are presented in Section 3.5.

3.3 Citation and Co-Citation Analysis

Citation analysis covers both the concept of citations and references. The two terms frequently are used interchangeably, although to be precise, each represents a different view in the citing or cited perspective (Egghe & Rousseau, 1990, p. 204). A *reference* is made within a citing document and represents an acknowledgment to another work. A *citation* represents the acknowledgment received by the cited document. Cited documents are generally older than the citing document, although in some cases references may be made to documents that are being published concurrently or that have yet to be published. The motivations for citing are varied. Often it is to acknowledge the contributions made by previous works that the citing work builds on. In the end, the act of citing is a subjective decision made by the citing author.

Researchers in scholarly communication have recognized that the act of citing and being cited creates a link between two documents, which defines a relationship. This relationship is not just limited to citing and cited documents. The set of references within a document also represents a relationship among the cited documents (see Section 3.3.2). Furthermore, two documents that cite a third document also may be thought of as having a connection to one another. Units of analysis in citation studies consist of the documents themselves, the author(s) of the documents, or less frequently, the higher level sources being cited (e.g., journals). Citation analysis can be carried out through the tedious task of tallying the references made within documents. Citation data collection has become more accessible and less labor intensive largely due to the efforts of the Institute for Scientific Information (ISI), which publishes the *Science Citation Index, Social Science Citation Index*, and *Arts and Humanities Citation Index.* With machine-readable reference and citation data now available through the ISI, citation data collection has become much more efficient.

3.3.1 Citation Measures

Citation measures may be as simple as counting the number of citations received by a given author, publication, or journal over a period of time. Like document relevance within IR systems, a citation is frequently treated as a binary value by the investigator, with no recognition of the significance of a citation or, more important, the citer's motivation for including the referenced work. At face value, citations are treated as uniformly positive recognitions of the contribution made by the author or work being cited, so the greater the number of citations an author, work, or journal receives, the greater the recognition.

Citations are made for many different reasons, which may affect the relationship between the cited and citing work, for example arguing against the cited work's findings. The practice of authors citing their own previous works, known as self-citation, is also well known (Snyder & Bonzi, 1998). In addition, citation studies do not always take into account the "success-breeds-success" phenomenon (see Section 3.8.2), wherein authors or works receive a disproportionately high number of citations because they are already highly cited. Conversely, the lack of a reference made to a work does not mean outright that there is no topical relationship between two documents. The citer may be unaware of the existence of the second document or barriers such as the language in which the second document is written may prevent the citer from recognizing a connection.

A number of techniques are used to represent and analyze citation data. These data lend themselves well to network analysis, where authors, documents, or journals and their citations may be represented as directed graphs to visually represent the connections between units (Egghe & Rousseau, 1990). Citation matrices are also useful for representing the strength of the citation relationship between the citing and cited sources.

The most widely used and, perhaps, controversial citation measure applied to journals is the *journal impact factor,* introduced by Garfield and Sher (1963). Researchers have since published many formulations of impact factors, with vigorous debate continuing on the merits of the different calculation methods used. Impact factors have also been applied to authors, groups of authors such as academic departments, and disciplines. In its general form, an impact factor (*IF*) may be calculated as

$$IF = \frac{\textit{\# of citations received by source during a specified time period}}{\textit{Total documents produced by source for that time period}} \tag{3.10}$$

In its classic form, a journal's impact factor is the number of citations the journal receives for articles published over the past two years divided by the total number of articles published by the journal during that time. Journal impact values for ISI-indexed journals, along with citation counts, appear annually in the publication *Journal Citation Reports.* Related to the journal impact factor is the journal *immediacy index,* which measures how quickly documents are cited by dividing the number of citations received by a journal in a given year for articles published in that year by the number of articles published that year.

3.3.2 Co-Citation Analysis

Co-citation analysis is used primarily to determine the existence of relationships between documents or authors. A *co-citation* is the common occurrence of two documents in the reference list of a third document. If documents are co-cited, they are assumed to be related in some way. The strength of this relationship is based on the number of documents that co-cite a document pair over a period of time. Small (1973) and Marshakova (1973) are credited with independently suggesting the use of co-citations as a measure of interdocument relatedness. The concept of co-citations can be extended to groups of documents, called literatures, where the literatures are based on authors, journals, subdisciplines, or even the overarching fields themselves. The observed patterns can be helpful in understanding scholarly communication patterns within and among the groups studied. As an assumed measure of interdocument relatedness, it also has applications for IR in determining document relevance.

The absence of co-citations between literatures also has been found to have research value. Swanson (1986, 1990) has investigated the absence of co-citations as the basis for revealing previously unknown causal connections. This can be expressed as one literature asserting that *A influences B*. In another literature, *B influences C*. Due to a lack of interaction between the two literatures, represented as an absence of co-citations, the possible connection that *A influences C* remains undiscovered. The possibility of missed causal connections has been found particularly in the medical literature, where subspecializations tend not to co-cite one another.

The related concept of bibliographic coupling, introduced by Kessler (1963), merits mention. *Bibliographic coupling*, also called *co-referencing*, is similar to co-citation analysis in that the strength of the topic relationship between two documents is measured. However, in bibliographic coupling this strength of relationship is based on the number of common references contained within both documents. So the more references two documents share, the more closely related the two documents are assumed to be. Bibliographic coupling studies are far more rare than co-citation studies.

Several data analysis methods may be used in co-citation studies. Most frequently, cluster analysis and multidimensional scaling (MDS) methods are used to explore the intellectual structure within a literature or sets of literatures. McCain (1990) provides an overview of applications of cluster analysis and MDS. In brief, units of study (authors, documents, journals, etc.) are organized into a matrix representing the pair-wise comparison of each combination of units. Co-citations are tallied for each pair. The totals for each pair represent the strength of the similarity between the two units. These values are normalized to a matrix of proximity values, for example, Pearson product-moment correlations. Cluster analysis will group units with high inter-correlations. Through hierarchical clustering, the strength of relationships between clusters may also be represented. Most statistical analysis packages will provide the option of using one or more clustering methods with MDS analysis. The MDS outcomes are represented as plots showing the relationship among units as physical proximities. Usually two-dimensional plots are used, but higher dimensions are possible, where each dimension corresponds to an influential factor to be interpreted by the investigator. It should be noted that these techniques are used for exploratory analysis resulting in supporting evidence but do not provide definitive proof of relationships or their origins.

3.3.3 Hypertext Links as "Sitations"

Citation concepts have been applied to hypertext systems, where hypertext links between documents can be thought of as a form of reference representing an acknowledgment of the linked document. Citation analysis methods have recently been applied most notably to the Web environment. The term *sitation* has been used by Rousseau (1997) to represent a hypertext linkage between Web sites, to distinguish between citations received by published works and hypertext linkages between two documents.

Clearly there are differences between the two concepts. Once a document is published in print form, it is permanently part of the research landscape, with no changes in the list of referenced items. Web documents can be more temporary due to the dynamic nature of the Web. Linkages within Web documents may change, or the document itself may disappear. References in printed documents also generally point to older documents. On the Web, document age is not an issue, making concurrent linkages possible. It also makes it possible to have sitation loops, where document A links to document B, document B links to document C, and document C links back to document A. In his study, Rousseau examines the distribution of domain names and links between Web sites, finding that both may be adequately modeled with a Lotka distribution.

The concept of a *Web impact factor* has been proposed by Ingwersen (1998), where the Web site and its individual pages correspond to journals and articles respectively. This impact factor is calculated as the number of link pages pointing to a given site/domain, both the external and internal links, divided by the number of pages on a given Web site. Like the standard impact factor, the Web impact factor may serve as an indicator of a Web site's significance.

3.4 Document and Co-Word Analysis

In Section 3.2.3, Zipf's law for document word frequencies was introduced. Informetric studies based on document attributes and co-word relationships within documents represent a departure from traditional studies, although the techniques used are largely the same.

3.4.1 Document Attributes

Document attributes include the document length in words or pages, referenced sources contained within a document, title word length, and the number of descriptors assigned per document. Document length studies have examined how the word or page lengths of documents such as journal articles change over time (Little, Harris, & Nicholls, 1990). The number of references within a document may similarly be examined within or across fields (Yitzhaki & Ben-Tamar, 1991). To normalize the number of references, document length is also factored in to account for differences in reference frequency due to document length.

Title content analysis as encapsulations of document topicality has received little study. Wilson (1999) points out that title length studies can take two approaches: title word length or title informativeness. Title word lengths include all words, whereas title informativeness studies focus on substantive words within titles, ignoring non-content-bearing words.

Finally, the level of assignment of subject terms/descriptors to documents, referred to as *indexing exhaustivity*, may be studied (Bird, 1974). Few terms assigned to a document are indicative of low exhaustivity, while the assignment of larger numbers of terms increases exhaustivity. Changes in assignment characteristics over time have also been studied (Chapter 5, Section 5.3).

Studies of document attributes have revealed that most, if not all, of the resulting distributions do not follow the same inverse relationship observed in classic informetric law studies. Instead, the distributions have modes greater than one term per document and more closely resemble Poisson-like distributions. This observation also applies to query exhaustivity studies. Potential distributions for modeling these phenomena are discussed in Chapter 4, Section 4.4.4.

3.4.2 Co-Word Studies

As with co-citation analysis, co-word analysis has been used to determine the strength of relationships among textual containers, whether the containers are full-text documents, their surrogates, fields within documents (e.g., titles, descriptors), or queries submitted to IR systems. Techniques for the analysis of word co-occurrence are generally similar to those used for co-citation analysis, consisting of cluster analyses and MDS methods.

Co-occurrence analysis of document content is usually performed on substantive keywords appearing in a bibliographic database record field such as the title, descriptors, or abstract. These fields best encapsulate the topicality of a document, although keywords from the body of text could be used as well. The benefits of co-word analysis can be mixed depending on the application. For example, Courtial, Callon, & Sigogneau (1993) applied clustering techniques using title word co-occurrence on patent data, which resulted in well-defined clusters of topics. Peat & Willett (1991), however, conclude that the co-occurrence of terms within documents in an IR system has limited utility for query expansion applications. Leydesdorff (1997) also observes that due to the ambiguities of language, co-word analysis of full-text document content has limited applications.

Co-word analysis can be applied to smaller containers of text, such as queries submitted to IR systems (see Chapter 6, Section 6.4).

3.5 Resource Utilization

Traditional studies of resource usage have centered on the document circulation process within libraries. Today, resource utilization may also extend to records accessed within databases, or hits on Web sites. This process is treated separately from citation analysis, which also can be argued to be a form of use, due to other confounding factors that may arise in the analysis of document usage that are not part of the citation process. Also, because the processes involved, at least for circulation data, are tied to a specific environment (e.g., a library or information center), to which the process of circulation is unique, the treatment will be brief.

3.5.1 Circulation Studies

Document circulation within libraries presents several challenges. First, one is dealing with tangible resources that cannot be borrowed by more than one person at one time. Second, the loan period for the circulation essentially means that an item cannot be circulated to anyone else until the item is returned. The length of the loan period will also affect how many times a document circulates over a given period of time. As with citation analysis, there will be a sizeable number of documents that do not circulate, called "dead items" or the "zero class" of circulations, due to their lack of availability or minimal interest to users.

Egghe and Rousseau (1990, sect. II.6) outline the three main shapes taken by circulation distributions when plotted on semi-logarithmic scales, with number of items circulated on the y-axis (logarithmic scale) and the number of times an item circulates on the x-axis. What results is a decreasing straight line, a line that is slightly concave, or slightly convex. They also outline a model to explain the observed straight-line phenomenon.

Straight counts of circulation recorded by electronic circulation systems will allow the investigator to determine the utilization of resources over a given time period but will not reveal changes in circulation patterns as the document ages, unless a record of when each document circulates is kept. In this case it is the obsolescence of the document that is of interest. Obsolescence concepts are dealt with in Section 3.6.

3.5.2 Electronic Resource Usage

Use studies also extend to the utilization of electronic resources such as database records, Web page visits, or digital libraries. Because of the recency of this area, little informetric research has been conducted on usage patterns of electronic records. The use of transaction logs of database sessions to understand usage behavior has been investigated for over thirty years. However, the primary studies to date have focused on transaction logs for specific resources (e.g., Jones, Cunningham, & McNab, 1998; Wolfram & Xie, 2000) or the Web as a whole (e.g., Nielsen [1997], whose Web site at http://www.useit.com also provides access to many other studies), but few studies in which model development was a key goal have been carried out to date. Usage studies will need to apply different ideas and assumptions than circulation studies because there are no loan periods and models based on queuing theory need not apply with multi-user access databases. However, single concurrent usage assumptions may need to be made in database environments where database updating will require locking individual records or documents from other users for the duration of the update to maintain database integrity.

Many issues associated with usage of electronic resources, particularly on the Internet, remain to be explored. Investigators examining these areas must recognize that the ideas and assumptions applied to informetric studies in the tangible, print-based world may need to be modified for the electronic world. See, for example, Egghe (2000), who outlines some of the difficulties associated with informetric analysis on the Internet.

3.6 Growth and Obsolescence

The growth of literatures and their obsolescence, also called *aging*, are treated in the same section because they represent the initial and final stages of the information life cycle. Growth studies investigate regularities in the creation of literatures or documents over time, which is equated with the growth of information. Obsolescence in informetrics refers to the decline in use of a document or in citations received by a document over time. Obsolescence could be easily treated as an aspect of citation analysis for journal articles or resource utilization for monographic sources, but the focus here is on the tail end of the information life cycle, where document usage or the number of citations received slows down to a point where for all purposes the document is no longer cited. Growth and obsolescence studies are also more time-dependent than most other areas of informetrics, where time is not treated as a variable but more as a boundary defining which data are collected. The focus of growth and obsolescence studies may be at the individual document level or may extend up to the journal, subdiscipline, or discipline level.

3.6.1 Literature Growth

Studies of literature growth have been conducted since the early days of statistical bibliography (Wilson, 1999) but have not been as abundant as other areas of informetrics. See for example Meadows (2000), who provides an historical perspective on general growth patterns in journal literature. The main obstacle has been access to appropriate data sets that are truly representative of the literature being studied and that exist for sufficiently long periods of time, from which regularities can be observed. In more recent years, bibliographic databases have provided primary sources for access to growth data. Price (1963) has been a notable pioneer in this area. He observed that the growth in the number of scientific periodicals since the mid-seventeenth century has been exponential. The same patterns have been observed for different disciplines, or specializations within disciplines. For example, Tabah (1992) observes that linear growth occurred in the literature of superconductivity from the 1960s to the mid-1980s, but exponential growth has occurred since that time period due to recent discoveries in the field that have prompted research growth.

Several types of distributions have been observed in growth studies. These are depicted in Figure 3.4. Growth data are frequently modeled in cumulative form so that values from subsequent years can be added to previous years, resulting in more dramatic graphs. A linear model is indicative of the steady production of documents within the subject area investigated. Exponential growth is representative of a very active area of research where increasing numbers of documents are produced over time. The exponential model, widely used in the biological sciences to describe population growth, is useful for modeling bursts in literature production. As with any population, exponential growth must slow as a result of declining resources, or in the case of literature growth, the lack of additional researchers to contribute additional documents. A third model that has been used that takes into account the slowdown in exponential growth is the S-shaped logistic model. The logistic model has its shortcomings and presents greater challenges for modeling data (Efthimiadis,1990). Other models that more flexibly model the above patterns have also been proposed. Egghe and Rao (1992) compare common models against twenty data sets from different disciplines. Generally, the greatest growth rates have been observed in the sciences. More recently, Saxena, Gupta, and Jauhari (2001) have examined six families of models for literature growth studies and argue that there is no one general model for all situations, but rather more appropriate models are determined by the situation.

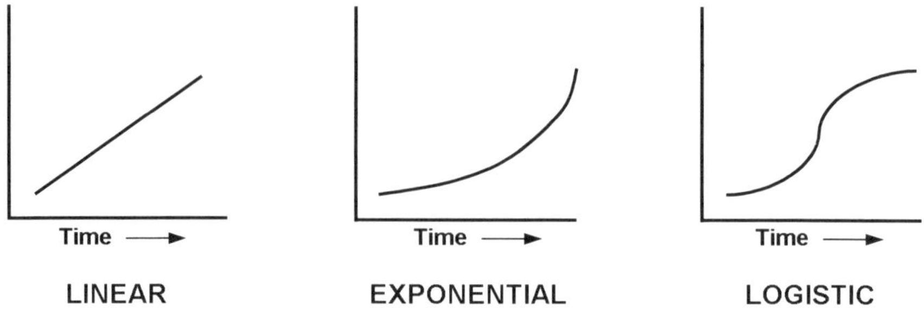

Figure 3.4. Examples of Literature Growth Patterns

Although growth studies have been primarily applied to literatures, the methods may be applied to other information production process environments, for example the growth of indexes in IR systems or the assignment of index terms in databases (Long, Barnhard, & Levy, 1967) or thesauri (Henry & Diodato, 1991) (see Chapter 5, Section 5.7).

3.6.2 Obsolescence of Literatures

Obsolescence involves the decline in use of documents over time. This is most easily studied using document citation counts, where the continued citations received by a document are taken as an indication of its value to a discipline. As new documents are published in the discipline, citation counts for a given document usually decline as the research front of the discipline moves on. Eventually a document may no longer be cited. It has become obsolete. Some documents, on the other hand, continue to see high levels of recognition long after their publication. They become citation classics, which authors will continue to cite in recognition of their contributions. Very few documents fall into this category. Within a literature group there are significantly more documents that are never cited at all, and although published, they remain unacknowledged.

For documents that receive sizeable numbers of citations, the distribution of citations over time is generally unimodal, with the mode dependent on how quickly document findings are cited after publication. The document begins to receive citations after an initial lag resulting from the publication delay of works citing the document and the time needed to carry out research influenced by the initial document. It is also possible that a document will remain uncited or rarely cited for long periods of time because its contributions are not initially recognized or valued by the research community. Over time, more researchers become aware of the document's value, so the citation count grows. As new documents contributing to the subject area are published, the citation focus shifts to these new documents, resulting in a decline of references being made to the initial document. Citation classics, however, enjoy continued recognition, with no indication of decline in citations for many years.

The concept of obsolescence itself is relatively straightforward, but there are two main approaches that may be used in collecting and analyzing obsolescence data. Measures used in obsolescence are usually tied to one of these approaches.

3.6.3 Synchronous versus Diachronous Studies of Obsolescence

Most obsolescence studies have used a synchronous approach, which examines the distribution of the ages of references appearing in a document set over a specified time, such as a year. This approach provides a cross-section of citing behavior within a literature for that point in time. Data are readily available for synchronous studies through citation indexes. Due to the skew observed in the distribution of citation ages, the "median citation age" is used as an indicator of how quickly a literature obsolesces. For example, in some scientific and technological disciplines, the median citation age is quite short because of the rapid turnover in developments, while in the humanities, the median citation age is usually much longer, indicating a slower rate of obsolescence. A measure used to describe the recency of citations in a document or document set proposed by Price (1970), called the Price Index, is the proportion of citations no more than five years old divided by the total number of citations. Several equations have shown some promise for modeling synchronous obsolescence data, most notably the generalized gamma distribution (Tahai & Rigsby, 1998) (see Chapter 4, Section 4.4.4).

Diachronous studies of obsolescence follow the citation behaviors of documents over time, usually from the time they are published. This allows researchers to track the citations received by documents as they age. As with growth studies, models have been proposed to describe the range of observed behaviors in citation distributions. Avramescu (1979) has proposed a continuous model with sufficient flexibility to fit flat distributions of rarely cited documents, unimodal distributions for documents with a distinct growth and decline of citations, and citation classics for which obsolescence is not observed for many years.

A hybrid method combining features of synchronous and diachronous methods, called diasynchronous obsolescence, may also be used. Diasynchronous studies make use of synchronous data collection methods over different time periods (Line, 1993).

Obsolescence can be thought of as analogous to radioactive decay. The term *half-life* in diachronous obsolescence studies is used as a measure of the time in which half of the currently cited literature is published

(Burton & Kebler, 1960). The definition may vary depending on the unit being measured, for example, citations received versus given (Diodato, 1994). The term is also occasionally used in synchronous studies.

Obsolescence studies are not without their critics, particularly because it can be argued that they may not measure "actual" obsolescence but rather "apparent" obsolescence. Results using synchronous and diachronous studies are often different and do not take into account the growth of literatures, which could affect citation counts received by a given paper. Whether synchronous or diachronous approaches are used to study obsolescence, the methods can be quite useful in identifying the practical shelf life of documents within disciplines, which can be used as a decision support tool in the development of retention schedules and space planning.

3.7 Science Indicators and Policy

The area of scientific indicators deals largely with the measurement and summarization of national, field-specific, or institutional productivity in science and technology activities. These areas of study fall primarily within the domain of scientometrics. The data employed in these studies will often go beyond sources of recorded discourse such as publications and scholarly communication, and may include data sources of economic and sociological interest. Results of scientometric research frequently lead to recommendations for science policy. Although overlapping with informetrics, the applications of science indicator research are peripheral to the main focus of this work and are presented very briefly. Geisler (2000) provides a much more detailed treatment of these areas.

3.7.1 Science Indicators

Science indicators are measures that provide a sense of the state of a scientific discipline or scientific activities within a geographic area (Diodato, 1994). Data collection and analysis techniques used in the development of measures are similar to those already discussed and may involve input and, more likely, output measures. A typical input measure is research and development (R&D) intensity, measured as the ratio of investments in R&D to the gross national product of a nation (Geisler, 2000). Output measures include metrics of economics such as funding received and employment data. Bibliometric measures dealing with citations, publication productivity, author productivity, and patent-based measures may also be applied. In the United States, the National Science Board's *Science Indicators* series publishes quantitative data on science and technology activities. With the growing interest in scientometrics, particularly through conferences sponsored by ISSI and other organizations, science indicator literature has expanded greatly.

3.7.2 Science Policy Development

Science policy development can be thought of as the qualitative recommendations that arise from the quantitative analysis of science indicator research. With recent focus shifts in national research funding in the sciences, at least in the United States, recommendations for sound science policy development may be made with supporting evidence from scientometric studies. Policy development also extends to more regional or local applications, for example, where promotion and tenure decisions for faculty members at colleges and universities are based in part on citation measures. Recommendations may result in strategies to address needs to increase the scientific workforce or to emphasize research areas where greater effort and support are needed. In a field that is sometimes criticized for being too theoretical and not very practical, the development of science policy serves as an important example of the application of informetric/scientometric methodologies.

3.8 Theory Development and Informetric Model Generalization

It becomes clear from a simple visual inspection of equations used in informetrics that many of the "reverse J-shaped" models used in different areas of informetrics are very similar to one another. The question arises whether the models developed for specific data measures may be generalized so that a unified approach may be adopted when undertaking informetric research. Also, with larger data sets now being fitted to traditional models, it becomes evident that traditional laws do not always apply, prompting the need for more sophisticated models that can account for a wider range of observed behavior. Once a better understanding of the range of observed phenomena has been reached, empirical regularities in recorded discourse lead to theory development to explain observed behaviors. Both of these areas have been challenging researchers for over fifty years. Considerable progress has been made in generalization and theory development, but consensus among informetrics researchers on the ultimate causes and explanations for observed behavior remains elusive, as does agreement on assumptions made in developing more generalized models.

3.8.1 Generalized Distributions for Informetric Modeling

The equivalence of many classic informetric laws and distributions has been shown by several authors. In particular, Chen and Leimkuhler (1986) derive a common functional relationship among the three classic informetric laws using an index approach that removes the gaps observed in the tail of the distributions. This is echoed by Bookstein (1990a, 1990b, 1997), who argues that many of the observed regularities in the biological and social sciences represent variations of a single regularity. He demonstrates the relationship between the Bradford Leimkuhler's laws, the Lotka and Zipf laws, and finally the Leimkuhler and Lotka laws. Egghe (1988) also has demonstrated the equivalence of a Bradford formulation with Brookes law and that Brookes law is asymptotically equivalent to Zipf's law. For an overview of earlier contributions to general informetric models, consult Hubert (1981), who analyzes general models proposed by Price (1976), Bookstein (1977), and Brookes (1977).

The need for generalized distributions with broad applications has resulted in the derivation of a number of more sophisticated models. In the pursuit of commonalities between different informetric phenomena, relatively simple models developed for specific data types evolve into more sophisticated models with additional parameters to make the models more flexible for a broader range of data. In addition, these models incorporate mixing distribution to better represent the variable nature of the phenomena studied. Functional forms of several such promising models such as the generalized Waring and generalized inverse Gaussian-Poisson (GIGP) distributions are introduced in Section 4.4.3.

The motivation for undertaking research can impact whether an investigator selects a dynamic, but challenging, distribution like the GIGP, or chooses a more parsimonious model that reflects the shape of the observed data but may not provide as good a fit. There is always the desire to simplify observed behaviors. Clearly, models most closely resembling the observed data patterns are preferable, but what of the underlying assumptions that resulted in the development of the models? The model that most closely fits the observed data sometimes is not the one that provides the strongest theoretical foundation for its use.

3.8.2 Theory Development

Many early models used in informetric studies provided no explanation of why the observed data behaviors exist. Theory development to explain observed regularities continues to be an important area of investigation within informetrics. Several general models have led to theory development of informetric phenomena. Among the earliest, Zipf (1949), in offering an explanation for observed regularities in human behavior, established "The Principle of Least Effort," where humans will minimize effort for different types of gains. The principle is argued to be responsible for many aspects of social interaction, including the use of human language in speech and text. The principle explains why short words are used more frequently than long words, and why we see the inverse relationship in the distribution of words, regardless of the language studied.

Price (1976) proposed a cumulative advantage distribution based on a classic urn model to explain the strongly inverse relationships observed in citations, author productivity, and journal productivity. In this model an equal number of red balls and black balls are placed in a series of urns; a red ball signifies "success" and a black ball signifies "failure." A ball is initially drawn from the first urn. If it is a red ball, the red ball is replaced and another quantity *c* of red balls is added. Balls continue to be drawn and replaced from the urn as long as a red ball is retrieved. If a black ball is drawn, the user moves on to the next urn. It is clear that half of the urns will result in an initial failure. But if a red ball is initially drawn, the probability of drawing a red ball the next time around increases. Observed regularities in informetric data, such as citations, publications, and resource utilization, have been attributed to the *success-breeds-success* phenomenon, which results in high success by a small number of sources. So, for example, in the case of citations, the likelihood of a document being cited increases if the document has already been cited. This phenomenon has also been referred to as the *Mathew Effect* by Merton (1968) in describing the added recognition bestowed upon scientists with already high recognition over scientists with lesser status who but have made comparable contributions. More recently, Egghe and Rousseau (1995) have expanded on the success-breeds-success principle by developing a general theory of source-item relationships that incorporate time-dependencies.

Among the more intriguing theoretical contributions are those by Haitun (1982a, 1982b, 1982c), who presented arguments for the existence of two types of distribution studies, called "Zipfian" and "Gaussian." Gaussian distributions are characterized by primarily unimodal characteristics based on normal distributions, representative of phenomena in the natural sciences. Human-centered activities, however, are characterized by Zipfian distributions, which are reverse J-shaped. It is an intriguing hypothesis but does not address some of the human-centered non-reverse J-shaped observed behaviors in informetrics.

3.8.3 Additional Challenges in Informetric Modeling

The quest for the ubiquitous distribution for modeling all informetric phenomena continues. Classic models have been found to be adequate for relatively small data sets. In today's electronic world where large data sets are readily available, most existing distributions often fall short, particularly failing to adequately model data in the tail end of the distribution. Most informetric models thus far have been univariate and have not taken into account the influence of important contributing factors such as time on the resulting distributions. Multivariate models, in which one variable is dependent on one or more other variables, are the future of informetrics, as are models that can deal with changes in distribution shapes over time.

The tremendous growth of electronic systems presents additional large data sets to which existing informetric modeling techniques may be applied. The comparative newness and broad usage of information environments such as the Web and communication tools such as electronic mail, mailing lists (e.g., listservs), and real-time communication tools present additional processes to which informetric models may be applied. Does the usage of these environments produce regularities similar to more traditional communication and publication outlets, or does the nature of the electronic medium result in other patterns requiring alternate models? To date, research efforts in these areas have been limited.

3.9 Summary and Additional Readings

From its beginnings as statistical bibliography, the field of informetrics has grown to include all aspects of the quantitative study of recorded discourse. The boundaries of informetrics and its subfields, however, continue to fuel debate. Whether one uses the label bibliometrics, scientometrics, or cybermetrics, a common foundation of methodologies exists to unite these cognate areas. As the field has grown, so have the sizes of the data sets studied. It is not unusual today to see studies consisting of millions of data items.

Informetric research has sometimes been criticized for being old wine in new bottles, with established methods simply being applied to new data sets to provide corroboratory evidence of the empirical regularities that are already known. There is value in this pursuit when combined with contributions on other fronts such as model and theory development. Theory development continues to provide new perspectives on informetric phenomena, although the connections between theory and practice have not always been made. Despite this, the future of informetric research is promising. Practical applications for informetrics abound, as this work will outline for IR research in subsequent chapters.

The reader is encouraged to consult additional sources for more detailed coverage of informetric topics. Only a small number of monographs have been devoted to informetrics as a whole or its allied areas. The primary monograph published to date is Egghe and Rousseau's *Introduction to Informetrics* (1990), which provides not only detailed coverage of the scope of the discipline but also mathematical and statistical concepts useful in informetric research. The authors make few assumptions about the reader's background in quantitative methods, but some knowledge of elementary statistics, algebra, and discrete mathematics is helpful. Wilson's (1999) chapter on informetrics in the *Annual Review of Information Science and Technology* (*ARIST*), although not a monograph, is strongly recommended for its thorough treatment of the field, its subspecialties, research trends, and extensive bibliography of informetrics research. Diodato (1994) has developed a useful reference work on key informetric concepts, providing examples of published research incorporating the concepts covered.

Other monographic works provide more specialized, in-depth coverage of the field. Borgman (1990) brings together research and overview papers on scholarly communication and bibliometrics, with an emphasis on citation/co-citation analysis and journal studies. More recently, the *Web of Knowledge: A Festschrift in Honor of Eugene Garfield,* edited by Cronin and Atkins (2000), contains chapters on informetric topics by leading researchers in the social sciences. Geisler's *The Metrics of Science and Technology* (2000) includes a chapter on bibliometrics; however, the term *scientometrics* is noticeably absent throughout most of the work. Leydesdorff's (2001) second edition of *The Challenge of Scientometrics* includes many chapters of interest for broader informetric study and other areas of information science. Baayen's (2001) detailed monograph on modeling word frequency distributions is recommended for readers with strong quantitative backgrounds. Although focusing on word frequencies, the topic coverage, which includes distributions for modeling data, assumptions of sample randomness, and model fitting techniques, provides valuable insights for informetric studies in general.

Several English-language journals merit mention for the publication of informetric research, although a number of non-English-language journals also publish sizeable numbers of papers on informetrics. Most notable of the English-language journals is *Scientometrics*, which, in addition to scientometric research, publishes bibliometric/informetric studies. *Social Studies of Science* also publishes scientometric research. Other key journals are *Journal of the American Society for Information Science and Technology*, *Information Processing & Management*, and *Journal of Documentation*. The electronic journal *Cybermetrics* (http://www.cindoc.csic.es/cybermetrics/cybermetrics.html) provides a forum for the publication of Internet-based studies. Finally, the proceedings of the biennial conferences of the International Society for Scientometrics and Informetrics contain papers on all aspects of informetrics. Proceedings have been published as monographs, conference proceedings, or special issues of *Scientometrics*.

4

Data Collection and Model Development Techniques

In mathematics you don't understand things. You just get used to them.

—John von Neumann (1903–1957)

4.1 Overview

As with any empirical study, informetric investigations are only as good as the data sets collected from which models are developed and understanding of phenomena is gained. The purpose of this chapter is to outline data collection and model development techniques used in informetrics. These techniques may then be applied to the observable IR system content and usage processes covered in Chapters 5 and 6. The chapter sections are organized around the activities needed to study quantifiable characteristics of IR system content and use.

Chen and Leimkuhler (1986) outline the four areas that have shaped informetric modeling research: equation formulation, parameter estimation, goodness-of-fit, and determination of the underlying explanatory mechanisms. Before models can be developed, data representing the information production process (IPP) being studied must be available. Relevant data may be extracted from a number of sources, both electronic and paper-based. Next, representation and storage of data for manipulation are determined. These may range from simple text files, to spreadsheets, to databases. From the raw data sets, data distributions are created. Based on the data distribution forms, candidate theoretical distributions to model the observed data are selected. Fitting techniques are then applied to determine appropriate parameters for each model and the goodness-of-fit that determines the best model.

The question arises why one would need to fit the data to a mathematical model, when the observed distribution is readily available. Mathematical models are used as generalizations of the empirical distributions. The models, at their most basic level, are used to describe observed behavior of the IPPs (see Chapter 3, Section 3.1.1) studied and are assumed to represent the characteristics of the larger population being studied. Second, they may serve as predictive tools, where given the probability of occurrence, one can predict the likelihood of a source with x items. Third, models can be useful in shaping explanations of observed behaviors.

Several assumptions are made in this chapter regarding the reader's familiarity with mathematical and statistical methods. Although the focus of this work is applied rather than theoretical, it is assumed that the reader has some familiarity with probability theory and an understanding of descriptive and inferential statistical methods. Familiarity with computer programming is needed to apply some of the data manipulation and modeling techniques covered, or statistical and mathematical modeling software also can be used.

4.2 Data Types and Sources

Data used in informetric studies of IR systems may come from several sources and may initially be text-based or numeric. Ultimately, all raw data will be converted to numeric format for analysis, whether collected manually from print sources or automatically from electronic sources. With enormous quantities of information now available in structured electronic databases, the process of identifying and extracting data has become much easier, although manual confirmation is still needed to assess data quality or to reveal possible outliers or glitches in the data set.

4.2.1 Sources for Data

The manual collection of data is always possible by going directly to print-based sources. Normally the raw data item counts within sources are not provided, requiring that these values be tabulated manually. Fortunately, with IR systems, data tabulation usually can be automated where the identification of items within sources is straightforward, although manual definition of search parameters may be necessary when selective extraction of database subsets is undertaken. Also, because electronic sources may not contain the full range of data needed, manual collection may still be required.

Electronic databases with structured content provide the most easily selected and manipulated data. Normally, data are partitioned into fields, making it easy to extract only the data of interest. Data of interest may be returned to the user by querying the system. Some systems will permit the downloading or logging of retrieved data in user-specified formats. Others may require successive screen captures. In either case, extraneous content may find its way into the raw data files, requiring editing. Data from highly structured bibliographic and full text databases are easily extracted through the use of search commands that allow field limiters along with search parameters (Wormell, 1998). These commands will vary depending on the database vendor (e.g., DIALOG, OVID, H. W. Wilson). For citation studies, the Institute for Scientific Information databases are invaluable for collecting citation and co-citation data.

Key issues investigators must contend with before extracting data from proprietary databases include the following:

- Will duplicate records/documents be an issue, particularly when searching across multiple database files with possible content overlap?
- Are there sufficiently well-defined fields available to limit documents retrieved, for example by author, subject/descriptor, source, keyword, or complete field for titles, or by publication date?
- Is output ranking by frequency of occurrence supported? This is especially useful for analyses examining highly productive IPPs.
- Are there any restrictions that limit the purpose for which the data will be used? It is always a good idea to contact the database vendors for permission to use data sets derived from their databases beforehand.

Ingwersen and Christensen (1997) discuss several database-specific examples from widely used database vendors showing how these issues may be resolved.

Increasingly, data from Web servers are being used as a source for database content studies. Bar-Ilan (2001) outlines the types of data collection that have been used to date for Web-based studies. Document sources are usually less structured, making the extraction of field-specific data more difficult. Most Web page documents at present do not make effective use of <META> tag features to provide a subject access point to the document. Searches based on the content of widely used tagged fields such as <TITLE> are supported by some search engines. Search limiters based on geography, Internet domain, or dates of creation/modification are also possible. For example, Rousseau (1997) demonstrated how data on the distribution of domain names and links could be extracted by using the "link:" limiter in the AltaVista search engine. Similarly, Larson (1996) performed a co-"sitation" analysis among Web sites available through AltaVista dealing with geographic information systems and satellite remote sensing. Given the volatility of the search engine market and the ongoing changes made to service features, data that could be collected at one time may not be available in the future.

Transaction logs of user data sessions are generally more difficult to obtain, unless one relies on search sources within one's control such as intranet search engines. These logs may contain user query formulations (Spink, Wolfram, Jansen, & Saracevic, 2001) or user browsing habits (Catledge & Pitkow, 1995). Commercial vendors are usually unwilling to share usage data with external researchers. Understandably, they wish to protect the privacy of their users. They also wish to maintain their competitive edge by not revealing any secrets of the inner workings of their service.

In some situations, human intervention may still be needed when decisions about data recognition and inclusion are ambiguous. An example of this is subject classification of queries submitted to an IR system. In Ross and Wolfram (2000) and Spink, Wolfram, Jansen, and Saracevic (2001), manual categorization was initially used to identify the subject content of Web queries. Automatic indexing routines could be applied to identify and include or exclude words based on linguistic rules (Pu, Chuang, & Yang, 2002), but ultimately in situations of uncertainty, human intervention may be needed.

The unit of data being studied can present problems for researchers, particularly in the newer areas of investigation dealing with the Internet, where units of measure may be ill defined. Jansen and Pooch (2001) review the numerous definitions and types of data used in IR research using traditional bibliographic IR systems, OPACs, and Web search engines. A comparison of studies from each category reveals the lack of equivalent metrics between the different types of systems, making comparisons across system studies difficult. Definitions for data units in Web-based user studies can be quite variable at this early stage of research, with analysis possible at three levels of user interaction: the session level, constituting the entire sequence of queries entered by a user; the query level, consisting of a string of zero or more characters used as the basis for a search; and the term level, where a term is delimited by nonalphanumeric characters. Within each of these levels other decisions remain. For example:

- User identifiers are most frequently tied to a specific computer as a "cookie," not to a specific person. Can it be concluded that all queries with the same identifier represent the same user? A case can be made for equivalence for personal machines, but not for public access machines that are shared by many individuals.

- If time data associated with queries are available, do queries submitted hours apart constitute the same session, or do they constitute a different session for the same identifier? What defines the boundary of a session? There is no standardized measure for what constitutes a session, so the investigator should indicate how a session is defined.
- Does one count the request for an additional page of results from a search engine as a new query, or is it simply a repeat of the initial query requesting the first set of results? From the user perspective, they are the same query and should be treated as such.
- Does a string of characters with no valid terms constitute a query? Both approaches are justifiable. If these strings constitute valid queries, then the count of queries with zero terms will be higher than if the strings were not identified as valid queries.
- For term definitions, do strings of characters such as e-mail addresses or uniform resource locators (URLs) that contain periods, slashes, and other nonalphanumeric characters constitute a single term, or multiple terms? Does one define a term by what the user intended or by how the system interprets what is entered? The search intent is for a singular object, but nonalphanumeric characters are usually treated as term delimiters. The investigator may wish to develop parsing routines that distinguish electronic address components from standard term delimiters.
- Does one treat words that can serve as search operators (e.g., AND, OR, NOT) as terms or strictly as operators? What if they are entered as part of a text phrase? The focus of the research may cause these tokens to be treated either way.

4.2.2 Sampling

Data sets used in informetric studies are assumed to represent a random sample of the overall population being studied (e.g., the study of author productivity of a subset of researchers in a given discipline) or the population itself (e.g., the study of the word frequency distribution of a document). These assumptions have implications for statistical validity and hypothesis testing (see Section 4.5). With today's largely electronic data sets, it becomes possible to include millions of observations within the data set. Even so, the population being studied may be too large to be included or identified. With very large data sets it becomes more difficult to model as a result of the increase in the sizes and the larger number of source types that need to be fitted. More opportunities are introduced for the observed distribution to fail being adequately fitted to theoretical models (see Section

4.5.5). Sampling provides an alternative to working with the complete population. A representative sample of the data population can reveal the overall characteristics without having to analyze many millions of observations. With such large populations, how can one ensure that one has selected a representative sample from which overall population characteristics can be determined? Several sampling options are available when complete data sets are difficult to obtain:

- **Linear systematic or straight sampling**: Every *n*th observation is included in the data set. This method has the advantage of being simple to implement. The main drawback is that it does not take into account possible clumping characteristics within the population.
- **Random sampling:** A subset of the original data set is randomly selected. Similar concerns exist as with straight sampling.
- **Stratified sampling**: This method uses proportional or disproportional representation of data from different categories of data. Key categories are first identified, from which straight random sampling is used within the categories.

A small number of studies have explored sampling methods for IR system data to estimate population characteristics and sizes. Henzinger, Heydon, Mitzenmacher, and Najork (2000) explore different methods for sampling Web URLs based on its hyperlink structure to be able to characterize overall Web characteristics. Through the use of random walks using hyperlinks, they devise a method that achieves near-uniform samples that take into account linking characteristics and document dependence that can skew samples.

Ozmutlu, Spink, and Ozmutlu (2002) have studied the impact of sample size on outcomes for the mean numbers of queries submitted per user based on study of queries submitted to a search engine. They developed an unbiased, proportional sampling technique based on Poisson arrival process assumptions for a large Web query data log. A Poisson sampling mechanism was suggested over a straight sampling method because the process of submitting queries to a search engine is assumed to be a stochastic arrival process, thereby giving each user session an unbiased opportunity for selection. Changes in sample characteristics were compared over ten different sampling rates. They demonstrated that relatively small sample sizes still preserve the overall characteristics of the complete data set when using this method. With classic reverse J-shaped informetric distributions, the height and tail of the distributions are directly affected by the size of the data set, but averages can still be similar to that of the complete data set.

One must also consider whether one samples at the informetric source or item level. The organization of the raw data may dictate which is feasible. Sampling at the item level will not provide a complete portrait of any single source if straight count sampling is used, whereas sampling at the source level reduces the number of sources included in the study set.

4.3 Data Storage and Processing

Several options exist for raw data processing and storage. Each has its own advantages and disadvantages. Options selected will depend on what types of analyses will be performed, the method used for the analysis, and the amount of flexibility needed in data manipulation. Computer applications used for numeric and textual data processing provide useful structures in which to store and manipulate raw data observations.

4.3.1 Raw versus Aggregate Data Storage

Whether one uses raw data or relies on aggregate data (i.e., the tabulated data representing the observed distribution) will depend on the type of analysis to be performed. In most cases, aggregate data are used by the processing routines for modeling purposes, whether data relate to frequency distributions or co-occurrence studies. The advantage of leaving data in their raw format is that in multidimensional IPPs the connections between sources and items are not lost. Each data observation retains its "identity" and is not lumped together with the other observations. Ultimately, data will need to be aggregated to develop distributions. Some storage mechanisms such as spreadsheet and database software can facilitate data aggregation.

4.3.2 Text Files

ASCII or text files are a very basic way of storing data requiring the least amount of storage space of the methods discussed. Data may need to be put in this form to be compatible with modeling routines developed by the user or borrowed from mathematical and statistical software libraries. Raw data or aggregated distribution data may be stored, depending on the routines used. Data stored in text files permit no internal mechanisms for processing the data. The files are simply a container for the data and require external mechanisms to perform any summarization or presentation of the data.

4.3.3 Spreadsheet and Statistical Software

Spreadsheet software has evolved to include many useful mathematical and statistical operations for at least preprocessing of data, if not for modeling purposes as well. The user-friendly plotting capabilities with logarithmic scaling alone make this software invaluable for some types of modeling techniques such as least squares estimation (see Section 4.5.3). Built-in tools for data consolidation and sorting, along with tools for the calculation of descriptive and inferential statistics, allow data analysis to be undertaken with minimal effort. Statistical software such as SPSS, SAS, or Minitab will provide a broader array of statistical options.

One drawback of spreadsheet software for large, raw data sets is that there is at present a limit of 64K rows of observations in most packages. This is not a problem for aggregate data already in distribution form where the number of unique data types usually consists of less than several hundred rows of data even for large data sets. For large quantities of raw data storage that exceed the limits of spreadsheet and statistical software, such as index contents or user log data records, DBMS software provides a better alternative.

4.3.4 Database Management Systems

Other than spreadsheet software, no structured storage mechanism other than relational DBMSs provides a comparable level of flexibility for the representation and aggregation of raw data. The ability to create tables and establish links between the tables permits easy access to all data of the information production process studied and establishes a connection between sources and items, particularly for multidimensional IPPs. Although highly usable for strictly numeric data, the advantages of using a DBMS for quantitative analysis are clearer for large textual data sets, where parsing and recognition of individual observations as types and tokens may be carried out using the programming capabilities built into many DBMSs. Once stored, tabulation of distributions can be easily performed using queries formulated with Structured Query Language (SQL).

As an example, consider the IPP of index term generation within an IR system. The IR system documents represent sources, which generate index terms as items. Within this environment a second IPP may also be studied, where each unique index term (i.e., the source or type) generates occurrences of the type (items or tokens). In the former case, the distribution of index term exhaustivities is studied, in the latter it is the distribution of index term frequencies. These data can be stored as a set of three tables within a relational DBMS. The original documents are initially stored in their own table, representing the raw data. Each document is parsed for terms. Recognized terms are then stored in a separate index term table. The relationship between terms and documents is clearly many-to-many (i.e., one document may have many terms and one term may be associated with many documents). By reducing this relationship to two one-to-many relationships required by relational DBMSs, the redundancy is eliminated. A third table is created to store the tokens and the identity of the original document from which the tokens came (see Figure 4.1). Observe that what results is similar to an inverted file structure. In essence, we have built a simple storage component for an IR system on top of a DBMS. Commercial textbase software such as Inmagic's DBTextWorks could also be used to isolate terms and tabulate term distributions, but manipulation of the indexes is limited to exporting them as text files and there is limited control over the definition of term delimiters.

PRIMARY SOURCE

Documents		
Doc_id	Content	Freq
1	A C	2
2	A B C G	4
3	D	1
4	A B G H I	5
5	E H	2
. . .	. . .	. . .
...	...	...

SECONDARY SOURCE

Terms		
Term_id	Term	Freq
1	A	3
2	B	2
3	C	2
4	D	1
5	E	1
. . .		. . .
...		...

ITEMS

Tokens	
Term_id	Doc_id
1	1
1	2
1	4
3	1
3	2
. . .	. . .
...	...

Figure 4.1. Sample Relational DBMS Layout to Analyze Index Term Data

More sophisticated database designs that include complete document representation within the database are possible. See, for example, Fernández, Cabrero, Zulueta, and Gómez (1993), who outline the construction of a relational database for informetric analysis using bibliographic and demographic data fields. More recently, Järvelin, Ingwersen, and Niemi (2000) have outlined a database model for storing bibliographic references and extracting data for informetric analysis. Their representation of bibliographic references as complex objects permits the study of author, journal, article, citation, co-citation, and term-based analyses.

Once the raw data have been processed, SQL queries may be constructed to tabulate the indexing exhaustivity and term frequency distributions. In the case of the term frequency distribution, the unique term "sizes" need only be tallied, with

```
SELECT Terms.Freq, Count(Terms.Freq) AS CountOffreq
    FROM Terms
    GROUP BY Terms.Freq
    ORDER BY Terms.Freq
```

For the indexing exhaustivity distribution the SQL statement would be:

```
SELECT Documents.Freq, Count(Documents.Freq) AS CountOffreq
    FROM Documents
    GROUP BY Documents.Freq
    ORDER BY Documents.Freq
```

The resulting output for each, respectively, will be a frequency distribution for the number of terms occurring once, twice, etc. and the distribution for documents containing one term, two terms, etc. The existing structure is also useful for determining co-occurrences between terms. A basic two- or three-table layout may be applied to a number of two-dimensional IPPs (author productivity, journal productivity).

Small (1995) provides additional details of relational database modeling for bibliographic data and demonstrates how SQL may be applied to perform citation network analysis within a relational DBMS environment.

4.3.5 Software Specifically for Informetric Analysis

There have been many examples of in-house and proprietary software developed since the late1980s that have been designed to tabulate informetric characteristics of primarily bibliographic data sets. These include the Bibliometrics Toolbox (available as freeware from ftp://ftp.u.washington.edu/public/tabrooks/toolbox/), which contains routines for Bradford analysis and indices of concentration, and DataView (http://crrm.u-3mrs.fr/commercial/software/dataview/dataview.html), which automatically analyzes bibliometric characteristics of tagged bibliographic data. Sotolongo-Aguilar, Suárez-Balseiro, and Guzmán-Sánchez (2000) cite further examples of software for informetric analysis and present a five-step methodology called MOBIS-ProSoft that relies on proprietary and in-house software to collect, convert, and analyze data. Additional examples of software for informetric research may be found on the *Cybermetrics* Web site (http://www.cindoc.csic.es/cybermetrics/links18.html). Many of the programs developed are application specific, that is, for the analysis of a specific type of informetric data such as author productivity or citation analysis, but for those applications they can be quite helpful.

4.4 Model Selection

The selection of an appropriate mathematical model to fit to observed data can be challenging. Although models initially selected may resemble the observed phenomenon, subtle differences between the observed distributions and those generated by the theoretical models may ultimately make the prospective model inappropriate. This does not become apparent until after the investigator has fitted the model to the observed data.

Model flexibility and tractability are dictated, in part, by the number of parameters to be estimated. The parameters will define the underlying characteristics of the distribution. Families of distributions may share common features but may be more suitable under different circumstances. An example of this idea is a set of related unimodal distributions that are widely used in data modeling—the Poisson, binomial, and negative binomial distributions. The density function forms for the Poisson, binomial, and negative binomial distributions are presented in Section 4.4.4. The Poisson distribution is used to model the likelihood of x events occurring where there is a constant probability for the occurrence of each event. It is a single parameter model such that the parameter value is equal to both the mean and variance of the distribution. A simple estimator for the value of the parameter then would be the sample mean of the data set being modeled. However, what if the observed variance of the data set is less than the mean? The fit for a Poisson model and the data set in this case likely would not be a good one. A binomial distribution, which can be used to model phenomena similar to the Poisson where data variances are less than the mean, would be more appropriate. It is a two-parameter distribution with more flexibility to model a wider range of observed behaviors. For informetric studies, the variance of unimodal-type data sets is often greater than the mean due to the long tails. In these cases, a binomial distribution may not be appropriate. The negative binomial distribution is a comparable two-parameter model, usable for distributions where the variance is greater than the mean.

Model selection should be based on the principle of parsimony or "simple is better." Usually distributions with fewer parameters are easier to fit. More sophisticated models with additional parameters will generally result in a better fit for the observed data because of the additional flexibility introduced by the extra parameter(s). Some theoretical distributions represent special cases of more generalized distributions, which contain a greater number of parameters. Questions arise whether the additional parameters are necessary and whether they significantly improve the model fit. Kinnucan and Wolfram (1990) demonstrate how distributions with additional parameters might not provide significant improvement in the fit of the data sets to merit selection of parameter-rich distributions. In these situations, the more parsimonious distributions to model observed behavior are sufficient.

Informetric data sets present modeling challenges not evident in other social scientific investigations based on normal or Gaussian distributions. The long or "heavy" tails found in most informetric data sets make modeling of the tail end of a distribution difficult due to the large gaps between the data observations on the abscissa for data represented in size-frequency form. Mathematical functions do not take these gaps into account. This presents a challenge for fitting the gap-ridden tails of the observed data to gap-absent outcomes of the models used.

The intended application of the model will also affect which model is ultimately most appropriate. If one wished to investigate the impact on the distribution resulting from changes in the shape of a reverse J-shaped model, a model containing one parameter that is responsible for the shape of the distribution would be more convenient than a model where the shape is dictated by two or more parameters that must be adjusted to achieve the same end. For example, the generalized inverse Gaussian-Poisson distribution (see Section 4.4.3), although quite effective in modeling reverse J-shaped distributions, becomes cumbersome because all three parameters affect its shape (Sichel, 1992). In this situation, a simple Zipf model (see Chapter 3, Section 3.2.3) with a well-defined shape parameter— the inverse power *b* parameter—may be more easily applied with variations of the *b* parameter.

4.4.1 Size versus Rank Model Forms

As discussed in Chapter 3, two primary approaches are used in the representation of data for informetric modeling: size-frequency and rank-frequency. Wilson (1999) outlines three other approaches: size-cumulative frequency, rank-cumulative frequency, and equal production groups. These three forms are not widely used or are reserved for specific types of analyses within informetrics. The size-frequency approach represents data in their tabulated format, where the size represents the number of items and the frequency the number of sources. In the rank-frequency approach, items are converted to ranks so that the source with the greatest number of items receives rank 1, with the number of items associated with the source representing its frequency.

There has been considerable debate over which method should be used (Tague, 1990). Brookes (1984a, 1984b, 1988) espouses the rank-frequency approach to data analysis. Hubert (1978, 1981), on the other hand, argues that there is no difference between the two approaches. Although the data sets using either approach may be comparable, employing the rank-frequency approach requires that the investigator be specific about the ranking method used because there are several ways to deal with the inevitable ties that occur in the data sets. Heine (1998) outlined five methods for dealing with ties in ranks for studying Bradford phenomena that result in different outcomes:

- **Arbitrary assignment:** where each tied observation is randomly assigned a separate rank value.
- **Mid-rank assignment:** using the mean rank for tied observations.
- **Next-in-line assignment**: using next-in-line values representing the lowest next available rank for all tied observations.
- **Last-in-line assignment**: using values representing the highest rank possible for the tied observations.
- **Sequential assignment**: with ranks being incremented singly, regardless of the number of ranks, tied items receiving the same rank (compare to Chen and Leimkuhler's index method, discussed below).

The method used for ranking will affect the form of the model ultimately selected. Because the size-frequency form does not require any data conversion, as is necessary with the rank-frequency form, the size-frequency form will be used for subsequent examples.

Variations of the size and rank approaches could also be used. Nelson and Tague (1985) developed a split size-rank model for index term distributions. Rank-based models perform better for the high frequency sources, while the size-based models are better for low frequency sources. By using a rank-frequency model for the few high frequency terms and a size-frequency model for the many low frequency terms, a good fit was achieved.

Chen and Leimkuhler (1986) introduced an alternate format that has shown merit but to date has not been widely adopted. Their "index" approach eliminates the gaps observed in the sizes or ranks by assigning each subsequent observed type or size an incremented value, so that the gaps are removed.

4.4.2 Continuous versus Discrete Models

Information production processes by their nature represent discrete events, so discrete models should be used. However, it is possible to use continuous analogs to discrete models (Rousseau, 1990), such as the Pareto distribution (see Chapter 3, Section 3.2.4), which is a continuous equivalent of a generalized Zipf model. The lognormal distribution (Cooper & Weekes, 1983) may take a reverse-J shape or one with a mode at greater than the minimal abscissa value. Many of the classic inverse power law models may be treated as continuous for large data sets; however, in practice, discrete input values (e.g., $x = 1, 2, 3, \ldots$) are assumed. With large numbers of sizes or ranks in large data sets, the distinctions between discrete and continuous forms become less noticeable. Continuous assumptions are useful for applying differential and integral calculus methods. For discrete models, summation techniques may be used (Wilson, 1999). One area of informetrics where the distinctions between continuous and discrete approaches do not seem to differ is in the graphical representation of plots; discrete model plots are almost always plotted as continuous curves. This is more for convenience and legibility of the distribution line.

4.4.3 Potential Models for Reverse J-Shaped Distributions

Most IPP distributions follow an inverse pattern, with many sources producing few items and few sources producing many items. They are represented by the classic informetric laws, where distributions are characterized by very long tails. Many distributions have been developed for modeling reverse J-shaped phenomena. Early models used in informetric studies are covered in Chapter 3 and include the Lotka, Zipf, and Mandelbrot distributions. The three-parameter Mandelbrot (see Chapter 3, Section 3.2.3) provides the greatest flexibility among these models. Additional derivations for Zipfian-type behaviors are discussed in Fedorowicz (1982b). Although easily managed, a primary drawback of some of the early models is that they lack a strong theoretical foundation. They may closely model the observed behavior but lack explanatory power.

More recently derived distributions have integrated probabilistic mechanisms to better model observed behaviors. Two of these distributions have been found to provide reasonable fits to a range of observed phenomena, the generalized inverse Gaussian-Poisson and generalized Waring distributions.

The generalized inverse Gaussian-Poisson (GIGP) distribution developed by Sichel (1985, 1992) has shown promise for a variety of informetric data modeling. The zero-truncated form of the equation (i.e., beginning at "1" instead of "0") takes the form

$$\phi(r) = [(\alpha / b)^{\gamma} K_{\gamma}(b) - K_{\gamma}(\alpha)]^{-1} \frac{[(\alpha^2 - b^2)/2\alpha]^r}{r^2} K_{r+\gamma}(\alpha), \quad r = 1,2,3\ldots \quad (4.1)$$

where $\phi(r)$ represents the probability of r occurrences of an IPP, parameters a >= 0, b >= 0, $-\infty < \gamma < \infty$, and $K_{\nu}(z)$ is the modified Bessel function of the second kind of order v and argument z. An overview of Bessel functions along with equation forms can be found in Abramowitz and Stegun (1972). Numerical software libraries such as those developed by the Numeric Algorithms Group (see http://www.nag.co.uk) contain routines for calculating Bessel function outcomes based on input parameters supplied by the user.

On the face of it, the GIGP does not resemble the traditional inverse power models of earlier generations of informetric distributions. It uses Poisson distributions that are combined with the inverse Gaussian distribution as a mixing distribution. Sichel indicates that many distributions previously used in informetrics can be shown to be special or limiting cases of the GIGP. He and others have successfully fitted data sets representing different types of informetric phenomena to the distribution. The model can also be applied to data sets with modes greater than "1." The complexities of the GIGP and other general models are enough to challenge even those well versed in informetric modeling and do not easily permit "on the fly" estimation of values for the parameters (see Section 4.5).

Sichel has demonstrated how the model may be used for different types of informetric data sets. Nelson (1989) has also fitted the GIGP to several data sets of IR term frequency distributions (see Chapter 5, Section 5.2). Similarly, Nelson and Downie (2001) found that the GIGP distribution best modeled the n-grams of music intervals (based on combinations of 4, 5 and 6 intervals) extracted from a database of more than 9,000 folksongs. Baayen (2001), however, encountered mixed success with the GIGP and concluded that it was not always the best distribution for fitting word frequencies.

A two-parameter case of the GIGP, called the inverse Gaussian-Poisson (IGP), also merits consideration. As a two-parameter distribution, estimates for the parameters can be more tractable. Ajiferuke (1991), in particular, found the IGP to be the best-fitting model for author collaboration distributions in a number of subject areas. The equation takes the form

$$p(x) = \left(\frac{2\alpha}{\pi}\right)^{1/2} e^{\alpha}(1-\theta)^{1/2}\frac{(1/2\alpha\theta)^{x}}{x!}K_{x-1/2}(\alpha), \quad x = 0, 1, 2, \ldots \quad (4.2)$$

where parameters $a >= 0$, $0 <= \theta <= 1$, and $K_v(z)$ is the modified Bessel function of the second kind of order v and argument z.

The generalized Waring distribution (Irwin, 1975) is a form of hypergeometric distribution that has shown promise for modeling long-tailed informetric data such as Bradford and Lotka-type distributions (Burrell, 1988; Nelson, 1989). The probability of x occurrences, $p(x)$, is determined by

$$p(x) = \frac{\Gamma(\nu+\alpha)}{B(\alpha,\beta)\,\Gamma(\nu)}\;\frac{\Gamma(x+\nu)\,\Gamma(x+\beta)}{\Gamma(x+\beta+\nu+\alpha)\,x!} \quad x = 0, 1, 2, \ldots \quad (4.3)$$

where

$$\Gamma(x) = (x-1)! \quad , \quad B(\alpha, \beta) = \frac{\Gamma(\alpha)\Gamma(\beta)}{\Gamma(\alpha+\beta)}$$

and parameters *a, ß*, and *v* are greater than zero.

The generalized Waring distribution has been applied to several types of reverse J-shaped data. Nelson (1989) demonstrated its applicability for modeling the distribution of index terms using six data sets. Burrell has proposed its use based on assumptions of variable productivity over time within and across individuals for Lotka data using a mixture of negative binomial processes. Note that the distribution has a starting point of $x = 0$, but most observed informetric distributions start at $x = 1$. One solution is to shift the equation so that x is replaced by $x - 1$. Ajiferuke (1991) and Wolfram (1992a) used this approach in modeling author collaboration and index term distributions respectively. Another solution, used by Nelson (1989), is to truncate the distribution by removing the $p(0)$ probability and then to divide subsequent generated values of $p(x)$ by $(1 - p(0))$.

Another probabilistic model based on a mixture of Poisson distributions has been developed by Bookstein and Swanson (1974). Their 2-Poisson model, used by Harter (1975a, 1975b) to fit the distribution of specialty terms appearing in technical literatures, draws on specific probabilistic assumptions for frequencies of occurrence of terms. The model postulates two document classes, representing different levels of treatment within each class of a subject area represented by a given term. The model recognizes that a term is treated differently by relevant and nonrelevant documents, defining two classes of documents. With this model, the proportion of documents in a document collection containing x tokens or term occurrences $p(x)$ is measured as

$$p(x) \quad = \quad \pi \frac{\lambda_1{}^x e^{-\lambda_1}}{x!} + (1-\pi) \frac{\lambda_2{}^x e^{-\lambda_2}}{x!} \qquad (4.4)$$

where parameters λ_1 and λ_2 ($\lambda_1 >= \lambda_2$) represent the mean number of occurrences of a given term in each document class respectively and p ($0 <= \pi <= 1$) represents the proportion of documents belonging to the first class (Harter, 1975a).

It should be noted that several distributions known for their Poisson-like modeling properties (Poisson, binomial, negative binomial) may also take a reverse J-shape with the assignment of a high value to the probability parameter, but fits to observed data sets are usually poorer than when using the above-mentioned models, particularly in the upper tail, where probabilities quickly approach zero (see Section 4.4.4). The generalized negative binomial distribution, however, may also have some application for reverse J-shaped data sets. Ajiferuke and Wolfram (submitted b) found it provided good fits for five data sets dealing with the frequency distribution of hypertext links on top-level Web pages from different high-level Internet domains, and outperformed the GIGP in two cases. The generalized negative binomial distribution takes the form:

$$p(x) = \frac{\nu\Gamma(\nu + \beta x)}{x!\,\Gamma(\nu + \beta x - x + 1)} a^{\nu + \beta x - x}(1 - a)^{x} \quad x = 0, 1, 2, \ldots \tag{4.5}$$

where $\nu > 0$, $0 < a < 1$, and $|a\beta| < 1$.

To summarize, key distributions to model reverse J-shaped data sets in increasing order of complexity but decreasing tractability are the Zipf/Lotka, Mandelbrot, generalized Waring, generalized negative binomial, IGP, and GIGP. A 2-Poisson model may also be useful for term frequency distributions.

4.4.4 Potential Models for Distributions with Modes Greater Than 1

As noted previously, most IPP distributions follow inverse relationships. However, there are notable exceptions, where observed distributions are unimodal with modes greater than 1. Obvious initial choices for modeling unimodal data sets include the Poisson, binomial, and negative binomial, and generalized negative binomial distributions. The Poisson distribution equation takes the form

$$p(x) = \frac{\lambda^{x} e^{-\lambda}}{x!} \quad x = 0, 1, 2, \ldots \tag{4.6}$$

with the single parameter $\lambda > 0$. The two-parameter binomial distribution provides additional flexibility:

$$p(x) = \binom{\kappa}{x} \pi^{x} (1 - \pi)^{\kappa - x} \quad x = 0, 1, 2, \ldots \tag{4.7}$$

where parameters $0 < \pi < 1$ and $\kappa > 0$. Similarly, the two-parameter negative binomial distribution, perhaps the most useful of the three for informetric data modeling takes the form

$$p(x) = \binom{\kappa + x - 1}{\kappa - 1} \pi^{\kappa} (1-\pi)^{x} \quad x = 0, 1, 2, \ldots \tag{4.8}$$

Note that there are different formulations for the negative binomial distribution. Setting κ to 1 results in the geometric distribution, also sometimes used in informetric studies. Shifting or truncation is necessary for modeling observed data sets with starting values of x = 1.

The application of continuous distributions may also be appropriate, particularly for large data sets with many observed data types. One potential model is the lognormal distribution

$$p(x) = \frac{1}{x\sqrt{(2\pi)}\sigma} \exp\left[-\frac{(\ln x - \mu)^2}{2\sigma^2}\right] \quad x > 0 \tag{4.9}$$

where μ and $\sigma > 0$ are parameters.

For similar unimodal data sets with a strong time component, such as found in diachronous obsolescence studies, several models have shown promise. Avramescu's (1979) continuous dual exponential model can be used for the full range of observed citation obsolescence distributions:

$$c(t) = C_0(e^{-\alpha t} - e^{-m\alpha t}) \tag{4.10}$$

where $c(t)$ represents the number of citations at time t, C_0 the amplitude parameter, a the age decrement parameter, and $m > 1$ the initial increment parameter. Egghe and Rousseau (1990, p. 268) presented the equation in a slightly different form. Other models that have been successfully fitted to diachronous data include the (discrete) negative binomial and the (continuous) Weibull distribution.

For synchronous obsolescence, the continuous lognormal, exponential, gamma, and Weibull distributions have been applied with varying degrees of success. Their equation forms are not included here, but may be found in Cooper and Weekes (1983, ch. 5). The more recently tested generalized gamma distribution used by Tahai and Rigsby (1998) shows promise. It takes the form

$$c(t) = \frac{\lambda\rho}{\Gamma(\theta)}(\lambda t)^{\rho\theta-1} e^{(-\lambda t)^{\rho}} \tag{4.11}$$

where *c(t)* is the number of citations at time *t*, ρ and *0* are shape parameters, and Γ*()* is the gamma function. It can be shown that the lognormal, exponential, gamma, and Weibull distributions are special cases of the generalized gamma distribution.

4.4.5 Potential Cumulative Growth Models

The growth of IR system indexes, documents sets, and access to resources requires a different set of distributions to model rates of growth. Like diachronous citation studies, they are also much more time-dependent than the other informetric models, As outlined in Chapter 3, Section 3.6.1, three general types of growth are observed: linear, exponential, and logistic.

The simplest, linear growth, is readily modeled with a simple linear equation of the form

$$F(t) = a + bt \quad x = 0, 1, 2, \ldots \tag{4.12}$$

where parameters a and b correspond to the start size at $t = 0$ and the growth rate respectively.

On the other hand, if exponential growth of IPPs is observed , a standard exponential distribution, may be used:

$$F(t) = ae^{bt} \quad x = 0, 1, 2, \ldots \tag{4.13}$$

where a again is the initial size and b is the growth rate. A three-parameter power model that combines the general form of the linear model with nonlinear growth was introduced by Wolfram, Chu, and Lu (1990) of the form

$$F(t) = a + bt^{c} \quad x = 0, 1, 2, \ldots \tag{4.14}$$

The c parameter introduces a nonlinear component to the growth when $c \neq 1$. Egghe and Rao (1992) studied this model more thoroughly by comparing its performance with several other distributions. They found it provided the best fit for concavely increasing growth.

A strict exponential growth model may suffice for initial growth, but eventually the growth may slow, requiring a model that can reflect these changes. Traditionally, a logistic distribution has been advocated (see Figure 3.4, page 58), but difficulties arise in the parameter estimation, and the inflection point is halfway between the initial and final observations (Wilson, 1999). Egghe and Rao also investigated a Gompertz model in their study, and found that it best fitted S-shaped data sets. The Gompertz distribution takes the form

$$F(t) \quad = \quad d\, a^{b^t} \qquad x = 0, 1, 2, ... \tag{4.15}$$

where a represents the initial size at $t = 0$ with parameters d and b.

More recently, Saxena, Gupta, and Jauhari (2001) examined six families of growth models, including those listed above, and demonstrated the similar performance of many models in fitting observed data, including polynomial models up to degree three. The authors concluded that no one model is ideal for growth studies. Rather, the nature of the data will dictate which model will provide the best fit.

4.5 Model-Fitting Techniques

Once candidate distributions have been selected, they must be fitted to the observed data distributions. Parameter values for the candidate models must be estimated such that the resulting distribution most closely resembles the observed data distribution. The form of the distribution selected may dictate the method of parameter estimation used, although there is almost always more than one way to estimate suitable parameter values. Four methods commonly used for parameter estimation are presented here: the method of moments, minimum chi-square, least squares, and maximum likelihood estimation. Each method has its own strengths and weaknesses for model fitting. Researchers continue to debate the merits of each approach.

4.5.1 Method of Moments

Moments represent specific types of summary statistics of a distribution such as the mean, variance, skewness, or kurtosis. The method of moments (MOM) relies on the moments of the observed data set as estimators of the moments of the theoretical model being fitted. Parameter values are estimated from formulas expressed in terms of the moments of the theoretical model. For example, for the Poisson distribution the moment estimator for the single parameter λ is the mean, represented by the sample mean of the data set being fitted to the Poisson model. Ajiferuke (1991) used multiple methods of parameter estimation for the fifteen distributions he tested for observed author collaboration distributions, including the MOM for several distributions.

With known estimators for candidate distributions, the MOM results in the least computational burden of the model-fitting techniques discussed. However, it may not be possible to calculate moments for some inverse power distributions because moments other than the mean may be infinite. Furthermore, the variances of moment estimators may not be as small as for other methods such as maximum likelihood, resulting in parameter values that are not optimal (Cowan, 1998). Still, moment estimators could be used to calculate starting parameter values in conjunction with iterative parameter estimation methods such as minimum chi-square.

Moment estimators for a number of discrete distributions may be found in Johnson and Kotz (1969).

4.5.2 Minimum Chi-Square

The goal of minimum chi-square (MCS) parameter estimation is quite simple—find the parameter values that result in the lowest chi-square goodness-of-fit value. Chi-square outcomes comparing observed and expected values resulting from the proposed model are used as an indication of the goodness-of-fit between the two data sets. The lower the chi-square value, the better the fit. Goodness-of-fit testing using chi-square tests is discussed in Section 4.5.5.

The process of parameter estimation using MCS can be computationally expensive, requiring calculations on many combinations of parameters to zero-in on the best parameter value combinations. For relatively simple models with one or two parameters where the range of likely values is relatively small, parameter values may be calculated through brute force manual tabulation using built-in routines in spreadsheet software or programming where combinations of parameter values may be entered. More directed programs that integrate numeric minimization algorithms, listed in sources such as *Numerical Recipes: The Art of Scientific Computing* (Press, 1989), or one of its programming language-specific editions, may be developed to reduce computational burden by directing how parameter values are sought. If available, mathematical libraries such as the Numeric Algorithms Group (NAG) software system, which contain readily available minimization routines (see chapter E04 of the NAG documentation) should be used. Routines are available for different functional forms that rely on different minimization algorithms (e.g., quasi-Newton, Gauss-Newton). Users will need to develop a shell program in a computer language such as FORTRAN to reference the NAG library and to calculate the resulting chi-square values for each set of parameters returned by the minimization routine.

A key advantage of MCS is that the process of parameter estimation and goodness-of-fit testing can be performed at the same time, unlike other methods where goodness-of-fit testing is performed as a separate step. Although computationally intensive, this burden is placed squarely on the computer instead of the researcher when minimization algorithms are used and does not require the derivation maximum likelihood or moment estimators. The process is also distribution-independent, where the same routine may be used for other models by simply substituting the new equation to be fitted. Researchers such as Sichel (1985, 1992) and Berkson (1978) favored the use of MCS over the other techniques such as maximum likelihood estimation. Sichel, for example, used a constrained MCS approach to fit observed data to the GIGP distribution. Other examples where MCS estimation has been used include Nelson (1989) for the generalized Waring distribution and Wolfram (1992a) for Zipf, Mandelbrot, and negative binomial distributions.

There are drawbacks to MCS, some of which are tied directly to the use of chi-square goodness-of-fit tests. These are discussed in Section 4.5.5. Unlike the other model-fitting methods, MCS lacks an elegant theoretical underpinning for the calculation of the parameters themselves. Also, when using any type of minimization routine, the investigator must be careful that the outcomes do not represent local minima. Some minimization routines rely on declining rates of descent to zero-in on minimum values. This may cause the routine to focus on a local minimum, when in fact deeper valleys with lower minimum values in the terrain of outcomes may exist. A robust minimization routine that can take local minima into account should be selected. Also, it is advisable for the investigator to run the minimization routine several times using different starting parameter values to determine if local minima have been encountered. Some minimization routines may use parameter values that produce overflows or underflows when being fitted as a result of asymptotes within the theoretical distributions being modeled. In these cases, boundaries for parameter value ranges must be set.

4.5.3 Least Squares

Linear least squares (LS) estimation is a useful method of parameter fitting for linear models or power models that have been linearized through logarithmic transformation of the distribution equation. Least squares estimation results in a model that minimizes the sum of the squared residuals (i.e., the random components that represent variations from the expected value) between the theoretical model and the observed data (Cooper &

Weekes, 1983). In essence, it is a linear regression analysis. The technique may also be applied to polynomial distributions using nonlinear LS techniques. Routines based on LS algorithms may be developed using similar sources as for MCS estimation, such as math libraries.

Spreadsheet software contains many routines to simplify mathematical and statistical data processing. Many have LS estimation abilities built-in for linear and basic power models that can be represented as trendlines. In Microsoft Excel™ this is accomplished by first plotting the observed data distribution using the XY plot feature. By invoking the "Add trendline" menu option and then selecting the "Power trend/regression" type and "Display equation on chart" option, a fitted equation in power form is displayed. An R-squared goodness-of-fit value, called the coefficient of determination, can also be displayed. This method is useful for distributions in which there are no gaps in the data set, for example growth studies where data are available over consecutive time periods, or data sets for which the most productive contributors at which gaps begin have been truncated. The use of the trendline option is not appropriate for long-tailed informetric distributions where gaps exist in the tail. The fitting method used by spreadsheet software only fits the non-zero values and ignores the gaps that occur in observed informetric distributions and their impact on the goodness-of-fit. The absence of these gaps on probability density distributions should be accounted for when determining goodness-of-fit.

Acceptable fits for LS estimation have been found when data sets have been truncated. For an example, Pao (1985, 1986) developed a methodology for tabulating the exponent (b) and numerator parameters (k) for Lotka distributions using LS and truncated data sets. Although R-squared values are usually used as a measure of model effectiveness for regression analysis and may be used for comparison purposes, as a goodness-of-fit measure they have limitations. Using R-squared values does not result in an indicator of whether the outputs of a theoretical model are statistically significantly different from the observed data. The use of another measure of goodness-of-fit is recommended in addition to the R-squared value.

4.5.4 Maximum Likelihood

In a nutshell, the maximum likelihood (ML) estimator for a parameter is that value that maximizes the probability of obtaining the observed data. To determine the value, one must initially develop a likelihood function for the observed data. This determination can become quite challenging for more sophisticated models. For example, it can be shown using calculus that for the Poisson distribution, the maximum likelihood estimator for the single parameter λ is the mean, just as it is for the moment estimator. Distributions with more than one parameter will require the derivation of multiple likelihood functions or the use of additional parameter estimation techniques. Maximum likelihood estimators have been developed for many distributions. Some likelihood estimators require simple formula substitution. Others require iterative calculations through numeric programming.

Maximum likelihood has been used by a number of researchers to model informetric phenomena. In fact, some authors recommend the use of ML estimators over other methods for certain theoretical models. Tague and Nicholls (1987) use ML estimation for the exponent parameter (b) of the Lotka model. The ML estimator b' for the b parameter is the sample statistic that satisfies

$$\frac{\sum_{i=1}^{n} \log_e x_i}{n} = \frac{\sum_{i=1}^{x_{\max}} (\log_e x)/x^{b'}}{\sum_{i=1}^{x_{\max}} 1/x^{b'}} \tag{4.16}$$

The k parameter can be estimated using the inverse of the Riemann zeta function $\zeta(b)^{-1}$ (Nicholls, 1989):

$$k = \zeta(b)^{-1} = \left[\sum_{x=1}^{\infty} x^{-b}\right]^{-1} \tag{4.17}$$

or through an approximation for the $\zeta(b)$ formula (Pao, 1985). Stein, Zucchini, and Juritz (1987), Nelson (1989), and Ajiferuke (1991) use ML to estimate the parameters of the GIGP distribution, which requires the use of iterative algorithms on the likelihood functions of a reparameterized form of the GIGP equation to make it more tractable.

From a computational perspective, ML estimation can have the greatest overhead, requiring first the determination of the likelihood function, if a derivation is not already available, followed by the implementation of iterative techniques to maximize the function. However, just as with MCS, math libraries can provide routines to perform the maximization. Goodness-of-fit results for ML are often superior to other parameter estimation routines.

4.5.5 Goodness-of-Fit Measurement

Just as with model-fitting methods, debate continues over the appropriateness of different methods used to measure the goodness-of-fit between observed and fitted theoretical distributions. The two primary methods in use are the chi-square (χ^2) test and the Kolmogorov-Smirnov

(K-S) test. A third method, using the coefficient of determination (R^2), is generally used for comparative purposes but also provides an indication of the closeness of the fit. Visual inspection of plotted observed and theoretical distributions may also be used as a crude estimator but provides no quantitative comparison or indication of statistical significance.

Measures of goodness-of-fit may be used for comparative purposes (i.e., to determine which among several models best fits the observed data) or to determine whether the outcomes of a model differ significantly from the observed data. Many authors have pointed out the difficulties of applying the latter purpose, which involves testing of the hypothesis that the observed data set (assumed to be a sample) is statistically significantly different from the developed model (assumed to represent the population). The question arises whether data sets used in informetric research truly represent random samples of a larger population. In some cases the samples drawn are not random but rather are incomplete representations of the population, or they may represent the complete population being studied (Chen, 1989). As an example, if one were to study the distribution of all index terms within an IR system, does this constitute the population of index terms, or does it serve as a representation of one of many possible index term distributions?

The most widely used method for goodness-of-fit, whether for hypothesis testing or simply comparison purposes, has been to apply chi-square testing. As a nonparametric method for categorical-level data, chi-square values are calculated using the standard formula:

$$\chi^2 = \sum_{i=1}^{n} \frac{(O_i - E_i)^2}{E_i} \tag{4.18}$$

where n is the number of categories or observed cells, O_i the count of sources within the ith cell, and E_i the expected count of sources in the ith cell. If used for hypothesis testing, the resulting χ^2 value is compared to the critical value for $n - k - 1$ degrees of freedom, where k is the number of parameters in the model being tested. It is interesting to note that the chi-square distribution used to determine goodness-of-fit is itself a one-parameter distribution that may be reverse J-shaped or Poisson-like depending on the parameter value. The standard χ^2 testing requirements of no more than 20 percent of expected cell counts containing less than five and no cells containing expected counts of less than one still apply. These requirements are cited as one of the primary drawbacks of chi-square goodness-of-fit testing. Cells from the tail of data sets must be collapsed to raise the cell counts, thus losing some of the key characteristics of the observed data set, along with a number of degrees of freedom. For hypothesis testing, the χ^2 test has also been found to be sensitive to large data sets with many cells. With even modest differences between observed and expected cells the cumulated cell values ultimately result in a large χ^2 value that causes the null hypothesis of no significant difference to be rejected (Nelson and Tague, 1985; Nelson, 1989; Ajiferuke, 1991).

The other method primarily used for testing goodness-of-fit is the Kolmogorov-Smirnov (K-S) test. The test compares the cumulative relative frequency distributions of the observed and expected data sets. The outcome of the test is dependent on the largest distance between the two distributions over all values. If the maximum difference exceeds a critical value based on the sample size, the null hypothesis that there is no significant difference between the two distributions is rejected. Unlike the χ^2 method, the K-S test requires no collapsing of data cells. The K-S test has been used to study Lotka (Coile, 1977; Nicholls, 1989) and Bradford phenomena (Qiu, 1990). With Bradford and other cumulative distribution data, the assumption of cell independence in χ^2 testing is violated because cumulated cell values are not independent of previous cell values. The main argument against using the K-S test for informetric data sets is its intended use for continuous data. Despite this, it is argued to be conservative if applied to discrete informetric data sets. The statistician Sichel (1992) argues that the K-S test is only superior to the χ^2 test if a sample size is less than thirty, which is rarely the case in informetric studies. Also, the K-S test relies on a single maximal divergence between the observed and theoretical cumulative distributions, unlike the χ^2 test, in which differences cumulate.

4.6 Summary and Additional Readings

Electronic data sources for informetric analysis have become readily available in recent decades. This is especially true for data from IR systems, whether the representation of print documents, the document creators, or the content of the IR system itself. There are many ways to extract and manipulate these data. With large databases available indexing terabytes of content, today's primary difficulty is not so much the lack of data but perhaps too much. Sampling techniques can be used to make these large data sets more manageable. Using structured access to data, such as is available through spreadsheet and statistical packages and DBMSs, powerful data manipulation and processing tasks can be readily accomplished.

The usefulness of any application of informetrics ultimately will be determined by how well the extracted sample data characterize the larger population, in addition to the adequacy of the theoretical models selected to represent that population. It is for these reasons that the process of data collection, model selection, parameter estimation, and goodness-of-fit testing must be carefully thought out. Through visual inspection of observed distributions and an understanding of the underlying mechanisms, candidate models may be selected. Each model-fitting technique has its merits but may not be appropriate in each circumstance. Ultimately, the model-fitting technique adopted may be dictated by convenience and tractability of the theoretical distributions being used as models. Finally, the goodness-of-fit testing technique used could affect whether a model is selected as most closely representing the observed phenomenon. There are no universal agreements on which methods are best.

There are several sources the reader may wish to consult to find out more about the topics presented in this chapter. Most of these sources are not geared specifically for informetric modeling, but the ideas presented readily translate to other disciplines and applications. Egghe and Rousseau (1990) devote several chapters in section IV of their monograph on informetrics to the treatment of modeling, with specific examples on fitting Bradford-type data. A recent source that is recommended for dealing with long-tailed distributions is the collection of papers edited by Adler, Feldman, and Taqqu (1998). The contributed papers deal with model-fitting techniques and applications from several disciplines that encounter skewed or heavy-tailed distributions. Many statistical methodology works geared for the social sciences will include a section on data collection and sampling methods. For a more mathematical treatment of available sampling methods, consult Sampath (2001). Additional details on model development and representation of general models may be found in Cooper and Weekes (1983) and Linhart and Zucchini (1986).

This chapter has presented only a subset of possible distributions useful for modeling in informetric studies. Other models may also be used. Univariate discrete distributions may be found in Johnson, Kemp, and Kotz (1993), who cover distribution characteristics, their interrelationships, and techniques useful for parameter estimation. Johnson, Kotz, and Balakrishnan (1997) provide a similar treatment for multivariate discrete distributions. The much earlier classic work by Johnson and Kotz (1969) on discrete distributions is also still useful and covers univariate and basic multivariate distributions, although it does not include more recent developments in distributions and modeling. Kraft and Boyce (1991) devote a chapter of their work to stochastic processes for library models, which also have applications for IR purposes. Functional forms of many discrete distributions are found in this chapter. Further details of model-fitting techniques and goodness-of-fit testing may be found in Cowan (1998) and Morgan (2000). Characteristics of nonparametric statistics and goodness-of-fit testing may also be found in Conover's (1999) monograph on nonparametric statistics.

5

Informetrics and IR System Content

The [Babbage] Analytical Engine weaves algebraic patterns just as the Jacquard loom weaves flowers and leaves.

—Ada Lovelace, 1843

5.1 Introduction

From an informetrics perspective, IR system processes can be thought of as collections of information production processes (IPPs). For convenience, these processes can be divided into two broad categories: (1) those regularities associated with the documents indexed by the system and the additional files that are generated from the storage process, and (2) those regularities that result from user interactions with IR systems. User and usage-based processes are dealt with in Chapter 6. The focus of the present chapter is those regularities that result from the storage of documents in the IR system, primarily for text-based content. Most informetric studies have involved textual IR environments, but other documentary media and their components could also be analyzed.

5.1.1 IR System Content

The contents of IR systems present a number of areas of investigation as products of recorded discourse, from the perspective of both the IR system as a container of documentary information and the sources and items that result from the IR processes that operate on those documents. Any identifiable unit stored within the system may be a candidate for study. For example, in highly structured document environments, attributes of stored documents that may be investigated include document length, field content, field entry length measuring co-authorship or title length, linkages between documents, and document collection growth. Processes enacted on documents during automatic indexing also result in measurable IPP sources, such as index term frequency and index exhaustivity distributions. Over time, and with the addition of documents to the IR system, the co-occurrence of index terms, index and postings file growth, and rates of term assignment also follow regular patterns. With newer distributed IR systems that index sources from different locations, a new unit of analysis becomes possible at the site or domain level.

As a purely academic pursuit, the study of informetric characteristics of IR systems results in a better understanding of information retrieval processes, the characteristics of the system content, and how they may be used. From a more pragmatic perspective, these findings can translate into applications for system design and evaluation (see Chapter 7).

5.1.2 Current State of Research

Investigations of the empirical regularities of IR system textual content have been undertaken since the earliest days of automated information retrieval. Studies of index term distributions on comparatively small sets of data are among the oldest, having resulted in numerous Zipfian-type distributions being proposed to model index content. Patterns in indexing exhaustivity, although equally longstanding, have not been as widely studied, with fewer models proposed. Term co-occurrence studies have been used in IR system design research to enhance system search capabilities. Growth studies of document collections and indexes have gained more prominence in recent years as technologies have permitted the economical storage of larger collection sets. The development of search and storage systems for full-text materials, particularly for Internet-based resources, has permitted much larger-scale studies of IR system content to be carried out. Distributed IR systems introduce the facet of document location, permitting the study of its impact on system content regularities, for which studies have only recently emerged.

5.2 Distribution of Index Terms

5.2.1 Overview

The distribution of index terms represents the most studied informetric aspect of IR systems. Index terms represent searchable alphanumeric units found within documents. Terms are usually delimited by nonalphanumeric characters and may consist of one or more words. To be included in an index, terms may be selectively chosen based on location in specific fields such as authors, titles, abstracts, or the main body of text in full-text systems. Automatic indexing will determine which words are included in indexes based on stopword lists or the calculated significance of a word. Often descriptors will be manually selected for bibliographic databases and will be based on established thesauri outlining valid terms, representing a controlled vocabulary.

Data are readily extracted by exporting index contents. In systems with field-specific indexing, index contents may be further broken down by field type, allowing the study of authors, title keywords, descriptors, or keywords from abstracts or the text of the document itself. The use of multifield indexes presented as a single searchable index with term occurrences in different fields representing different document types can affect the term distribution because the same term may appear in more than one field. The investigators must decide whether the field indexes should be treated separately, or if occurrences of the same term in different fields constitute distinct term types.

5.2.2 Term Distribution Research

Studies of the distribution of indexing vocabularies that recognize their Zipfian nature date back at least to the early 1960s (Schultz, Schwartz, & Steinberg, 1961; Houston & Wall, 1964). Figure 5.1 plots the distribution of 4,234 descriptors appearing in 2,500 bibliographic records dealing with library and information science in size-frequency form. Even with only a few thousand documents and terms, the number of term sources and items causes the data points to hug the axes unless a semi-logarithmic or complete logarithmic transformation is used on the data. With a simple Zipf model, the transformed data should follow a straight line. Notable departures from the straight line appear at the tail end of the distribution, which represent the most frequently appearing terms.

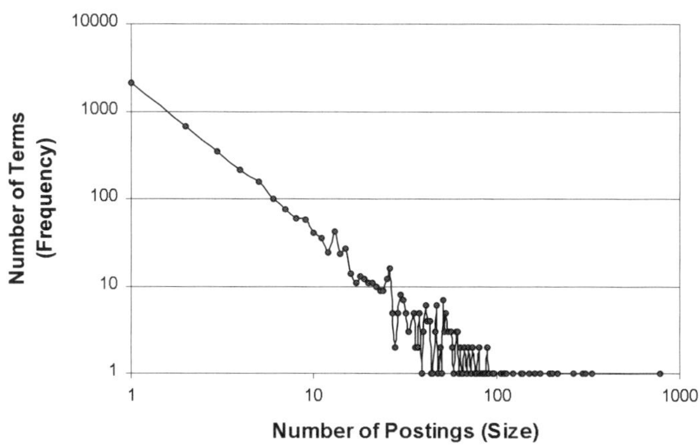

Figure 5.1. Term Frequency Distribution

Numerous theoretical models have been applied to term distribution data sets over the past forty years. Houston and Wall (1964) applied a lognormal model with little success. Bennett (1975), using a size-frequency data set, modeled index term data from two bibliographic databases using the Zipf distribution. The poor fits in the tail were attributed to the relatively small frequencies of occurrence of the index terms, but subsequent research by others would show this was often the case even with larger numbers of terms. Nelson's (1989) fitting of the generalized Waring and GIGP distributions to six data sets demonstrates the feasibility of these models for fitting index term distributions. The reasonable fits of a Mandelbrot form of the Zipf model for two of the data sets fitted by Nelson indicate that it should not be excluded from consideration. Earlier, Nelson and Tague (1985) employed a split model using the size-frequency form of the Mandelbrot distribution to model low frequency terms and a log-rank distribution (a generalization of the Bradford distribution) to model the most frequently occurring terms in rank-frequency form, obtaining reasonable fits. The mixing of the two approaches, however, presented challenges in estimating the crossover point between each approach. Zipfian distributions have also been applied to some nontextual database environments.

With today's larger data sets, adequately modeling index term distributions has become more challenging. Data sets may consist of more than 100,000 distinct terms with millions of postings. Consequently, model fitting with data sets containing large ranks/sizes and frequencies may produce goodness-of-fit outcomes that exceed critical values, thereby causing the theoretical model to be rejected. In this situation, one is limited to relying on the best-fitting theoretical model tested, even if the fit is less than ideal.

5.2.3 Characteristics of Term Distributions

The relationship between the number of types (terms) and tokens (postings) in a Zipfian-type distribution will influence the shape of the term distribution observed. The fewer tokens per type, the steeper the distribution will be, indicating a greater proportion of singly occurring terms. Conversely, with a larger number of tokens per type, the distribution will be a shallower, more gently descending curve with a greater proportion of higher frequency terms. This relationship is demonstrated in Figure 5.2, where plots for hypothetical examples of shallow, mid-range, and steep distributions are represented. Each distribution has a maximal size value of fifty occurrences for the most frequent term.

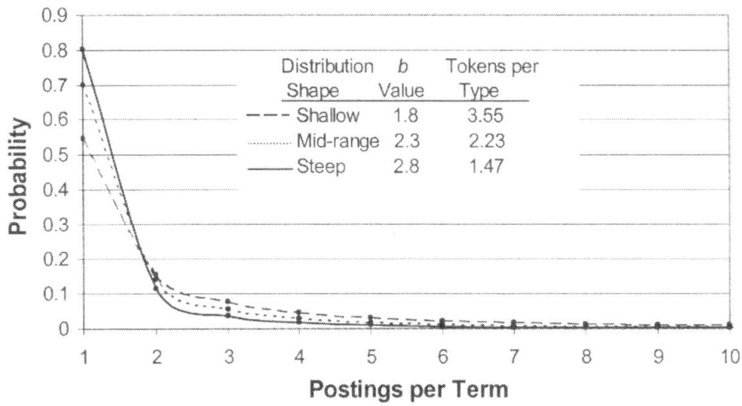

Figure 5.2. Three Sample Term Frequency Distributions

Often informetric studies focus on the most frequently occurring terms. For IR purposes, these frequently used terms provide little discriminative capacity in distinguishing one document from another. From this perspective, they represent prime candidates for stopword list membership. The estimation of maximal Zipf size values can be useful in determining the greatest number of tokens (x_{max}) likely to be encountered within a data set based on a sufficiently sized sample. Tague and Nicholls (1987) provide an estimation technique for the maximal size of a Zipf distribution and expected relationship between types and tokens. Summaries of resulting maximal values for different *b* parameter settings and numbers of term types are provided in tables.

The distribution of index terms may affect retrieval weights that are assigned to document terms. A classic term weight assignment measure for a given term in a document, called the inverse document frequency (*idf*), weight relies on the frequency of occurrence of a term across all documents:

$$idf_k = \log\left(\frac{N}{freq_k}\right) \tag{5.1}$$

where $freq_k$ is the number of documents in which term k appears and N is the total number of documents. Low frequency terms across documents are assigned a higher weight for retrieval purposes than are high frequency terms because the rarity of the term allows the system to identify a smaller number of documents of potential relevance. The term weight may also be calculated by multiplying the *idf* value by the frequency of the term within the document (*tf-idf*), to take into account the importance of a term within a document (assuming frequency implies importance):

$$tf\text{-}idf_{ik} = freq_{ik} \, x \, idf_k \tag{5.2}$$

where $freq_{ik}$ is the frequency of term k in document i. The frequency of the term within the document will affect the weight, with a higher frequency within the document indicating its significance. Within full-text documents, the term frequency within the document should intuitively also follow a Zipfian distribution and will contain more terms than a document surrogate. The highest weights will be assigned to infrequently occurring terms across documents that occur with higher frequency within a document.

The frequency of appearance of a term within a document will affect the number of postings associated with the term if proximity searching is supported. Because each occurrence of the term in the document will be recorded as an offset, the number of postings associated with a given term will be determined by dual Zipfian generation processes, where the frequency of occurrence both across documents and within documents will follow a Zipfian distribution. From a space design perspective, knowledge of the term distributions followed provides an indication of the space needed to house term indexes (see Chapter 7, Section 7.3.2).

The relationship between types and tokens has information theoretic implications as well, where the retrieval of the greatest amount of information may be determined by the term distribution (Zunde & Slamecka, 1967). In information theory, information is quantified as the likelihood of receiving messages of a given probability within a communication system (Shannon & Weaver, 1959). Using principles of information theory, Zunde and Slamecka derive a function for the optimal frequency distribution that results in the maximum average amount of information per term, represented by

$$p(t) = \frac{\left(1 - \frac{1}{\bar{t}}\right)^{t}}{\bar{t} - 1} \qquad (5.3)$$

where $p(t)$ represents the probability of occurrence of terms with $\bar{t}$ postings and is the average number of postings per term.

5.3 Indexing Exhaustivity/Term Assignment

5.3.1 Overview

Document indexing exhaustivity, or the number of terms assigned to a document, has been less frequently studied than term distributions, although characteristics of exhaustivity have been known since the earliest days of term distribution studies. Schultz, Schwartz, and Steinberg (1961) observed that rates of term assignment per document within two studied databases were unimodal with a mode greater than 1, but did not attempt to fit the data to any mathematical models. A sample of descriptor assignment exhaustivity for the same data set as in Figure 5.1 appears in Figure 5.3.

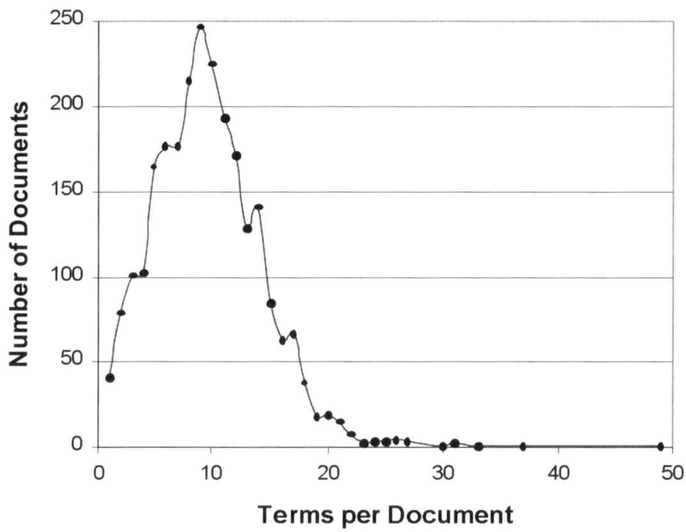

Figure 5.3. Indexing Exhaustivity Distribution

The study of indexing exhaustivity can be approached from two different levels of focus. Selective study of exhaustivity can be applied to the subject-oriented fields of structured documents such as descriptors, where human decisions have usually been made for subject assignment. For complete document indexing, exhaustivity may include all nontrivial words from all searchable fields determined by IR automatic indexing algorithms, thereby greatly increasing the number of access points for a given document. The average number of terms assigned per document in this case can quickly become quite large and will be dependent on the length of the overall document, not just the document subject field.

5.3.2 Indexing Exhaustivity Research

Fewer models have been proposed for fitting exhaustivity distributions. Bird (1974) uses Poisson, binomial, and negative binomial distributions, with some success for each depending on the nature of the distribution based on the relationship between the mean and variance of the data sets (see Chapter 4, Section 4.4.4). He also attempts to fit the continuous lognormal distribution with limited success. Since then, researchers such as Nelson and Tague (1985) and Wolfram (1992a) have also applied shifted forms of the Poisson, binomial, and/or negative binomial distribution, with varied success. The steepness of ascent and descent of the theoretical distributions does not always adequately model those of the observed distributions. However, for general modeling purposes such as computer simulations of IR systems where means and variances are known, the negative binomial distribution is usually the best to use. It does not appear that more dynamic models have been tested on exhaustivity data.

5.3.3 Characteristics of Indexing Exhaustivity Distributions

The tails of exhaustivity distributions are generally much shorter than term distribution tails for large data sets. The reasons for this are evident in how data are cumulated. The addition of documents to an IR system results in potentially many new tokens being added to the system as a result of the indexing process. It is much more dependent on the number of documents in the system whereas exhaustivity is more dependent on the indexing policy or the length of an individual document. Because exhaustivity data focus on the tally of the terms contributed and not the terms themselves, each document contributes only a single observation to the data set. As a result of the smaller number of types encountered in exhaustivity data sets, each new document is more likely to contribute to the amplitude of the distribution instead of new size values to the end of the tail.

There are trade-offs to be considered when deciding on the level of exhaustivity to be used in an IR system. Lower levels of exhaustivity produce fewer tokens and possibly types, resulting in smaller system storage requirements. They also result in fewer access points by which to retrieve a document, which could affect system recall. Higher levels of exhaustivity will result in more tokens and types and added access points for the retrieval of documents. However, by having more access points and greater potential for overlap in the number of common terms shared among documents, the ability to differentiate between documents during retrieval can be affected, particularly in vector-based retrieval environments (Wolfram & Zhang, 2002).

5.4 Term Co-Occurrence

5.4.1 Overview

Two index terms co-occur with one another if they are both indexed within the same document. By definition, co-occurrence can only exist if the document is indexed by at least two terms. The number of co-occurring pairs is directly affected by the indexing exhaustivity within a document, such that for n distinct terms per document, there will be $n(n-1)/2$ combinations of term pairs. In systems where field searching is possible, terms may even co-occur with themselves.

The concepts of term dependence and independence are central to co-occurrence studies. Binary independent models assume that the probability of two terms co-occurring is no greater than what chance would predict. Binary dependent models assume that some term pairs will co-occur with greater or lesser frequency than what chance would predict. Researchers have argued that term independence assumptions are unrealistic because some terms clearly will be more likely to co-occur with one another than with other terms (Salton, Buckley, & Yu, 1983; Nelson, 1983). Others cite that the percentage of terms where binary dependence holds true is small enough to ignore. The classic probabilistic information retrieval model, for example (see Chapter 2, Section 2.2.3), is based on a binary independence assumption, although dependence influences may be factored in (van Rijsbergen, 1977). Calculating the influence of binary dependence can be computationally quite expensive, but it does more realistically model dependencies among terms. When conducting co-occurrence research, researchers should indicate whether binary dependence or independence is assumed in their models.

5.4.2 Term Co-Occurrence Research

Distributions of term co-occurrence frequency, that is, the frequency with which two distinct terms co-occur with one another, follow a reverse J-shape, so that very few term pairs co-occur with great frequency, whereas most pairs co-occur infrequently (see Figure 5.4). Although it is possible to incorporate all non-co-occurring term pairs, that is, all possible term pairs for which the frequency of co-occurrence is zero, which will likely represent the largest tally, in practice only term pairs co-occurring at least once are studied. The lack of co-occurrence will be affected by the indexing exhaustivity, where higher levels of exhaustivity will increase the number of possible co-occurring term pairs and may reduce the number of non-co-occurring pairs.

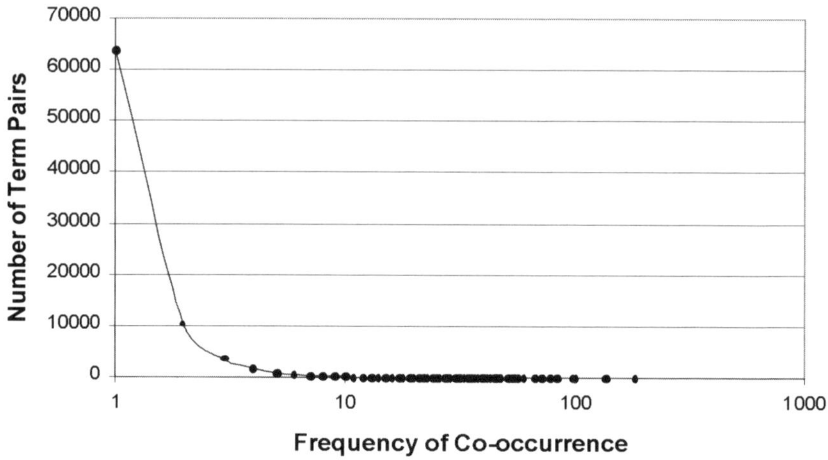

Figure 5.4. Distribution of Term Co-Occurrences by Unique Term Pairs

Nelson (1983) provides a survey of models that have been used to describe term occurrences. Models that have been suggested or fitted have included the Poisson (Jacquesson & Schieber, 1973), hypergeometric (Switzer, 1965), Bradford (Griffiths, 1975), and Zipf (Nelson & Tague, 1985). Zipfian models have been fitted most frequently, with mixed results. Models assuming binary independence underestimate the number of singly co-occurring pairs. Nelson and Tague (1985) demonstrate that a better theoretical fit is obtained when binary dependence is incorporated into the models fitted. Using a simulation methodology, they found that a second order binary dependence model produced a better fit than a binary independence model. However, even the dependent model still underestimated the number of singly occurring pairs.

Another approach, used by Tague, Nelson, and Wu (1981) and Nelson (1983), is to initially randomly select a term and to generate subsequent terms within the document based on a Zipf distribution of co-occurrences. Other efforts to model dependence influences have included van Rijsbergen (1977), who used a tree structure of term relationships, and Salton, Buckley, and Yu (1983), who developed a model for calculating binary and higher degrees of dependency using the Bahadur-Lazarsfeld expansion (BLE). Losee (1994) further investigated the impact of different degrees of dependence assumptions and the resulting retrieval improvements in a probabilistic IR system environment using the BLE. Based on experimental results, Losee concludes that incorporating dependence probabilities beyond degree 3 resulted in diminishing improvements in performance that did not merit further computation.

5.4.3 Characteristics of Term Co-Occurrence

The complexity of the relationship in term co-occurrences can be demonstrated by plotting the term co-occurrences based on the frequency of occurrence of each term. Intuitively, frequently occurring terms should co-occur frequently with other frequently occurring terms because their occurrences are distributed across a larger number of documents than are less frequently occurring terms. Likewise, the large number of uniquely occurring terms should co-occur frequently as a whole with other singly occurring terms. However, for terms of mid-range frequency, a wide range of co-occurrences is observed. Figure 5.5 demonstrates the relationship of term co-occurrence between term types of different sizes for the earlier data set consisting of 2,500 records and 4,234 terms, with an average of 9.6 terms assigned per record. Because of the symmetry between the co-occurring term pairs, only half of the plot is needed. There is a great deal of variability in the co-occurrences. In general, the large number of tokens generated by the few frequently and many singly occurring terms results in the highest number of co-occurrences.

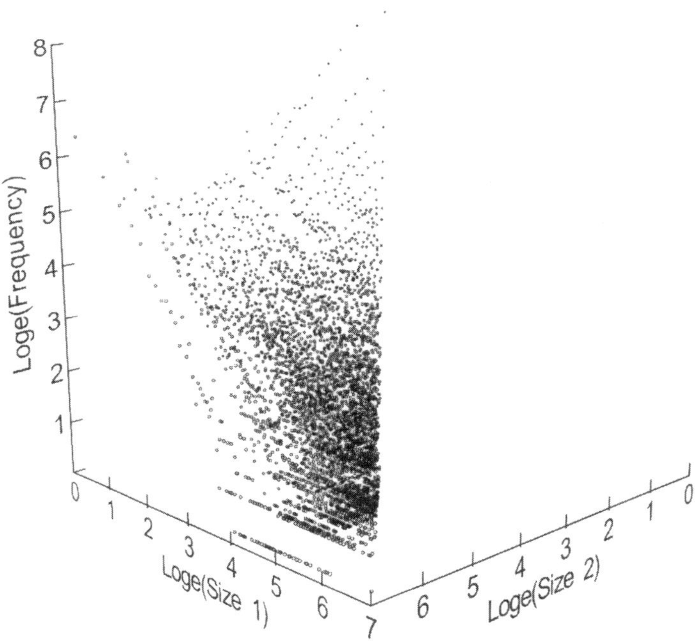

Figure 5.5. Distribution of Term Co-Occurrences by Term Frequencies of Occurrence (Sizes)

A high level of co-occurrence between two terms provides an indication of a relationship between the two terms. Knowledge of these relationships can be applied to IR system design. Applications have included the automatic generation of thesauri, query expansion, and automatic indexing. The significance of co-occurrence contributions, however, has been debated, because comparatively few term pairs in a term set generate high degrees of co-occurrence. Jacquesson and Schieber (1973), using a similarity co-efficient based on the number of co-occurrences of a term pair divided by the total number of documents containing either term, found that 0.14 percent of all term pairs produced a co-efficient value of more than 0.1. Peat and Willett (1991) demonstrated the limited gains achieved in retrieval effectiveness when co-occurrence data are incorporated into query expansion. Terms with high degrees of co-occurrence tend to be those that occur frequently anyway, and added terms do not improve the ability of the query to discriminate between relevant and nonrelevant documents.

5.5 Document Citations and Hyperlinks

5.5.1 Overview

Chapter 3, Section 3.3 outlined how references and citations create important connections between documents. The primary assumption upon which citation and co-citation analysis is based is that references to other documents or the co-citing of documents within another document create a topical connection among these documents. Information retrieval systems that incorporate document references and citations may then use these connections in the calculation of interdocument similarities.

The concepts of reference, citation, and co-citation may be extended to the hypertext environment. A hypertext link originating from one document pointing to another, called an *outlink*, is comparable to a text document reference. From the receiving document perspective, the acknowledgment it receives as a result of the link is called an *inlink,* representing the equivalent of a traditional publication citation. Two documents that receive inlinks from the same document are considered to be *co-linked.* A document that links to another part of itself is an internal link or a self-sitation. The similarities between references/citations and outlinks/inlinks make it possible to conduct investigations into the IPP equivalents in the hypertext environment. Because linkages define the structure of a hypertext system, one may study the frequency distribution of outlinks and inlinks per document. The distribution of co-linkages, like co-citations, may identify the strongest relationships among documents.

5.5.2 Research on System and Linkage Structure

The concept of citation and co-citation has been used in bibliographic IR research to help provide additional information on which to determine document similarities and ultimately the potential relevance to user queries. For example, bibliographic coupling (Kessler, 1963), or the determination of the similarity of two documents based on the number of references they share, serves as a simple way of grouping documents. Similarly, references given, citations received, and co-citations provide additional sources by which the relatedness of documents may be calculated. Croft and Thompson (1987) have demonstrated the benefits of incorporating citation data. However, apart from citation databases such as those produced by the ISI and the freely accessible NEC ResearchIndex or CiteSeer (http://citeseer.nj.nec.com), reference and citation data are generally not promoted by commercial bibliographic database services.

Studies examining the structure of hypertext environments, particularly the Web, have emerged since the mid-1990s. A number of techniques have been applied to the modeling of hypertext structure. Larson (1996) uses co-sitations (co-linkages) as an equivalent to co-citations to conduct a multidimensional scaling analysis of Web sites dealing with geographic information systems, earth sciences, and remote sensing. By tallying the number of pair-wise co-linkages from the collected sites, a correlation matrix of co-linkages among the sites is created. The resulting two-dimensional map reveals four distinct clusters of Web sites and their proximity relationship to one another. The two axes generated from the plot define the topical distinctions among the clusters, with sites at the center of the plot signifying the central importance of sites dealing with more general topics. Larson's research demonstrates the feasibility of using methodologies from co-citation analysis to study the relationships among Web sites. Like more traditional co-citation analyses, which are generally used at the disciplinary or subdisciplinary level, these methods are likely to be feasible only with well-defined subsets of the Web.

Pirolli, Pitkow, and Rao (1996) outline techniques based on structural topology and textual similarities between documents to organize Web pages based on categories, node types, and node relevancy. Through the use of linear equations and spreading activation models based on hyperlinks between documents, in combination with textual similarities and hyperlink usage patterns, additional documents likely to be relevant may be identified.

Wolfram (1996) examines interdocument linkage structure in a specialized bibliographic record hypertext system where descriptors with frequencies of occurrence greater than one served as paths of linkages to permit browsing of records sharing a common descriptor. The length of each path was the frequency of that descriptor, with the last document connecting back to the first document, and the descriptor exhaustivity for terms occurring more than once in the collection representing the number of outlinks from, or inlinks to, each document. Three models of descriptor co-occurrence were tested against the observed distribution of co-occurrences: a binary independent model of expected co-occurrences; a basic simulation model that assigned exhaustivity values, then descriptor frequencies to each document; and an enhanced simulation model that incorporated likelihoods of terms of a given frequency co-occurring with one another based on document exhaustivity. The enhanced model provided the best fit of the three tested but still underestimated the number of infrequently occurring terms, as had the other models. Even with such a highly structured hypertext environment, the development of an adequate model for the relationship between documents was elusive.

The complexity of a hypertext system with a large document collection is readily apparent to anyone who has tried to navigate the myriad of linkages that interconnect documents within such a system. The Web serves as the ultimate example of such a complex environment. With billions of interlinked Web pages, the structure of the Web is almost unimaginable. It has been estimated that the diameter of Web—that is the number of links to get to any point on the Web—may be as little as nineteen links or button clicks (Albert, Jeong, & Barabasi, 1999). Egghe (1997) proposes the use of a fractal model, where the fractal dimension serves as a measure of the complexity of the hypertext system. The fractal dimension (D) is defined as

$$D = \frac{\log N}{\log N + \log\left(\frac{1+\mu}{\mu}\right)} \qquad (5.4)$$

where N is the total number of documents and μ the average number of hyperlinks per document. The author indicates that, at present, there are no applications for such a measure.

In addition to overall structure of a hypertext system, one may study document-level features such as the distribution of inlinks and outlinks. The concept of inlinks and outlinks may be defined at different levels of granularity depending on the unit of measurement used and the definition of the boundary between what constitutes an internal or external link. As an example, a hypertext link may refer to a location within the referencing document itself. If an outlink is defined to be a link to another document, whether on the same Web server or elsewhere, this would be considered an internal link. At a higher level, an outlink may only refer to links to documents outside the referencing document's server or located at a different

Internet Protocol address. Finally, an outlink may refer to references made to documents outside the referencing document's high-level domain (e.g., a document within the .edu domain linking to a document in the .gov domain).

Inlink and outlink frequency distributions have not been widely studied to date. Rousseau (1997) investigated the distribution of inlinks to a set of Web sites dealing with informetrics. The initial frequency distribution could not be initially modeled to any classical informetric distribution. It should be noted that more than 70 percent of the sites did not receive any inlinks from outside sources. By assuming an implicit link from each site to itself, in essence removing the class of zero links, the observed distribution could be fitted to a Lotka model (or size-frequency form of a Zipf model). Adamic and Huberman (2001) fitted the distribution of inlinks and outlinks for Web sites, finding that both fitted an inverse power law (i.e., essentially Zipfian) for sites containing at least several dozen inlinks or outlinks. The relationship breaks down for smaller numbers, where the proportion of sites with a smaller number of inlinks and outlinks is overestimated. Ajiferuke and Wolfram (submitted b) have investigated the frequency distribution of outlinks using data sampled from top-level Web pages across five high-level domains (.com, .edu, .gov, .net, .org) and from sample pages within individual Web sites. The authors found that GIGP and generalized negative binomial models provided the best fits for the top-level Web page data. A Zipf model fitting was not attempted because it could not reflect the observed zero class. The outlink distribution data collected from individual Web sites revealed much more variable distribution forms. The observed bimodal and multimodal distributions could not be adequately fitted to any theoretical unimodal model without using a mixture of models over different parts of the observed distributions.

5.5.3 Characteristics of Hyperlinks

If one were to represent a set of print-based documents as nodes in a directed graph, with the references serving as edges within the graph, the graph would not contain lengthy circuits (i.e., a path of edges that ends at the same node where it started) because of the time differential in publication between citing and cited documents. At best, it may be possible to have a circuit consisting of two edges representing two concurrently published documents that cite one another. Hypertext systems, however, can make it possible to have circuits of any length up to the total number of documents within the systems if all documents in the system are treated as concurrent. In growing hypertext systems, where the modification of existing nodes and links is not possible, then the system would be comparable to a print-based environment without circuits.

Paths defining circuits within a hypertext system provide avenues for searchers to investigate. However, if the path is too long, there may be little benefit in its availability. The number of inlinks received by a document can serve as an indicator of the document's significance, just as citations received are thought of as indications of merit. The most visible example of the impact of inlinks can be seen in the Google search engine (Brin & Page, 1998), which, among other measures, relies on the number of inlinks received by a document to determine its relevance ranking. Within a year of its introduction in 1998, Google quickly became one of the leading search services available on the Internet, and the service of choice for many searchers.

The concept of a self-sitation is fundamentally different than a self-citation in the print world, although it can be equally problematic. A *self-sitation* is a self-referential document link, which is not observed in traditional citations, where other documents by the same author may be cited but not the same document. There may be design reasons for a document to supply one or more internal links, for example to quickly take the reader to another part of the document without having to scroll through additional content.

5.6 Other Document Attributes

Knowledge of the regularities of document attributes has applications in space planning for IR system content and potentially the design of file structures to house documents or their surrogates (see Chapter 7, Section 7.3). Universal generalizations of these properties may not be possible given the differences found across IR systems and their content, particularly for environments in which documents are not highly structured.

5.6.1 Term Lengths

Word lengths have been studied for many languages. For the English language, Kučera and Francis (1967) found the average word length to be 4.7 characters. However, this value includes repeating words. Because term files will house only distinct terms, or there may be a small number of repetitions of a given term in the file as a result of its appearance in different fields, the average length of a term will be higher. The distribution of term lengths will also be affected by the term inclusion policy, where short terms consisting of a small number of characters may be considered stopwords and will not be indexed. Subject-based terms, as opposed to keywords, may consist of more than one word in some IR systems, thereby increasing the average term size. By removing repeating words from the Kučera and Francis data set, Heaps (1978) found the average term length increased to 8.1 characters.

5.6.2 Field Lengths

For structured database environments, analysis at the field level can be revealing of properties associated with individual fields. For most IR systems, field lengths are variable, unlike traditional database management systems where they are usually of a prespecified length. Knowledge of basic statistics of field properties can be helpful in deciding whether the contents of a field should be indexed and can reveal implications for space requirements for inverted files for each field.

Analysis of field lengths may be undertaken at different levels of detail. For space requirement calculations, analysis will likely take place at the character or byte level. Distribution data will be revealing of the concentration of field lengths, with minimal and maximal values, but mean values and standard deviations are usually sufficient. Ayres and Yannakoudakis (1979), for example, have explored character-level field properties of bibliographic records stored in MARC (MAchine Readable Cataloging) format, a tagged field format widely used to catalog bibliographic records. The MARC format includes fields with very little variability (e.g., ISBN number) and those with considerable variability (e.g., document title). The authors also tabulated a rank-frequency distribution of unique subfields used in the MARC records studied. The distribution followed a strong inverse relationship, but it did not conform to a classic Zipf distribution when converted to a log-log format. Similarly, Williams and Schefner (1976) earlier analyzed MARC record characteristics over two time periods to determine the frequency of use of different MARC field tags and if changes occurred in the use of the tags over time.

Field analysis from a linguistic perspective is more useful when performed at the word or term level. Typically, a word-level analysis is performed on fields with no notable clumping of words. Examples of where word-level analysis would be used include title or abstract length distributions. Terms, on the other hand, may consist of one or more words. Complete author names or multiword descriptors that are not broken down to their individual words serve as examples of multiword terms that may be treated as singular units by some IR systems. In these cases, distributions would be tabulated based on the number of terms, not individual words. Whether word-level or term-level analysis is performed, each can be useful in estimating the space requirements for postings files or the size of individual field indexes.

5.6.3 Document Lengths

Document length analyses can be similar to field length studies. Although the primary unit of interest is the document as the source, the items generated that serve as the basis for measurement may be at the field, word, or character/byte level. At the character or byte level, the range of document sizes indexed by an IR system can be studied. With today's multimedia-based IR systems, the definition of document length becomes more complicated. Does one only include textual content, or are multimedia components embedded within documents also included? Multimedia components are stored as separate files for documents found on the Web. Do these then constitute separate, measurable documents? For studies examining document requests or downloads on the Web, the nontextual files, which are retrieved along with the textual components to which they are associated, must be included. If, on the other hand, the purpose of the study is to analyze indexable content in a text-based IR environment, then external nontextual documents would not be included as part of the data set. Whether the system stores the full text of the document or an abbreviated representation will affect the variability in document length. Document surrogates, with their more structured content and possibly extended abstracts, will have less variability than full-text systems, where documents of all conceivable lengths are possible.

Several units of measure for document length are possible, but what is actually feasible? The study of the number of fields used per document can provide a rough approximation for the level of structure within a document set where a set structure may not be in place. Lengths based on word or character/byte count distributions in large, diverse databases may be treated for practical purposes as continuous, given the range of values encountered. Word counts, in particular, may not be readily available, and document sizes may only be reported in terms of kilobytes or megabytes. With diverse document sets, values expressed in these larger terms should be sufficient to discriminate document sizes for modeling, particularly because space estimations rarely need to be specific down to the byte level when dealing with today's gigabytes of content. Due to the fineness of the granularity of measurement, continuous models may be used to represent document-length distributions. Candidate continuous models may include the Weibull, Pareto, logistic, and lognormal distributions (see Cooper & Weekes, 1983, ch. 5).

5.6.4 Document Persistence

Traditionally, bibliographic and full-text IR systems have relied on collections of documents that are static or simply grow in number. Unless there is an error in the document representation, or duplication, there is no need to remove or alter the document set that has already been indexed. Many IR systems now index dynamic environments, such as on the Web or organizational intranets, where there is turnover in the collection content, which requires that indexed documents be revisited periodically to determine changes in document content or availability (i.e., removal or change in location).

Recently, the lifespan of documents in these dynamic environments has been studied. Bar-Ilan and Peritz (1999) have examined the longevity of Web documents dealing with the topic of informetrics over a five-month period, with a follow-up a year later. They examined the persistence of Web documents in addition to the appearance of new documents and disappearance of existing documents. The investigators observed that approximately two-thirds of the documents found initially were still available during the follow-up period. Similarly, Koehler (1999) followed a sample of Web URLs weekly over the course of a year for continued availability and change. He developed two measures for Web-based document persistence: permanence, or the ability to access a document at a given or forwarded URL over time, and constancy, or the rate of change. The study reveals that although most documents have undergone changes, about 75 percent were still accessible at the same URL.

The distribution of frequency of changes of specific documents over a given period of time does not appear to have been investigated to date. This is admittedly more difficult to study than taking snapshots of document states at specified time intervals.

5.7 Database and Index Growth

5.7.1 Overview

The growth of literature collections such as journals, journal articles, monographs, and abstracting services that index journal articles represents an example of a one-dimensional IPP. These were studied even prior to the availability of electronic databases. The electronic medium, however, offers a more convenient method for studying the same phenomena. With an effective representation of system growth, one can predict future system resource requirements and plan accordingly. Size and growth studies of Internet search services and their coverage have been in vogue since the mid-1990s, with publications having appeared in the scholarly and popular literature (Huberman & Adamic, 1999; Lawrence & Giles, 1998b).

Many IR systems will add documents or records without deletion or modification unless there is an error in the document representation that needs correction. This is especially true for systems indexing bibliographic records, where the record content itself is never invalidated, although the documents the records represent may obsolesce. More recently, this notion of constant growth with no deletions has changed with Web-based IR systems, where content is constantly changing. Documents are created and removed from the Web, requiring regular updating of search engine indexes, but even with disappearing documents and Web sites, the general growth trend is predicted to continue sharply upward for the near future.

Growth investigations may focus on different components of an IR system, with each component potentially experiencing different rates and types of growth. Most studied is the rate of document growth, or rather the rate of growth of the addition of new documents indexed by the IR system. In addition, the growth of terms to the index may be studied. As new documents are added, new terms not currently appearing in the index may need to be added. Even if an indexed document contributes no new terms to the index, postings will be added to the postings file. Finally, with distributed IR environments gaining popularity, the growth of sources that contribute documents may be studied. In terms of the Internet, this could be represented by the growth in the number of Web servers or the number of domains available for indexing.

5.7.2 Research on IR System Growth

Models for document growth may incorporate any of the distributions discussed in Chapter 4, Section 4.4.5, particularly for linear or exponential growth. Because IR systems are not typically treated as systems with upper size limits, the use of S-shaped distributions for document growth may be inappropriate. If an S-shaped cumulative document distribution is observed, this may be a sign that the system is not keeping up with document growth by indexing fewer documents than expected.

Index and postings file growth is directly dependent on the number of documents and the content of the documents themselves. The growth rate in the number of index terms is highest when documents are first added to the new system. This growth then slows as more documents are added and fewer new term types are encountered. In early studies of dictionary buildup, Schwartz (1963) and Long, Barnhard, and Levy (1967) observed that index word growth followed a convex growth pattern. After the introduction of about 40,000 words of text, approximately 2,500 different words had been introduced, with a slowdown in growth for subsequent text, although even after 100,000 words, new words were still being added to the dictionary. Long, Barnhard, and Levy also compared the stability of word frequency, which establishes stable ranks for the different words. The twenty-five highest frequency words' ranks stabilized to their final rank after about 10,000 words, whereas words of lower frequency, such as a rank of 100, stabilized to its final rank after about 80,000 words. Heaps (1978) noted that for English texts of at least 20,000 words the increase (D) in the number of distinct words is related to the total number of words (N) such that

$$D = kN^{\beta} \qquad (5.5)$$

where k and β are constants.

5.7.3 Characteristics of IR System Content Growth

Document growth is measured by the number of documents indexed over time (e.g. monthly, yearly). Growth in space requirements to store documents can also be measured, but this is influenced by the distribution of document lengths (see Section 5.6.3). The growth of the document corpus itself will depend on external factors to the system such as document availability or indexing policies defining which documents are indexed.

Modeling the observed convex growth of index terms is more easily performed in cumulative form. Working at the individual document level in noncumulative form with large data sets is problematic, particularly given the "lumpiness" of the data with short-term variations. Grouping of documents into clusters of additions to the system may be needed to smooth out individual variability. In distributions without gaps, the use of LS model fitting using linear regression analysis on logarithmically transformed data presents a convenient way to determine growth rates (see Chapter 4, Section 4.5.3).

An example of the convexly increasing cumulative number of distinct terms with added documents is presented in Figure 5.6, representing the 2,500-record set from above, indexing only descriptors. Because the pool of terms consists of a more limited, controlled vocabulary, the rate of growth decreases more rapidly than in a free text indexing environment where a wider range of terms is encountered. Rates of decrease in the addition of terms may also be affected by the indexing exhaustivity, where higher rates of exhaustivity make it possible to introduce new index terms sooner in the growth of the document set. Index growth can continue at higher rates in distributed environments, such as the Web, even with sizeable indexes with many term types already in place. With multilingual content there is the ability of indexing systems to include a broader range of types of text, including URLs and e-mail addresses as potential terms. So, in practical terms, there is no upper limit to the size of an index if such a system continues to index new documents. Because these distributed environments do not store most of the indexed documents but merely point to them, determination of space requirements for document growth is not a vital concern, but the impact of this growth on the size of indexes that provide document access is of greater interest to developers of distributed retrieval services.

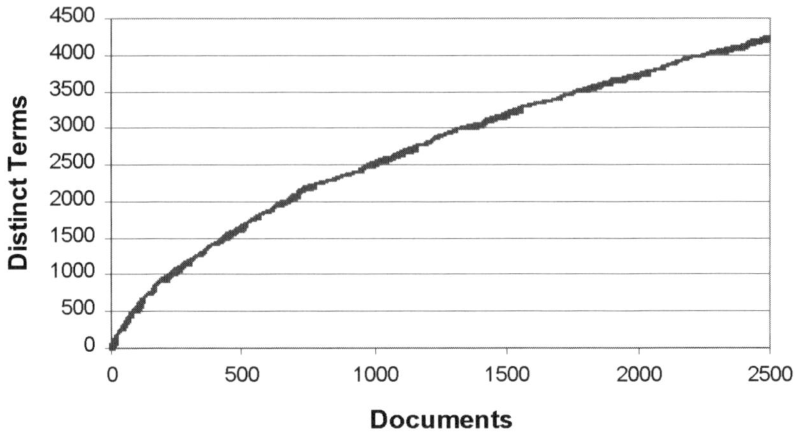

Figure 5.6. Term Index Growth versus Number of Documents

The growth of the postings file will more closely match the document growth pattern. Unlike the variable addition of new index terms as the number of documents grows, there will be a stable addition of tokens introduced by each document, each of which will be included as postings in the postings file. The average number of postings per document will only change if the average document length changes or there is a change in the indexing policy for documents. The indexing policy can affect the number of indexed fields within structured documents, and the search abilities that affect the number of postings, such as proximity searching, where each occurrence of a term within a document ultimately becomes a posting, will influence how quickly the postings file grows.

Today's distributed IR environments present new high-level units of measurement for growth analysis. With Web and file transfer protocol servers providing access to billions of documents, one can examine growth at the server or Internet domain level. Internet growth studies appear in the general scientific literature on a regular basis, and many services now exist that collect statistics related to Internet hosts and usage. This rate of growth from the system perspective, or from the user population perspective for that matter, has been phenomenal. The rate of growth of the number of hosts that constitute the Internet since the late 1960s has continued to be exponential, with over 170 million hosts as of early 2003 (Internet Software Consortium, http://www.isc.org/ds/). Within the course of a single decade, the number of Web servers has grown from a few internal servers to approximately 30 million worldwide (see, for example, the Netcraft Surveys Web site at: http://www.netcraft.com/survey; Adamic & Huberman, 2001). This growth can also be reflected in the increasing numbers of Web sites or pages over time. Other measures as indicators of the growth of document collections, such as the increase in the number of search services available, do not serve as a good indicator due to the volatility of the existence of individual services over time.

5.8 Domain-Level Analysis in Distributed Environments

5.8.1 Overview

So far, IR system properties associated with the documents themselves have been discussed. With distributed sites for IR system access, informetric analysis at the site or domain level has become feasible. A domain is a uniquely identifiable location in a distributed environment such as an Internet Protocol address, usually associated with a file transfer protocol server or Web server. Domain-level analysis may also be undertaken at higher levels of domain, such as at the organization type or national level (e.g., .edu, .org, .us, .de).

Web and file transfer protocol servers provide access to a collection of documents that are accessible to IR systems that index local and remote resources. The distribution of resources per domain, such as the number of Web pages, provides an indication of the total indexable content available and allows the system manager to determine the range of processing needed to index available domains. The collection of domain size data may be approached from two perspectives: the distribution of the number of documents/pages available on each domain (server-dependent) or the distribution of documents indexed per domain (IR system index-dependent). Pages per site distribution studies are beginning to appear in the literature.

5.8.2 Domain Analysis Research

The relative newness of domain-level investigations means that there are at present few studies that have investigated the nature of the domain size distributions. Rousseau (1997) investigated the distribution of top-level domains for Web sites indexed by the AltaVista search service that deal with informetrics, scientometrics, or bibliometrics. The top-level domain affiliation of the resulting 343 documents was tabulated into a domain distribution. The observed distribution was found to fit a Lotka distribution. Web search service evaluation sites such as Search Engine World (http://www.searchengineworld.com) publish statistical findings of different search engines, including the high-level domain distribution for Google (http://www.google.com).

Adamic and Huberman (2001) investigated the distributions of several domain-level data aspects for Web sites, including the number of pages indexed per Web site, using data from infoseek.org and archive.org. By plotting the number of pages (i.e., text files) per site against the proportion of sites containing that number of pages using a logarithmic transformation on each axis, they were able to fit an inverse power law distribution ($1/x^{\beta}$), although the values of the β parameters for these data sets are not reported. The slightly convex plot of data would indicate that a more general model is needed to adequately fit site size data. The use of theoretical distributions used in informetric research merit investigation for what appears to be an inverse relationship with a long tail.

5.8.3 Characteristics of Domain-Level Analysis

The distributed nature of domain-level data can present more data collection challenges than system-specific data analysis where the complete data set is readily available. This is comparable to more traditional print-based informetric studies where investigators are dealing with a potentially incomplete data set because of the lack of availability or awareness of additional relevant sites.

Adamic and Huberman (2001) noted that most Web sites consist of a small number of pages whereas very few consist of millions of pages. It appears this relationship is reverse J-shaped. The definition of what constitutes a Web site was not provided, but a completely inverse relationship based on the number of Web pages would mean the most frequent number of pages per site is one. This would seem small for an Internet domain, but perhaps not for the number of top-level Web pages per site. If one could demonstrate the applicability of a Lotka/Zipf model for domain distributions, the lack of fit to these models within a search service index could indicate the lack of comprehensive indexing by the system. Further research is needed to better define the characteristics of the distribution of domains over the Web or within search service indexes.

5.9 Summary and Additional Readings

The recognition of the existence of empirical regularities in IR system content goes back to the earliest days of automated IR research. These regularities in document content, whether the frequency distribution of index terms, indexing exhaustivity, connections between documents, or local/global growth of document collections, provide valuable input for understanding the mechanisms underlying IR and are invaluable in the design and evaluation of IR systems. The search for models to adequately describe system content often proves to be as challenging as in any other area of informetric study, demonstrating that although one may be studying what appears to be a clearly defined process, sophisticated social underpinnings affect how these processes may be generalized.

Few works on IR have incorporated significant components of informetric characteristics of system contents and their impact on IR system design. Heaps' monograph (1978), although lacking coverage of recent developments in IR, devotes a chapter to vocabulary characteristics of database documents and their applications for systems development. Losee (1998) also recognizes the importance of the characteristics of natural language and its impact on IR system processes. Although this is not presented specifically within an informetrics framework, the work does raise a number of important issues in theoretical information retrieval and how they are affected by term and query characteristics.

Developments in Internet-based services and reports of system content and their use can be found on a number of Web sites. Due to the volatility of Web site availability, the continued availability of current system statistics cannot be guaranteed. Search Engine Watch (http://www.searchenginewatch.com), for example, provides freely available and subscription-based information and insights into different publicly available IR services. For a perspective that is more library and information science oriented, Search Engine Showdown (http://www.searchengineshowdown.com) provides summary figures and analyses of search features and relative sizes of many popular services. Other resources for growth data in particular include the Matrix.Net Web site at http://www.matrix.net and Internet Software Consortium (http://www.isc.org).

6

Informetrics and IR System Use

One picture is worth ten thousand words.

—Old proverb

6.1 Introduction

Until the 1980s, informetric study of user interactions with IR systems focused almost exclusively on document circulation (see Chapter 3, Section 3.5), and to a lesser degree on query characteristics. With a growing recognition of the importance of the user in IR system design and evaluation have come many opportunities to study regularities in the way users interact with IR systems. To date there have been fewer user studies in these areas than system studies, but the area is rapidly developing. Many of the features studied in the IR systems themselves have equivalents in system usage. Units of analysis extend from the query term level, to the query itself, up to the user search session consisting of one or more queries. Regularities in search modifications and system browsing also present promising topics for investigation to better understand overall user interactions with IR systems.

6.1.1 IR System Use

A primary difficulty associated with user studies of IR systems has been the lack of available data. Nelson (1988) outlines four methods that may be used to collect user data: (1) surveys of users, (2) case studies using unobtrusive observation, (3) recorded search logs, and (4) online monitoring and tabulation. User data collection has usually been an afterthought in many systems. Those systems that do store usage data are generally proprietary, and data are unavailable to researchers. Other data collection methods introduce bias concerns. For example, data collection using post-search survey instruments is useful for eliciting user responses. However, such instruments may not represent actual search behavior but rather the behavior the user wished to report. Experimental studies involving unobtrusive observation to collect user search data are notorious for being time consuming and can create in the interests of experimental control an artificial environment that is not representative of real-life searching.

As commercial interest in IR systems has grown, so has recognition of the need for market research analyzing how users interact with the systems and their content. Today's systems can create immense log files of usage data, recording, among other features, queries entered, search features used, time spent conducting a search, and browsing patterns. Personal demographic information may also be requested or gleaned from the users. Ultimately, usage logs cannot reveal why users engage in the behaviors they do, unless the system used specifically asks this of each user.

6.1.2 Issues Associated with User-Based Data

The collection and availability of a wide range of user data raises both research and ethical issues. With so much data available, the processes being considered, the sources, and the items they generate must be well defined. Jansen and Pooch (2001) compare user-centered measures used in IR research in different types of systems. They find little overlap in the types of usage and performance metrics applied in OPAC, "traditional" IR, and Web-based IR user studies. Even among the newer Web-based studies there is little common ground on which to base comparisons. A common ground begins with a list of assumptions and definitions of what is being studied in user-based research. The definition of the data units for investigation is more clearly defined for system content data because the system processes create the data elements being studied. For analyses related to querying of IR systems, transaction logs of user sessions usually serve as the source from which query data are collected. These transaction logs must be processed manually or by some automatic means developed by the investigator. In this case, before analysis can begin the concepts term, query, and user session must be defined. Several key questions, outlined in Chapter 4, Section 4.2.1, must be asked. Another more limited option is to have the system tally counts of requests for resources or index term usage within the system. This method provides less context than transaction logs, but the data are more readily available and can be easily tabulated. Even with definitions of data elements, measures for those units must be determined. For example, does one measure a user search session by the number of queries or the amount of time taken?

Identification of and distinctions between users can be problematic. In single user systems, users, the queries they submit, and the search sessions they build may be identified by the starting and ending points defined by options to start or end usage of the system. In large proprietary IR systems that handle simultaneous requests, users may be identified by login information, where users are required to sign into an account. Internet Protocol addresses, which will more likely coincide with a given site and not a specific user, can also be used. Finally, for anonymous search environments such as public search engines on the Web, IR systems may deposit cookies on a given machine to track search submissions over time. At best, cookies can only identify searches originating from a given computer and not a specific user, particularly if a computer is publicly available for use by many people.

The study of system usage raises the same ethical issues inherent in all social research, which are not present in system-centered research that does not incorporate user experiments. Of primary concern are assurances of confidentiality and user privacy (Cooper, 1998). An example of this is data collected from public systems such as Internet-based search engine query and browsing data, where users may be unaware that their activities are being recorded. When using a computer there is an assumption of privacy and impermanence of one's transactions unless hardcopies are created. In reality these data are increasingly being collected to gain a better understanding of user search habits and interests. To protect user privacy, these data are not shared with others, or if they are, any information linking search data to specific individuals is removed. Numeric identifiers may be assigned to observations to allow linking of data to a given source, but nothing more.

6.1.3 Current State of Research

Informetric study of IR system usage has been more limited than system content research. Most user-based research until recently has focused on summary statistics without examining the full range of observed behaviors. Published research has related primarily to the use of in-house resources within specific organizations from systems such as OPACs or other internal bibliographic databases. As user session logs and database content statistics have become more widely available and are increasingly being viewed as valuable data for market research, the frequency with which these studies have been published has increased, especially since the mid-1990s. As have other areas of informetric study, much of this research has been spurred by the growth of Internet-accessible search systems. There are several advantages to studying the use of remotely accessible systems: (1) It permits the collection of larger data sets because of the broader potential user population, (2) it expands the demographic array of users and increases geographic diversity, and (3) findings may be more easily generalized.

Studies of Web-based services have appeared with increasingly regularity, including Web-based OPACs of library holdings (Cooper, 2001), vendor-based bibliographic and full-text databases (Wolfram & Xie, 2000), and Web search services such as AltaVista (Silverstein, Henzinger, Marais, & Moricz, 1999), Excite (Jansen, Spink, & Saracevic, 2000), and Fireball (Hoelscher, 1998). The Excite data sets, in particular, have resulted in a number of published studies of query and search characteristics of end users on the Web. The present array of research constitutes an initial foray into Internet user studies, with many areas still to be explored in detail.

6.2 Distribution of Query Terms/Term Usage

6.2.1 Overview

The system usage analogue of document index term frequency distributions is the distribution of query terms. A key distinction between the two is that query terms are not limited to the terms defined by the document contents. Conceivably, users may enter any term they wish, although terms consistent with the index vocabulary must be used to retrieve any documents. Also, unlike index terms, which have already been identified by the system, query logs will need to be parsed by the investigators. The definition of what constitutes a term must be specified before this can happen. For convenience and efficiency, transaction logs can be processed electronically by parsing queries on a character-by-character basis. Parsing routines will require rules to identify terms. Terms are usually assumed to begin and end with alphanumeric characters, although exceptions may need to be made in the case of e-mail addresses and URLs, unless each component is treated as a separate term.

Another method of recording the use of terms in queries can be system implemented, where a tally is kept of each index term usage in a query. The primary advantage of this approach is that no additional parsing is necessary to identify terms, and counts of each term's use are already tabulated. The drawbacks of using this approach are that there is no way to connect the co-occurrence of terms in queries because query data are not kept. Just as with other resource utilization tallies (Section 6.7), the data reflect cumulative usage over time but not potential changes in use over time unless the tallies are reinitialized periodically. Finally, term tallies only reflect the usage of query terms for which there is a corresponding index term in the system. In this case, the data set collected is more accurately described as the distribution of index terms used, as opposed to the distribution of query terms used. The use of nonindexed terms remains unknown, unless they are added to an exception file housing nonindexed terms, with its own counts.

6.2.2 Research on Query Term Distributions and Term Usage

The few studies that have investigated the distribution of query terms reveal a classic reverse J-shape, with most terms occurring once or twice and few occurring many times. Jansen, Spink, and Saracevic (2000) fitted the query term distribution taken from approximately 50,000 queries to a rank-frequency Zipf model using least squares estimation on a logarithmic transformation of the data set. The fit was poor, particularly for the frequently occurring terms located at the low end of the distribution. In subsequent studies of additional Excite data sets from 1997, 1999, and 2001, the authors found that approximately 57 to 62 percent of terms entered were unique (Spink, Jansen, Wolfram, & Saracevic, 2002). Ajiferuke and Wolfram (submitted a) attempted to fit the 1999 and 2001 Excite data sets to several additional models, including a zero-truncated GIGP, which produced the best fits of the models tested, but still with significant chi-square goodness-of-fit outcomes.

Several studies incorporating data from index term usage tallies have also appeared. Bennett (1975) studied searches performed on a medical database and concluded that the frequency of term occurrence in an index cannot be used as a reliable indicator of its frequency of use in searches. Nelson (1988) also examined the correlation of term usage and term indexing frequencies for an OPAC. He modeled both term indexing frequency and frequency of use in a cumulative form of the Bradford distribution using nonlinear LS, resulting in high R^2 values for each. Both Spearman's rank and Pearson's correlation coefficients were calculated against term index frequency and frequency of use, resulting in a significant outcome for both; however, significant variation existed as revealed by a scatter plot of the data. Wolfram (1992a) incorporated term usage data from the same system in a simulation of IR system usage by taking into account total usage for terms of each distinct term indexing frequency. When tallied, the many terms of low indexing frequency are used most often as a whole, with terms of greatest indexing frequency also seeing high usage. The terms of mid-range frequency, for the most part, were used less, although much variation existed, making modeling to a theoretical distribution unrealistic. Existing studies that have modeled query term distributions have rarely gone beyond traditional Zipf distributions.

6.2.3 Characteristics of Query Term Distributions

The nature of the distribution of query terms by itself merits investigation, but for some researchers the focus on specific parts of the distribution holds more interest. For example, the most frequently used query terms are of interest to determine what searchers are looking for. For systems with specialized content, such as subject-specific bibliographic databases, this may be less of an issue. However, for public systems indexing a broad range of subjects that are searched by general audiences, a basic understanding of common search interests can be gained by examining the most frequently entered search terms. In the case of Internet search engines, service marketers may wish to target advertising to users based on the popularity of search terms. As an example, the thirty most frequently entered search terms from the May 2001 query log of Excite appears in Table 6.1.

Table 6.1. Most Frequently Entered Terms in the Excite Search Engine (From a Set of 500K Distinct Queries from May 2001)

and	129,170	music	2,563
of	16,972	download	2,523
the	11,637	university	2,405
free	11,472	state	2,248
in	9,594	lyrics	2,226
for	5,894	or	2,142
sex	4,851	home	2,099
pictures	4,311	games	2,064
to	4,252	software	2,007
new	3,918	American	1,979
a	3,556	stories	1,965
nude	3,417	porn	1,947
pics	3,025	college	1,923
on	2,986	county	1,870
de	2,853	car	1,843

Note that many of the terms serve as search modifiers or are words that provide no indication of subject content on their own. There is a danger in trying to extrapolate user search interests based simply on the frequency of individual search terms. A term by itself may not provide a context for the query. For example, the first noun appearing on the list (sex) does not necessarily indicate that it is the most popular search topic. In fact, as a term it appears in less than 1 percent of the data set queries. Likewise, an adjective such as "adult" provides no context because it may appear in a query dealing with "adult material" or "adult education." Most queries consist of two or more terms (see Section 6.3), requiring that at least binary query term co-occurrence be analyzed if the emphasis of the research is on subject content (see Section 6.4).

The analysis of the many terms appearing only a few times can be just as revealing of search behavior, particularly for error analysis. Changes in the number of distinct terms over time can provide an indication of shifts in search behaviors. For example, in the Spink, Jansen, Wolfram, and Saracevic (2002) study comparing changes in searching over three data sets from Excite across four years, there were shifts in a number of areas. During that time the number of unique terms (types) for each comparably sized data set increased by approximately 29 percent, indicating that there has been growth in the range of terms being entered. Additional data sets are needed over a longer period of time to determine whether this is a trend.

6.3 Terms Used per Query

6.3.1 Overview

The number of terms used per query can provide a rough indication of the amount of effort users are putting into the formulation of their queries. It will be a function of the system capabilities and the search features supported. For example, in systems that support query expansion, fewer terms may need to be entered to produce the same outcome as a system that does not support query expansion. Unlike the distribution of terms assigned per document (see Chapter 5, Section 5.3), the terms used per query are not an indication of exhaustivity because user query contents are theoretically not confined to the system indexing vocabulary. The number of terms counted per query will depend on the definition of a term and how search operators are handled. In systems that permit word-based search operators (e.g., AND, OR, NOT, NEAR), are the operators considered to be terms? Without a context, it may be difficult to determine if a word is being used as a search operator or a search term. In this situation, it is easier to treat all entered words as terms. In some systems these operators may be replaced with nonalphanumeric characters (+,-,!), making their identification and exclusion easier.

6.3.2 Research on Terms Used per Query

The distribution of terms used per query can be reverse J-shaped in the case of environments in which most users simply enter single term queries. It is more likely that the distribution will have a mode greater than one, with a mean dependent on the sophistication of the search population. Unlike indexing exhaustivity distributions, the distribution of terms used per query has not been as widely studied. Wolfram (1992a) collected query data for three system environments (bibliographic citation, full text, and OPAC) as part of an IR system design study using simulation techniques. The observed distributions for each set were fitted to shifted forms of the Poisson and negative binomial distributions. The negative binomial model resulted in adequate fits for two of the three data sets using chi-square goodness-of-fit tests at an alpha level of .05. The data sets were small when compared to more recent studies, consisting of up to 300 queries.

In a study of a very large set of queries consisting of approximately one billion search requests submitted to the AltaVista search service, Silverstein, Henzinger, Marais, and Moricz (1999) found the mean number of terms per query to be 2.35. Approximately 80 percent of queries made no use of word or symbol operators. More recently, as part of the analysis of approximately one million queries submitted to the Excite search engine, Spink, Wolfram, Jansen, and Saracevic (2001) looked at the empirical distribution of terms entered per query. The data were not fitted to any theoretical models, but the distribution was unimodal with a mode of two terms per query and a long tail consisting of very few queries. An example of the distribution of terms per query for queries submitted to Excite in May 2001 appears in Figure 6.1. The mean number of terms per query is 2.6. This distribution, representing more than 500,000 nonrepeating queries, as a whole cannot be adequately modeled by a negative binomial distribution; however, samples of 500 queries taken from the data set can be fitted to a negative binomial model at an alpha value of .05. Ajiferuke and Wolfram (submitted a) fitted the 1999 and 2001 data to several models, including a zero-truncated GIGP, but with poor results for all models. The reason for the poor fit stemmed from the nature of the observed distributions. The GIGP was able to fit the first two classes (the number of one- and two-term queries) very well but could not account for the sharp drop thereafter in the number of terms used per query.

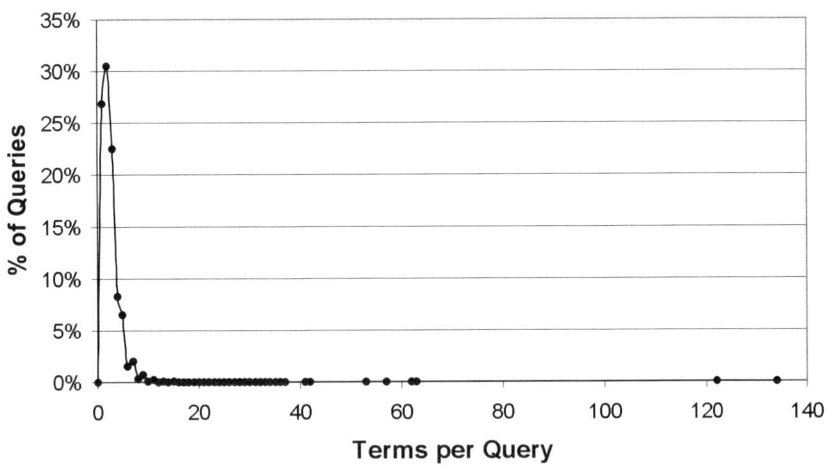

Figure 6.1. Terms Used per Query (Excite Search Service —Data Collected on May 4, 2001)

6.3.3 Characteristics of Terms Used per Query

The nature of the distribution will depend on factors that include the user characteristics, the type of IR system, and the type of searching supported. The small average number of terms used per query found in Web search engine studies contrasts with the higher average values of seven to fifteen terms per query found by Jansen, Spink, Bateman, and Saracevic (1998) in a review of four studies dealing with more traditional bibliographic databases. Generally, more experienced searchers used more terms per query than did novice or inexperienced searchers. Systems that support Boolean operations will contain on average more terms than those that do not. However, findings from the Excite studies reveal that few queries make use of Boolean operators (Spink, Jansen, Wolfram, & Saracevic, 2002). Systems that support natural language queries will clearly contain more words per query as a result of context phrases such as "Where can I find . . ." or "What is the . . . ". As more data sets become available over a longer period of time, it will become possible to track changes in general user search behavior over time. For example, in Spink, Jansen, Wolfram, and Saracevic (2002) the authors found that the use of Boolean operators grew between 1997 and 2001, from approximately 5 to 10 percent of queries, but the number of search terms remained relatively stable, from 2.4 to 2.6 terms per query, during the same time.

The average number of terms per query, although often unimodal, will likely be less than the indexing exhaustivity, and the observed range is likely to be higher as a result of the defined rules for indexing documents and relative freedom in formulating queries. One must also consider whether the system to which queries are submitted places limitations on the number of terms processed, thereby curtailing lengthy queries. This assumes, of course, that users are aware of these limitations. In the case of the Excite studies, even though the service processed only the first ten query terms, and the vast majority of users entered far fewer than ten terms, some queries contained dozens of terms. What emerges from the available literature on Web search services is that most users are generally unwilling or unable to formulate sophisticated searches using more than three terms (see Chapter 7, Section 7.5).

With an understanding of user query formulation habits, designers can estimate the average size of queries and the range of processing that will be needed to execute entered queries. It is also a key component of IR simulation models that incorporate user search behavior.

6.4 Query Term Co-Occurrence and Topic Analysis

6.4.1 Overview

Analysis of co-occurring query terms, like co-occurrence analysis of index terms, can provide insights into relationships among terms. In this case, the co-occurrence of terms arises from the user's perspective and is not based on automatic indexing rules or human indexers familiar with vocabulary control. Co-occurrence analysis also provides a useful quantitative tool for understanding the more qualitative aspects of the topicality of queries. Information retrieval service developers are understandably interested in how their systems are being used for searching and for what purpose. Co-occurring term pairs or higher combinations of terms will provide a better indication of topicality for multiterm queries than single terms alone, although it is the complete query that provides the best indication of topicality. Topic analysis of queries based on the complete queries themselves can present challenges. Manual analysis of query content can be quite time consuming, requiring that samples of large query logs be used for the analysis. Both approaches have been used.

Different informetric methods are used to study query term co-occurrence. Model fitting of co-occurrence frequency distributions can be useful in summarizing overall co-occurrence behavior and examining dependency relationships within the data sets. Exploratory techniques such as cluster analysis and multidimensional scaling are helpful in identifying patterns in query relationships.

6.4.2 Research on Query Term Co-Occurrence and Topic Analysis

Wolfram (1999) examined term co-occurrence characteristics of approximately 293,000 multiterm queries submitted to the Excite search engine. The observed frequency distribution for distinct term pairs followed a reverse J-shape. It was fitted to size-frequency forms of the Zipf, Mandelbrot, and generalized Waring distributions. None resulted in an adequate fit, causing the author to conclude that, although conforming to a classic inverse relationship, the distribution was not Zipfian.

In another study using the same data set, Ross and Wolfram (2000) used the thousand most frequently co-occurring term pairs to identify relationships among query topics using cluster analysis and multidimensional scaling. The analysis of term pairs allowed a larger representation of queries than individual query analysis alone would permit. Term pairs were categorized into one or more of thirty content areas. Using cluster analysis, the authors identified well-defined subject areas of searching at the six-cluster level (sex, computers/gaming, education, products and services, formal information needs, and informal information needs). An example of cluster organization from this study appears in Figure 6.2. Multidimensional scaling in two and three dimensions revealed a similar grouping of subject areas, with dimensions in the three-dimensional plot defining the continuum of search topics defined by personal to institutional interests, general to specific, and leisure/informal to formal information requests.

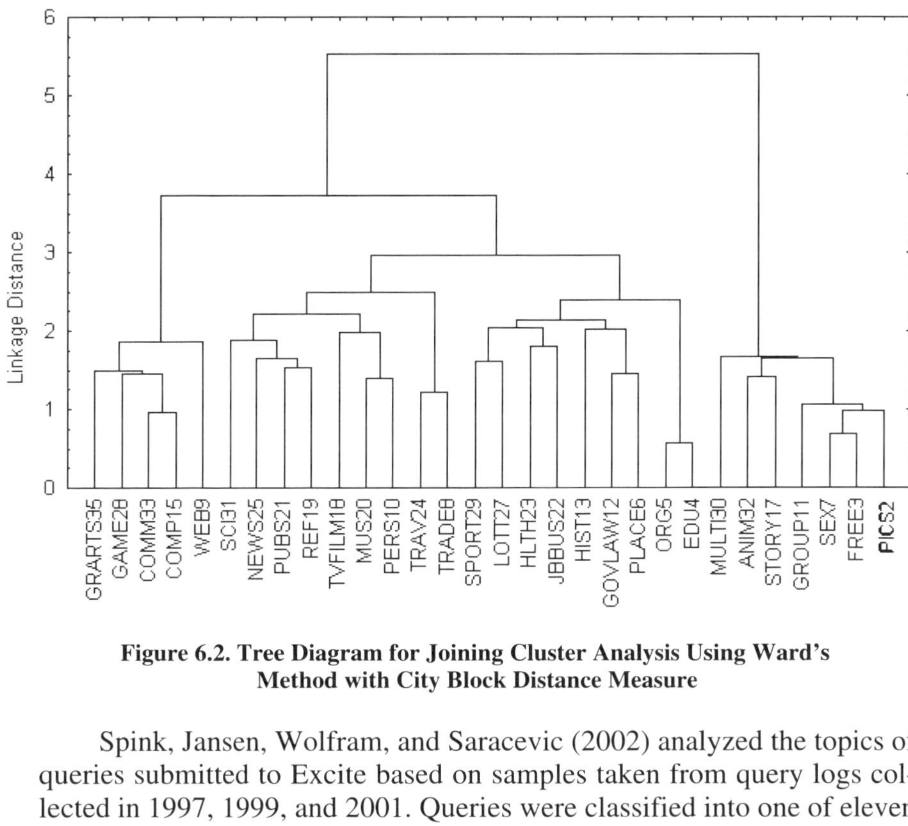

Figure 6.2. Tree Diagram for Joining Cluster Analysis Using Ward's Method with City Block Distance Measure

Spink, Jansen, Wolfram, and Saracevic (2002) analyzed the topics of queries submitted to Excite based on samples taken from query logs collected in 1997, 1999, and 2001. Queries were classified into one of eleven categories. The distribution of query topics shifted noticeably over the four-year period. In 1997, the two most frequent categories for searches, constituting approximately 37 percent of all queries, dealt with entertainment/recreation and sexually related topics. Within the 1999 and 2001 data sets, the two most popular categories, representing about 35 percent of all queries, were commerce/travel/employment and a general information category of people/places/things. The two most popular categories in the 1997 query set dropped to a combined 15 percent of all queries in the 1999 and 2001 sets. In an earlier study (Spink, Wolfram, Jansen, & Saracevic, 2001) the authors noted that for the 1997 data set, the distribution of query topics did not coincide with the distribution of subjects on the Web found by Lawrence and Giles (1999). The distribution of search topics appeared now to be converging with the content of the Web.

More recently, Pu, Chuang, and Yang (2002) used term co-occurrence in queries submitted to three search services to automatically categorize query terms into a set of thirteen predefined main and eighty-five subcategories without significant human intervention. Query terms new to the system were categorized based on co-occurrences with existing terms with known categorization. By relying on an initial set of queries and terms that were manually classified, the investigators were able to efficiently categorize submitted queries with a relatively high percentage of agreement with human experts. The ability to rapidly categorize queries makes it possible to efficiently analyze subject distributions over time.

6.4.3 Characteristics of Query Term Co-Occurrence and Topic Analysis

As with index term co-occurrence, the frequency with which the most frequent term pairs co-occur declines rapidly. Wolfram (1999), in his Excite query term co-occurrence study, found that 98 percent of term pairs co-occured fewer than ten times. The twenty-five most frequently meaningful co-occurring pairs (i.e., those containing at least one noun and not just combinations of semantically empty words such as operators) accounted for approximately 1 percent of the 1.3 million term pairs in the data set, but frequency of occurrence had already dropped below 350 occurrences by the twenty-fifth ranked meaningful pair.

Silverstein, Henzinger, Marais, and Moricz (1999) also examined frequencies of term pair co-occurrences for a subset of 10,000 terms used in 313 million queries submitted to AltaVista. They found high positive correlations between certain term pairs. Most often these pairs were parts of phrases. Higher level co-occurrences on three- and four-term combinations using the correlated term pairs with single terms and other term pairs were also examined, again resulting in combinations of terms being used as parts of phrases, resulting in the highest correlations depending on the word grouping used.

Preliminary findings of shifts in search topics submitted to general subject search environments such as Web search engines offer intriguing glimpses into changes in popular searching. Additional data sets over longer periods of time are needed.

6.5 Query Frequency Distribution

6.5.1 Overview

The frequency with which specific queries are entered by different users can provide insights into the scatter or concentration of user search interests. From an information seeking perspective, the study of the most frequently submitted queries to a public search service can provide a snapshot of popular culture at that point in time. Study of the changes in queries submitted over time may provide insights into seasonal and longer term changes in users' information needs.

Definitions for query equivalence need to be established. Are two queries, each submitted by different users, considered to be equivalent only if they match on a character-by-character basis? If one user includes an extra space between terms, but in all other respects the query contents are similar, does this constitute a different query? Or if the same terms and operators are used, but in a different order (e.g., "information and science" versus "science and information") , are the queries equivalent? System handling of queries and term ordering may need to be considered, where preceding terms are assigned higher weights or importance than subsequent terms, thereby negating any notion of query equivalence.

6.5.2 Research on Query Frequency Distributions

Published studies of the distribution of queries submitted to IR systems are relatively new and coincide with the availability of Internet-based search services. Some services such as Google and Lycos will post a list of the most frequent queries they receive during a given week. The sheer volume of queries submitted to most services makes reporting anything but the most frequent queries impractical.

Silverstein, Henzinger, Marais, and Moricz (1999), in their study of queries submitted to AltaVista, reported the twenty-five most popular queries submitted over a forty-five-day period. All but three of the queries consisted of single terms, with the remaining three queries consisting of two terms. These queries represented only 1.6 x 10^{-7} percent of unique queries, but constituted 1.5 percent of the total queries submitted. A collapsed distribution of the query frequencies was reported for queries that occurred once (63.7 percent), twice (16.2 percent), three times (6.5 percent), and more than three times (13.6 percent) over the 154 million query set used. The average query frequency was 3.97 appearances per query.

Wolfram (2000b) examined characteristics of queries submitted on a single day to the Excite search service in 1997. Fourteen of the top twenty-five queries appearing in the Excite set matched the AltaVista set.

Unlike the AltaVista study, approximately 90 percent of queries were found to be unique in the data set. Of the 400,000-odd different queries in the data set, only 18 occurred more than 250 times. The differences in the time frame between the collection of the Excite and AltaVista data sets likely contributed to the number of unique queries observed in each. With the longer data collection time period, the probability of a unique query being submitted again would increase, although new unique queries also would be entered during this time.

6.5.3 Characteristics of Query Frequency Distributions

It is not surprising that the most frequently entered queries would consist of only one or two terms. If using character-by-character equivalence to compare queries, the likelihood of different characters or typographical errors being entered increases with the addition of characters to the query.

The rate of descent of the query frequency distribution in size-frequency form, in terms of the percentage of queries occurring once or twice, appears to be steeper than other observed system data such as term distributions, at least for short time frames. The range of resources indexed by the system studied will play a role in the types of queries entered. For systems indexing general topic resources such as are available on the Web, OPACs, or general subject bibliographic databases, wide variation in queries can be expected. For systems that index subject-specific content, the amount of variation in query submissions is less clear in the absence of empirical data but may be less diverse. Of course, with topic specific databases, the diversity in queries may be equally broad if queries entered in these systems are more specific.

6.6 Queries per User/Session

6.6.1 Overview

The duration of search sessions can be quantified using discrete or continuous units of measure. Most often, user session duration is measured in temporal units (seconds, minutes) to describe the completion of each query or series of search tasks (see, e.g., Cooper [2001]). From an IPP perspective, the idea of the search task (source) producing temporal search lengths (items) does not work well with the discrete nature of most informetric processes, although continuous models conceivably could be used. Session duration may also be measured in terms of the number of queries a user submits to an IR system. Again, query logs must be able to identify the start and end of a user session, either through system mechanisms that identify and store starting and ending points, or through user identifiers for multi-user systems that store query data for many users.

A session will consist of one or more queries, although it is possible for users to submit blank queries to some systems as the entirety of their session, perhaps signaling usability problems with the system. When measuring session length as a function of queries submitted per user, the definition of what constitutes a query must be considered. For example, consider the following hypothetical sequence of queries:

Begin session
1. cosmogony
2. cosmogony AND "eighteenth century"
3. Laplace AND cosmogony
4. Laplace AND origin AND "solar system"
5. Kant AND cosmogony
6. cosmogony
7. Tahiti AND vacation

End session

Does the session contain six or seven queries? The first and sixth queries submitted are the same. For most informetric processes, the order of item production is not considered; only the tally of items is counted. However, for query production there may be repetition of queries later in the session that are not requests for additional pages, as in some search engine query logs. Furthermore, sessions may be defined by the number of distinct search topics introduced during the session, where queries that represent modifications of the same search topic are not treated as separate queries. Technically, search topic level analysis for sessions is possible, but it is impractical for large search sets unless query classification can be automated.

Another definitional problem can arise when one collects data over long periods of time. Most existing studies have considered the number of users to be equivalent to the number of sessions. If user identifiers can be tracked but no indicator of the starting or ending point of a session is recorded, does one consider all queries submitted by the same user identifier to be part of the same session? If time stamps of query submissions are recorded, do subsequent queries submitted at later times from previous queries, for example, submitted many minutes or hours apart, merit consideration as a part of a different session? If so, what time frame defines the separation of sessions? In this regard there will be a distinction between the number of queries a user submits and the number of queries submitted per session. With search engine data logs that keep track of user identifiers, the number of queries associated with an identifier may be exceedingly large for what a single person is capable of performing. An example of this was revealed in one of the Excite data sets, where one identifier appeared more than 100,000 times over the course of eight hours. In this case the "user" was a meta search service submitting queries to Excite. Such lengthy search sessions should be removed to avoid skewing the data.

Within a user session, the patterns of query modification may also be investigated for sessions consisting of more than one query. In the case of time-stamped query submission by identifiable users, one may examine changes in the number of terms entered by the user from one query to the next. More specifically, the number of distinct search topics may be analyzed as well.

6.6.2 Research on Queries Submitted per User/Session

Several studies have examined session duration from the perspective of the number of queries submitted for OPACs and Web search engines. To date it appears that there have been no investigations into applicable distributions to model the range of session lengths observed. Larson (1991) examined six years of transaction logs of the University of California's MELVYL online catalog. Over the period covered by the data, there was a slight decline in the number of command searches conducted per session, ranging from 3.1 down to 2.8 searches per session for each year's data. Cooper (2001) studied usage patterns of the Web-based MELVYL catalog, including presearch and actual search activities based on sixteen months of usage data. Over the course of the data collection period, the author reported an average of about three searches per session.

Using the 50,000-query Excite data log, Jansen, Spink, and Saracevic (2000) examined the distribution of queries submitted per user. Two-thirds of users submitted a single query, with approximately 98 percent of users submitting five or fewer queries. The larger Excite data sets from 1997, 1999, and 2001 revealed lower percentages of single query sessions, with averages ranging from 48.4 to 60.4 percent, and overall 1.9 to 2.5 queries per user. The maximum size of search sessions increased over the course of the data sets to the point where sessions of greater than 100 queries were treated as multiple users or automated requests, and ignored. Although not fitted to any distributions, a log-log transformation of the observed distribution data revealed that it cannot be adequately fit by a simple Zipf model due to its convex shape once transformed. Silverstein, Henzinger, Marais, and Moricz's (1999) AltaVista study reveals a similar percentage of single query sessions (63.7 percent), with a mean of 2.0 queries per session. Jansen and Pooch (2001), in their survey of IR evaluation studies, reported the longest search sessions with "traditional" bibliographic IR systems, with a reported range of seven to sixteen queries per user per session in the studies surveyed.

Investigations in query modification over the duration of a session reveal that users generally work incrementally in their formulation and modification of queries such that the number of terms added or deleted to a subsequent query is usually quite small and is approximately normally distributed, with a mode where no new terms were added, but existing terms were modified (Spink, Wolfram, Jansen, and Saracevic, 2001), followed by the addition of one term or subtraction of one term. Over all modified queries, 99.2 percent of queries either added or subtracted five or fewer terms from the previous query. Silverstein, Henzinger, Marais, and Moricz (1999) also examined query modification and noted that just over one-third of modifications involved totally changing the query.

6.6.3 Characteristics of Queries Submitted per User/Session

One observation that emerges from session analyses of end user searching of public IR systems, whether search engines on the Web or OPACs, is the brevity of most sessions. Most users typically do not submit more than a handful of queries per session. For example, Millsap and Ferl (1993) reported that more than three-quarters of remote OPAC users submitted five or fewer queries per session. Unfortunately the motivation for discontinuing a session cannot be determined from the transaction logs alone. The user may have adequately met his or her information needs within the session or may have chosen to search another system due to low recall or frustration in using the system. From a system designer's perspective, the user's motivation for ending a search would be helpful in determining system effectiveness, but that cannot be determined without user feedback. For systems where multiple sessions by the same user id can be identified, the number of repeat visits by the user may serve as an indicator of the user's ability to locate relevant information, following the business adage "a satisfied customer is a repeat customer." But these studies are done without being able to determine if machine identifiers correspond to a single user or many users. The shortness of searches has implications for marketing. For advertisers who support public systems, it becomes clear that the window of opportunity to inform users of products based on new query screens is small, unless advertisements are constantly refreshed on a given screen, which many advertising-driven services do.

6.7 User Searching and Browsing Patterns

6.7.1 Overview

With the growth of user-centered IR systems research have come opportunities to study regularities in the process of user searching and browsing. Marchionini (1995) describes a continuum of information seeking behavior that users engage in by combining searching and browsing strategies. Analytical search strategies are generally goal-oriented and systematic. These are represented by strategies such as database selection and query formulation, discussed in previous sections. Browsing is more informal and opportunistic and may involve scanning, observing, navigating, and monitoring. Where so merited, each type of strategy may be quantified and analyzed as an informetric process. Information seeking theory can provide direction in the study of how users interact with IR systems. To date, analogies have been used to describe the processes. For example, Pirolli and Card (1995) have introduced the concept of information foraging, particularly for the Web environment, to provide a framework for how users optimize information gain, just as hunter-gatherer societies would forage for food.

Browsing behaviors include the number of returned hits that users investigate, which is also roughly approximated by the number of pages of hits users request from a given query to systems that return results in blocks of records. In hypertext systems, the length of the path of linkages investigated or the number of "clicks" representing node visitations provides an indication of user persistence in browsing.

6.7.2 Research into Browsing Regularities

Few mathematical models have been developed to describe user browsing behaviors within traditional IR systems once searches have been conducted. Like session-level analysis, most models have been based on time as opposed to discrete actions taken by users. For search engines, hits are usually returned in groups of pages representing a set number of hits, usually ten per page, but some systems will permit the return of 25, 50, or 100 hits. As part of the Excite studies, the authors tabulated empirical distributions of the number of pages users viewed per query (Spink, Wolfram, Jansen, & Saracevic, 2001). In the case of the Excite data, duplicate queries submitted in succession by users were treated as requests for additional pages of the same query or were identified by a rank field that indicated whether the query represented the first request by users or subsequent requests. The distribution for the 2001 data set is roughly Zipfian, with approximately 73 percent of all queries having only one page of results viewed by users, with about 95 percent of all queries having fewer than five pages. Roughly 1 in 5,000 queries involved browsing of more than fifty pages of results. Across the three Excite data sets, about 1.7 pages were viewed per query on average. Ajiferuke and Wolfram (submitted a) fitted the 1999 and 2001 Excite data for page requests per query to several theoretical models. Although the best fits for each model resulted in significant chi-square outcomes, the zero-truncated GIGP and Zipf models produced the best fits, respectively.

Montgomery and Faloutsos (2001) analyzed general Web browsing based on data sets gathered from user computers and not servers. The unit of analysis is the number of URLs viewed per month per user machine, measured over a thirty-month period. They found a 2.4 percent growth in the number of URLs viewed per user per month, representing a doubling of browsing behavior every thirty months. Measured on a session basis, the authors found that the increase in the number of sessions and not the length of each session accounted for the growth over time. Therefore, users revisit Web sites frequently.

Usage patterns of a Web-based OPAC have also been studied (Cooper, 2001; Chen & Cooper, 2001). Using forty-seven variables, Chen and Cooper were able to identify categories of users with a high degree of success based on usage patterns alone, with no demographic data.

There have been two notable studies of the development of mathematical models of search path length in hypertext-based systems. Qiu (1994) investigated the distribution of path lengths for a general and specific search task undertaken by users in a microcomputer-based hypertext system. Shifted forms of the Poisson and negative binomial distributions were tested, with the negative binomial distribution providing an acceptable fit for the observed data. In a related paper, Qiu (1993) investigated search state patterns at a higher level using Markov models. A second-order model best fit the overall observed behavior.

Huberman, Pirolli, Pitkow, and Lukose (1998) have also examined regularities in user surfing patterns on the Web. The authors derived a two-parameter inverse Gaussian distribution to asymptotically model the probability of the number of links L a user will follow on a Web site, $P(L)$, before a stopping threshold is reached:

$$P(L) = \sqrt{\frac{\lambda}{2\pi L^3}} \exp\left[\frac{-\lambda(L-\mu)^2}{2\mu^2 L}\right] \tag{6.1}$$

with mean μ and variance of μ^3/λ. Reasonable fits to the theoretical distribution were obtained for three data sets using regression analysis. For one of the data sets, examining search path length within a given Web site consisting of more than 8,000 documents, the mean number of clicks/pages was 3.9. This is considerably less than the average of 39.5 clicks/pages found by Qiu in her more specialized, smaller system and highlights the impact of the users or system content on browsing behavior.

6.7.3 Characteristics of Searching and Browsing

Considerable variation is observed for browsing both within individual systems and across different types of systems. The Web search engine studies of pages of hits browsed reveal that most users do not look much beyond the first or second page of results. Again, the motivation for users to discontinue retrieval of additional pages is unknown. Users may be satisfied with the results returned with the first page. They may be searching for a single relevant site, making the return of large numbers of hits unnecessary. Users may be settling for what the search engine returns, assuming that the best sites to meet their information need will not appear on subsequent pages. Finally, users may give up on a search out of frustration if relevant results are not returned within the first few hits. This evidence of minimal browsing, at least for the Web, is supported by Huberman, Pirolli, Pitkow, and Lukose (1998), who observed brief browsing within Web sites once users arrived at the site.

There also does not appear to be any relationship between the effort users exert in formulating queries and the number of pages of results they browse on the Web. Wolfram (2000b) examined the distribution of pages browsed in relation to the size of the query submitted, measured by the number of terms input. The distribution of pages browsed for queries that contain one through ten terms did not differ significantly, with the mean number of pages per query ranging from 1.6 to 1.8 pages.

User motivation for searching will undoubtedly influence browsing. In the Web environment precision appears to be more important for end users who wish to receive quick results. Professional online searchers using bibliographic or full-text databases, on the other hand, may be more interested in recall, where the aim is to maximize the number of relevant items retrieved, not just the top few. Additional user search path length studies are needed to determine the impact of system content and user demographics on browsing behaviors.

6.8 Resource Usage

6.8.1 Overview

The study of resource usage data offers an alternative to search logs for studying how users request or make use of information system content. As with other complex systems, resource utilization processes may be investigated at different levels of analysis. Examples of quantifiable processes include the number of hits or site visitations a networked location receives over time, or the transfer of bytes handled by a given site per unit of time. On a more specific level, the number of requests for specific documents such as bibliographic records, Web pages, or file downloads can serve as an indication of resource popularity or demand. If simple tallies only are kept of resource usage, then usage characteristics by specific entities/users will be unknown. If the purpose of the data analysis is to develop a distribution of request frequencies, then the simple counts will suffice. However, site analysts often are also interested in seeing who is requesting resources and their origin. The dual nature of resource usage processes, involving a requestor and a requested resource, makes it possible to study frequency of use by given users when login information or IP address data are available to identify users. Growth in site visitation or in specific user visitation of given sites also offers opportunities for investigation.

6.8.2 Research on IR Resource Usage

Analysis of resource usage has become especially popular for market analysis of Web sites. Resource usage can also have implications for caching of frequently accessed documents for improved response time. Nielsen (1997b) notes that the rank-frequency distribution of hits per month distribution for pages on the Sun Microsystems Web site is largely Zipfian, at least for the most frequently accessed pages. The lower than expected number of hits for low ranking pages is attributed to the paucity of accumulated pages of low-frequency interest. Crovella, Taqqu, and Bestavros (1998) also note that the distribution of document accesses could be modeled by a power law, such as that of Zipf, and has implications for caching. In Qiu's (1994) study of hypertext search path lengths, the author also investigated the frequency distribution of specific node visitation and found that for the closed hypertext system studied, a Zipf distribution adequately modeled the observed distributions of visits per node. In Montgomery and Faloutsos (2001), the similarity of URL usage to the Zipfian pattern of word usage is highlighted. Huberman, Pirolli, Pitkow, and Lukose (1998) reach a similar conclusion in their study of Web site usage.

Wolfram and Xie (2002) have analyzed resource usage of the EBSCOhost database service by users of the state of Wisconsin BadgerLink information service. Usage data collected by EBSCOhost included requests for specific databases, searches conducted by identifiable users, visitations by users, and requests for specific resources such as titles of periodicals indexed within the databases. From a resource demand perspective, the classic relationship between demand and resources was observed. Data collected over a six-month period and then cumulated by frequency of use reveal that a small percentage of the titles accounts for the most use (see Figure 6.3). The number of requests made for EBSCOhost resources by different originating points is also strongly reverse J-shaped, even more so than requests for specific resources. The size-frequency distribution of the number of requests based on known IP addresses over the same period appears in Figure 6.4. Ajiferuke, Wolfram, and Xie (submitted) fitted the resource request frequency distribution and the site visitation by IP address data to several theoretical models. A simple Zipf model provided the best fit in both cases, outperforming both the GIGP and generalized negative binomial models. Although the calculated goodness-of-fit chi-square outcomes were significant, the resulting models were reasonable given that each fitted data set contained more than 200 cells.

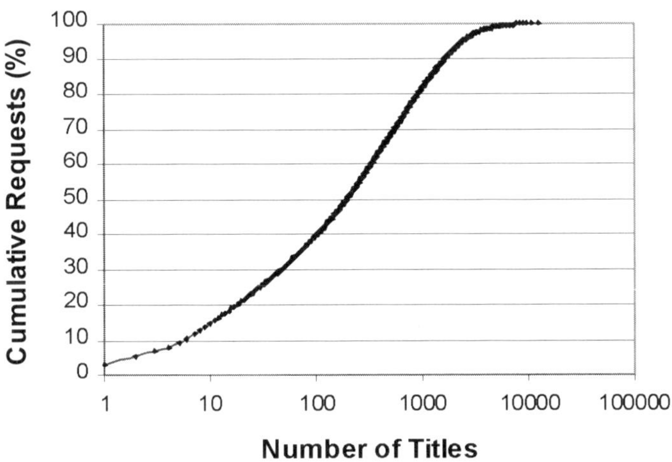

Figure 6.3. Cumulative Requests for BadgerLink EBSCOhost Abstracts by Source Title

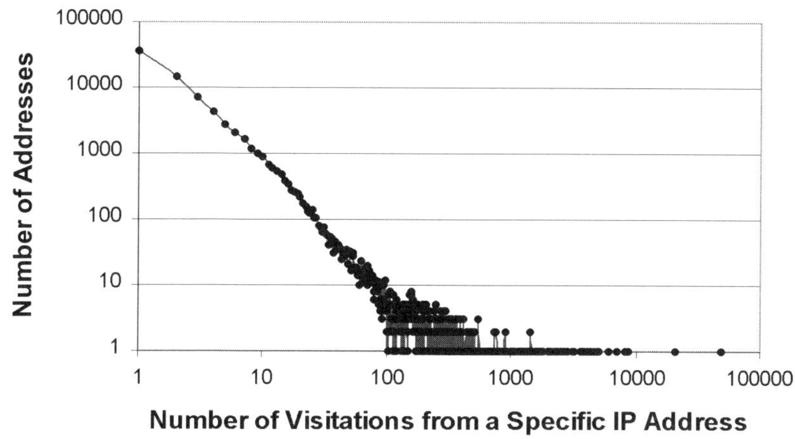

Figure 6.4. BadgerLink EBSCOhost Site Visitation Distribution by IP Address

6.8.3 Characteristics of IR Resource Usage

The frequency of resource usage will depend on the access methods available to locate documents. In a nonhyperlinked environment, usage will be solely based on the IR system's retrieval mechanisms. In systems that also support hypertext linkages, added opportunities are made available to users to discover documents. The more inlinks a document receives, the more opportunities exist to select the document. Nielsen's observation of a Zipfian distribution for site visitation raises some interesting questions for the future. With different rates of growth for the content of the Web and the number of users who access the Web, in addition to the growth in existing usage over time as reported by Montgomery and Faloutsos (2001), the impact on site visitation over time has yet to be determined. From the individual user perspective, the impact of Web growth on specific site visitation merits further investigation. Currently the growth in use by individual users is exponential, but given the finite amount of time and resources users have to search for information, this growth must decline at some point. From this follow implications for site developers who are competing with growing numbers of sites for regular user visitation.

6.9 Summary and Additional Readings

User interactions with IR systems from user transaction and resource access logs can be quite revealing for regularities in user behavior but do not reveal user motivations or attitudes toward IR systems that may account for observed behaviors. Sources such as Belew's (2000) monograph on cognitive perspectives on search engine technology acknowledge the importance of these regularities and their implications for IR system design, but in-depth investigations into many of these areas have been lacking. For coverage of Web user and usage behavior, Huberman (2001) provides a nontechnical presentation of observed regularities with examples of empirical distributions. The current dearth of literature examining the informetric characteristics of IR system usage at different levels of analysis presents many areas of investigation for researchers. The fitting of usage data to a range of models beyond a traditional Zipf is needed to better determine distribution characteristics and their underlying mechanisms.

Published summaries of most frequent user queries, search terms, and Web site visitations have appeared regularly in the print and electronic literature with the rise in popularity and influence of the Web. Some search services such as Google will post summaries of the most frequent queries over a given time period (see http://www.google.com/press/zeitgeist.html). Trends in worldwide Internet usage, growth, and advertising may be found at the Nielsen/Netratings Web site (http://www.nielsen-netratings.com). Links to collections of figures by various Internet marketing organizations are available from Cyberatlas (http://cyberatlas.internet.com). Access to online published articles may be found at the NUA Web site (http://www.nua.com). A useful repository of Web user surveys is available from the Graphics, Visualization and Usability Center at Georgia Tech (http://www.gvu.gatech.edu/user_surveys). Although not reporting results specifically in formats useful for informetric analysis, these end user surveys can provide insights into search and browsing behavior that can help to interpret observed regularities. The initial public interest in what end users search for on the Internet appears to be losing its novelty, although from a research perspective, changes in search patterns are still of great interest.

7

Applications

Nothing tends so much to the advancement of knowledge as the application of a new instrument.

—Sir Humphrey Davy (1778–1829)

7.1 Introduction

If bibliometrics/informetrics has been accused of anything by casual observers, it is that the field is too theoretical and abstract and lacks applications. In its defense, the discipline represents more than frequency distributions and citation counts. With an understanding of the regularities of IR system content and use, there are numerous applications. Many fundamental concepts long applied in IR research have a basis in informetrics, although this connection is often lost. Unaware of these characteristics or regularities in IR systems, researchers and practitioners in allied areas have been reinventing analytical methods that are central to informetrics, without realizing that many of the regularities observed have long been known to apply in other information media formats. Other applications of informetric concepts, such as those used in automatic indexing and query expansion, are so fundamental to the design of IR systems that this association with informetrics goes unmentioned.

Applications of informetric methods for IR systems have appeared in the research literature over the past few decades. With the wider availability and implementation of IR technologies to accommodate a broader array of audiences, interest in informetric applications has increased. Potential applications range from IR system simulation, to design issues at the lowest levels of system development for more efficient access and storage, all the way up to system search and interface features to better match user search behaviors. Applications also extend to an evaluation of system performance and to the targeting of services by developers and advertisers. Most of the applications to date, and the majority of those discussed in this chapter, have focused on efficient and effective systems design and development issues of benefit to systems administrators. User and usage applications are of more recent origin, with detailed exploration now emerging. Each of these applications is dealt with in turn.

7.2 Modeling and Simulation of IR Systems

7.2.1 Overview of Computer Modeling and Simulation

Computer simulation involves the use of computer programs to model the behavior of real-world systems, from which conclusions or insights may be drawn (McHaney, 1991, p. 2). Simulation is useful in environments where analytic solutions to problems are not available. Simulation techniques have been used to model many complex systems, including biological evolution, weather patterns, social phenomena, and the movement of astronomical bodies. These techniques can also be applied in the study the dynamics of interactions and processes in IR systems.

At the heart of any computer simulation will be a model to generate the range of behavior of the phenomenon studied. Models for IR system processes are derived from the characteristics outlined in previous chapters. Based on initial assumptions, simulations can serve as predictive tools for the phenomena in controlled environments, where initial conditions may be used to determine system outcomes when controllable access to the real phenomena is not possible or impractical.

Simulations can be divided into discrete event and continuous methodologies. In continuous simulation, changes in the simulation model are generally dependent on the passage of time. Examples of where continuous simulation models would be used include high-level biological systems or the analysis of physical motion among several gravitationally bound objects. Calculations are broken down into time slices at which point the state of the attributes of the system studied is recorded. Future states are calculated based on previous states taken at each time interval. For the simulation of most computer-based processes, including IR systems, models are based on the execution of discrete events, for example the submission of a query to an IR system or the arrival of a customer in a queuing simulation. Although time may pass, it is the event that triggers actions prompting system changes. A third category that often overlaps with discrete event simulation is Monte Carlo simulation, which relies on the generation of random numbers but where time is not a consideration. Simulation models may also be deterministic (i.e., nonprobabilistic influences) or stochastic, that is, they incorporate random components. For IR system simulation, the outcome of stochastic processes are most revealing of system dynamics.

The development and analysis of computer simulations require some familiarity with several fields. First, computer programming skills are desirable, although some commercial software to conduct simulations may not require substantial programming background. Programming languages such as SIMSCRIPT, SIMULA, SLAM, and GPSS have been specifically developed for simulation purposes, but more general programming languages may also be used. Second, the developer should be familiar with basic probability and statistical methods. The simulation outcomes will only be as good as the models used to represent the processes studied, no matter how sophisticated the programming. Finally, the developer should be familiar with the processes studied to help evaluate whether the statistical models are truly emulating the real-world phenomenon being studied.

Many works have been written on computer simulation techniques, emphasizing the mathematics and statistical methods, the models, or the systematic process of simulation development. The second edition of Ross's (1997) work on simulation takes a probabilistic and statistical analysis approach to the generation and analysis of simulations. Bennett (1995) emphasizes continuous simulation techniques in his work, with a chapter devoted to discrete event simulation. A practical perspective on the steps involved in carrying out simulation experiments can be found in McHaney (1991). Chapter 1 of McHaney's work also provides a useful summary of simulation techniques. Chapter 8 of Kraft and Boyce's (1991) monograph on operations research for libraries and information agencies is also recommended for its succinct introduction to simulation concepts and applications.

7.2.2 Modeling Characteristics of IR Systems

Chapters 5 and 6 introduced how informetric models may be used to summarize characteristics of IR system contents and their use. These characteristics serve as building blocks for the development of simulation models.

Computer simulation of IR systems can be used for two types of investigations, as outlined by Tague, Nelson, and Wu (1981). First, it can be used to study effective methods to represent documents and queries or user information needs. This is a more logical model for comparing document indexing and search formulation. Second, simulation can be used to study the efficiency of methods for the storage and retrieval of documents by analyzing retrieval performance when using different types of file structures. Both approaches have been used, but the latter has proved more pragmatic, providing applications that overlap with several other sections of this chapter.

The process of simulation execution using Monte Carlo random number generation is relatively straightforward. It may be summarized algorithmically using the following steps:

```
Begin simulation
        Initialize input parameters and model conditions
        While end condition is not reached
                Generate random number(s)
                Use random number(s) as input to simulation model
                Determine new system state
                Store resulting values
        Loop
        Report results
End simulation
```

The end condition will usually be a maximal value for the number of iterations for the simulation such as a specific number of documents or index terms generated or the number of queries processed.

The key to discrete event simulations with random components is the ability for the system to generate pseudo-random numbers ("pseudo" because they are not truly random). This feature is available in many of today's programming languages as a built-in function. Values returned are usually between 0 and 1 and are derived from the computer system clock. The ability to provide a seed value or to randomize output values ensures that different sets of numbers are produced for each simulation run. The returned value represents a probability for the output of the simulation model being studied. From the output, the corresponding input value is calculated.

Most of the informetric models introduced in previous chapters represent probability density functions for the phenomena studied when one removes frequency magnitudes, leaving probability values for each source type. Each random value generated corresponds to a cumulative probability value for the number of items. Based on the number of items, the source type is determined. To determine the corresponding source, the density function *f(x)* must be converted into a cumulative form *F(x)*. For continuous distributions, this may be accomplished using integral calculus, where

$$F(x) = \int_{0\,or\,1}^{\infty} f(x)$$

For discrete distributions, summation is used, where

$$F(x) = \sum_{x=0\ or\ 1}^{\infty} f(x)$$

Because informetric models are usually presented in a form such that the input corresponds to a source type and the output corresponds to items generated, the distribution must be reversed so that the output corresponds to the source type, called a generator function. The generator function may be developed using one of several methods (Devroye, 1986, ch. 3). With tractable equations, model inversion of the cumulative distribution can be used, where instead of $F(x)$ being returned, $F^{-1}(x)$ is returned. For more sophisticated models, where cumulative forms and inversion of the model are impractical, one can cumulate the values of $f(x)$ for $x = 1, 2, \ldots$ so that $F(x) < U(0,1)$, where $U(0,1)$ is the random value between 0 and 1. The returned value of x represents the source type corresponding to the random value.

Consider a Poisson model with a mean of 5.0 that is used to generate indexing exhaustivity source values for a document set. The cumulative probability distribution is represented in Figure 7.1. Each exhaustivity source value appearing on the x-axis has a range of probabilities associated with it. Any generated value that falls within that range will be assigned the associated exhaustivity source value. Take for example a pseudo-random generated value of 0.43. The associated exhaustivity source value for this generated value is the first number of terms with a cumulative probability value that exceeds the generated value. In this case, 0.43 falls between the cumulative probability value for three terms (0.265) but is less than four terms (0.441). Therefore, a generated pseudo-random value of 0.43 corresponds to four terms. Similarly, a generated value of 0.98 falls between the cumulative probability value for nine terms (0.968) and ten terms (0.986). So the corresponding exhaustivity source value is ten terms. Note that for this Poisson model, differences in cumulative probability values for mid-range exhaustivity source values are greater than for small and large exhaustivity source values, making it more likely that a generated value will fall into ranges that correspond to mid-range exhaustivity source values.

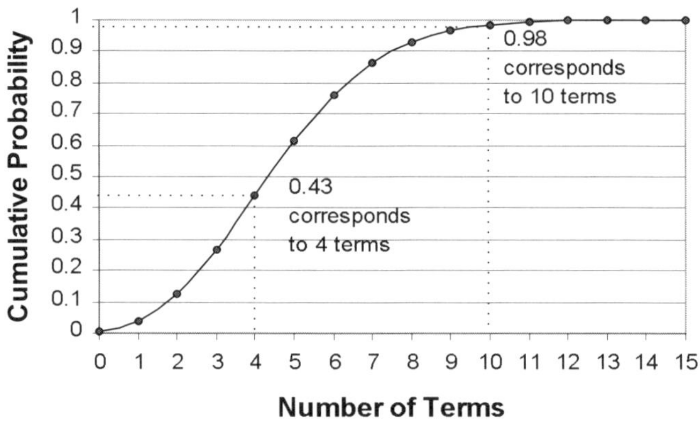

Figure 7.1. Cumulative Probability Poisson Distribution for Indexing Exhaustivity (Mean = 5 Terms)

To reduce computational overhead, during the simulation execution probability ranges and corresponding x values may be stored in lookup tables that can be searched. For reverse J-shaped density functions, the majority of generated values will correspond to source sizes of one or two, making a sequential search of the table stored as an array efficient. For models with large numbers of source types or high modes, it is more efficient to rely on binary or indexed search capabilities. Where no theoretical models can be adequately fit to observed data distributions, generators based on the cumulative form of the observed distribution and corresponding probabilities may be used. Depending on the complexity and number of system processes being modeled, more than one generator function may be used in a simulation model. For additional methods used in random variate generation, consult Devroye (1986) or Morgan (2000).

The use of simulation to generate hypothetical components of IR systems can be found in a number of IR studies. Research into IR system simulation, and more generally IR services that are not necessarily automated, dates back to the early 1960s, with different components being modeled. Aspects of IR systems that have been simulated have included index term assignment based on term distributions and indexing exhaustivity (Griffiths, 1978; Nelson, 1982), index term dependencies (Nelson, 1983; Nelson and Tague, 1985), user query formulation (Wolfram, 1992a), and document matching (Gordon, 1990). In most of these studies, simulation was used as a tool ultimately for system design and evaluation, discussed in subsequent sections.

Investigators must be careful about how probabilities are used to model the processes being simulated. In the case of term assignments based on the term distribution, probabilities must be calculated at the token level, not the type level. Probabilities represented by the term frequency distribution alone correspond to the type level, where the frequency of occurrence of a given type is not factored into the probability that the term will be selected. In this case, the most frequently occurring terms, which represent unique types, have a probability of *1/N* of being selected, where *N* is the total number of unique types or distinct terms. The actual probability of selection should correspond to the probability of the token of a given type being selected, which is the frequency of occurrence of the term divided by the total number of tokens over all terms.

7.2.3 Complete Simulation Models of IR Systems

The simulation of complete IR systems is an ambitious undertaking requiring the integration of several subsystems that interact with one another. Computational limitations prevented experimentation with larger scale simulations in early investigations, resulting in small-scale studies. Heine (1981) provides a summary of key early studies from the 1960s and 1970s and discusses issues in the simulation of IR systems and services. Problems associated with the simulation of IR systems are also discussed in Tague, Nelson, and Wu (1981).

At a high level, an IR system can be modeled as a set of processes. Cooper (1973) developed a simulation model to be used as a tool for designing and evaluating literature search systems. The model consists of five parts, containing a thesaurus generator, document generator, query generator, search routines, and evaluation routines. Each generator was defined by a series of parameters. For example, the thesaurus generator was bound by the size of the vocabulary, the word frequency distribution, the number of word classes, the assignment of words based on classes, and measures used to determine the similarity between two words. Experiments in system generation using hypothetical situations are conducted and compared based on system features and performance. The author recognizes that the model serves as only a first approximation of an overall simulation model, particularly because the interactions between the different system processes are not well understood even at the time of the study. Similarly, Griffiths (1978) examines the development of an overall simulation model based on term distribution characteristics taken from an operational IR system and attempts to incorporate user relevance judgments into relevant and nonrelevant classes. Tague, Nelson, and Wu (1981) more formally define their model of an IR system as a quintuple consisting of a set of document descriptions, query descriptions, rankings for the document set, a retrieval function, and an evaluation function. They also highlight problems encountered in modeling the different components of the overall model.

Differences in outcomes between the simulation models and operational systems indicate that existing simulation models require further refinement to more accurately model the complexities of IR system processes. For this reason, high-level, conceptual model simulation studies have given way in recent decades to more pragmatic studies that focus on specific parts of the IR processes. Information retrieval simulation research has gone through cycles of increased interest and neglect based on the application of new developments and their exhaustion until the next breakthrough occurs.

7.3 File Design and Space Planning for IR Systems

At the most fundamental level of IR system development are concerns related to the physical storage of and access to system content. Even with faster hardware and inexpensive, large capacity storage media, efficient access to indexes and documents remains an important consideration, particularly given the enormous amount of content now available for indexing by IR systems whether available on the Internet or through large bibliographic database utilities. Optimal access can be supported through the use of efficient file structures that take into account index characteristics and how indexes are used. Access is usually defined in nontemporal terms, which tend to be hardware specific, by using the number of block accesses from disk required to retrieve desired content, with minimal block accesses being the goal. In addition, both indexes and documents may be compressed to further improve access and transfer time. Space planning continues to be important for system managers. Estimation of existing space requirements across large installations as well as future needs as systems grow can be facilitated by informetric analysis. Trade-offs between efficient access and space requirements must be considered.

7.3.1 File Organization and Data Structures for Optimal Access

Chapter 2 introduced the process of document retrieval in an inverted file environment used by Boolean and related model IR systems. Several file structure options are available to support inverted file access to indexes, the contents of which ultimately point to specific documents for retrieval. Other models for IR systems, such as small-scale vector space model implementations, may not need elaborate file structures, but the informetric characteristics are still useful in determining access possibilities based on the number of terms and postings housed by the system. Other access methods, such as the use of signature files, will ultimately depend on the content of the indexes and the number of documents indexed, which will influence the size of the signatures used.

Analysis of file structure performance has been a long-standing area of research by computer scientists. When contemplating a candidate file structure, most often access issues are considered. However, from a system growth perspective, the implications for updating the system content also must be taken into account. Recall that for most traditional IR systems where content is additive, the cost of deletions using a given file structure is less of a concern. However, for dynamic environments with constantly changing documents, the cost of deletions and updates cannot be ignored.

An inverted file supported by a tree or hashing structure has been the most widely used method to access term index content within IR systems (see Chapter 2, Section 2.3.3). Comparisons of different inverted file structure's performances are usually limited to the identification and loading of index terms and possibly postings. Beyond this stage, the retrieval overhead for documents or their surrogates is generally the same and therefore is not considered. Tree structures, such as a B-tree and its variants, or a trie, permit fast access to index contents by dividing up indexes into more manageable subcomponents as nodes of the tree. As the number of nodes grows, access time will increase minimally. With a B-tree of order *m*, each new level added to the tree, which only increases the number of block accesses by one, will increase the number of nodes available by a factor of *m*. The total number of levels of the tree (*L*) of order *m* containing *T* terms can be calculated as

$$L \leq 1 + \log_{\lceil m/2 \rceil}\left(\frac{T+1}{2}\right) \tag{7.1}$$

where $\lceil N \rceil$ is the lowest integer greater than or equal to *N* (Knuth, 1973). However, one concern with tree structures in dynamic environments where insertion of new records and deletion of existing records is commonplace is the rebalancing of the trees to maintain optimal access (Rosenberg & Snyder, 1981). Depending on the number of branches per node, hashing structures, relying on "buckets" into which terms are inserted, in theory could provide the least number of block accesses with a sufficient number of buckets so that only one disk access is needed to retrieve the bucket contents. In hashing, a hash function is used to assign each term to one of *N* buckets. By using a perfect hash function, terms will be randomly but equally assigned to different buckets. With some hashing implementations there is concern related to the overflow of buckets with the addition of records, thereby requiring extra disk accesses to retrieve bucket contents. Chapter 13 of Frakes and Baeza-Yates (1992) discusses several hashing implementations.

Regardless of the structure adopted, the location of the indexes, whether stored partly or completely in fast access semiconductor storage such as main memory or comparatively slower disk access, will also significantly affect retrieval performance. The blocking factor (i.e., the size of the system retrieval unit measured in bytes), where controllable, will also influence retrieval. Given today's very large indexes, main memory storage of complete indexes may not be possible, making disk storage of parts of indexes necessary. Although having lost some of its appeal to Web-based systems in recent years, the use of slower access CD-ROM-based systems continues to make efficient index access vital.

The impact of indexing characteristics on retrieval performance in inverted file environments has been studied extensively. Several researchers who have conducted studies have already recognized the importance of the nonuniform distribution of search terms in estimating retrieval performance (see, e.g., Bookstein, 1973, 1974; Hill, 1978; Siler, 1976). Specifically, Sampson and Bendell (1985) demonstrate the impact of different Zipf distribution shapes of index keys (i.e., terms) on minimum block accesses by varying the exponential parameter. Christodoulakis (1984) also discusses the implications of assumptions in evaluating retrieval performance, including those of uniform attribute appearance within files, attribute co-occurrence independence, query uniformity, and uniformity in the number of records appearing within each block. Fedorowicz (1987) developed a comprehensive access time model for the retrieval of records in an inverted file system based on individual user queries, search operations used, index searching, and central processing unit processing times. Differences in processing queries of varying sizes are recognized, but the number of terms per query is assumed *a priori*. The study relies on actual search times and, unlike most other performance studies, provides a direct comparison with searches undertaken in an operational IR system. Wolfram (1992a, 1992b) constructed a simulation model based on models for index term distribution, terms used per query, and term selection within queries to compare retrieval performance and space requirements in three different database environments (OPAC, bibliographic, full text). The performance of six file organization methods (four variants of Balanced Implicit Multiway [BIM] tree structures and two hashing structures) under different combinations of five term distributions, five term selection models, and three index term totals was studied. The simulation results from this study demonstrate the preferred usage of specific file structures under different term distribution and term selection environments. Under shallow term distribution conditions, with smaller proportions of infrequently occurring terms, a chained hashing structure with postings stored in separate files provided the fastest access for all three database environments, regardless of the term selection condition. For steep term distributions, with a high proportion of infrequently occurring terms, a modified hashing structure with postings stored in the same bucket as the term was preferred under two term selection conditions (the empirical and equal term selection). A double BIM+-tree, with the most frequently occurring terms stored in main memory and the remaining terms stored in a separate tree on disk, performed best for the remaining three term selection conditions (equal term type usage, direct relationship between term size and selection, and mid-frequency preference). Brown, Callan, and Croft (1994) also note that over 90 percent of inverted lists in their data sets accounted for less than 10 percent of the total inverted file size. Because the larger postings lists were accessed more frequently, they were situated to provide the most efficient access.

Performance analysis may extend to distributed environments where system content is accessed from remote sources. Tomasic and Garcia-Molina (1993) examined response time in a simulated distributed IR environment using parallel query processing under different hardware organization environments. They note that the performance was strongly influenced by the inverted file organization, with a system index organization that divides part of the processing tasks among the remote hosts for partial answer sets and the local host for final consolidation of sets of postings.

Sornil and Fox (2001) have studied inverted index partitioning schemes for a parallel processing environment. Partitioning may be based on three approaches. Term partitioning locates all postings for a given term on the same processing node. Document partitioning groups all posting for the same document on the same node. The authors propose a hybrid scheme, that relies on a hybrid of document and term-based partitioning. The performance of each method was tested using data based on the TREC collection. Simulations were performed using different partitioning assumptions based on node size, inverted list chunking, and processing. Term usage in queries were based on assumptions of percentage utilization of the most frequently occurring terms (e.g., 80-20, where the 20 percent of the most frequently occurring terms see 80 percent of the use, 70-30, 60-40, and uniform usage). The authors demonstrate the superior performance of the hybrid partitioned inverted index over the varied conditions tested.

In addition to inverted file structures, signature files, using bit string representations of documents (see Chapter 2, Section 2.3.3), have been used as a text retrieval method. Instead of relying on term indexes and postings lists, document access is facilitated through pattern matching of bit strings. Implications of the importance of the informetric properties of the indexing process, however, have not been widely explored. Indexing exhaustivity and term distributions will affect the creation of signature bit strings. With higher levels of exhaustivity, more terms are represented in the signature, increasing the proportion of bits in the signature that are set to "1." To better disambiguate the signatures, longer signatures should be used, which increases the processing time.

The frequency with which some queries are entered into an IR system may justify the preprocessing of queries by storing postings associated with a query in a readily accessible area of computer storage to reduce processing time. Of the top twenty-five queries submitted to Excite during one-day periods in 1997, 1999, and 2001, nine of the queries (chat, games, horoscope, hotmail, maps, porn, sex, weather, Yahoo!) appear in all three data sets, with the other queries within each set reflecting variations of the most popular queries or topics of popular interest at that point in time. On the whole, the twenty-five most frequent queries in each data set constitute roughly 2 percent of all queries submitted to Excite during the time period. Regular preprocessing of these queries in anticipation of their being submitted may result in a small improvement in system performance.

7.3.2 Space Estimation and Planning

With Zipfian term frequency distributions, and similar regularities in term lengths and document properties, it is possible to realistically estimate existing and future space requirements to house system content and it associated indexes. Tague (1988) demonstrates how the Zipfian nature of term distributions can be used to determine the number of terminal nodes in a B-tree implementation of the index, the number of entry tokens (postings), the maximum length of a postings list (see also Tague and Nicholls, 1987), and the relationships among these values. For example, assuming a Zipfian distribution of terms, *f(x)*, where *f(x)* is the number of term types with x postings, the number of terminal nodes required to house the n distinct terms in an m-ary B-tree is directly related to n / m, such that

$$n = \sum_{x=1}^{x_{\max}} f(x) \qquad (7.2)$$

where x_{max} is the size of the most frequent word type. Similarly, the total number of postings, p, associated with n types is

$$p = \sum_{x=1}^{x_{\max}} f(x) * x \qquad (7.3)$$

With x_{max} postings as the maximal size, one could easily estimate the maximum number of blocks needed to house and retrieve the most frequent term, as well as the average blocks per term. The nature of the Zipfian distribution will directly affect the amount of space needed to store postings. With a shallow distribution, additional space will be necessary and will require, on average, a higher number of block accesses to retrieve postings over environments with steeper term distributions consisting of a higher percentage of uniquely occurring terms.

In addition to performance analysis, discussed in the previous section, Fedorowicz (1981a, 1981b) developed a model to calculate storage requirements for a bibliographic database index (index file and postings file) using a tree structure to facilitate access to terms (header file). Of note are the considerations given to the impact of the Zipfian term distribution on index space requirements and that of blocking factors on space requirements. Wolfram (1992b) also looked at the space requirements needed to house the simulated file structures and notes that retrieval structures based on hashing provided the best space economy, particularly with steeper term distributions, where the space savings were much larger than for tree-based structures. Clearly the number of buckets associated with the hashing structures will influence the retrieval and space requirements. The author finds that there is improvement in retrieval efficiency obtained by increasing the number of buckets on the generated data sets, but with diminishing returns and increases in the space requirements. Similar space and retrieval computations may be made for actual document storage, although the distribution of document length may not be Zipfian.

Relational database management table design can also benefit from the repetitive characteristics found in text-oriented databases. Brooks (1987, 1988) notes the benefits of relational database normalization for the storage of names from thirty bibliographic databases and telephone directory letter categories. Most of the thirty data sets that are examined result in space savings when a two-table design to remove name redundancy is used, although the majority of the bibliographies do not benefit from the two-table design.

Space requirements estimation for current systems can be straightforward in comparison to estimating future space requirements based on system growth. Many of the aspects of IR system growth have already been addressed in Chapter 5, Section 5.7. Well-designed retrieval systems should be able to scale up to handle additional content. With linear growth in documents, estimation of space requirements for the documents themselves, if centrally housed, or for postings files in distributed systems, can be easily extrapolated. However, the impact of linear document growth on the term file will depend on the maturity of the database index and the propensity for the addition of new term types to the system.

Traditionally the growth of bibliographic database contents and their corresponding indexes, although possibly nonlinear, has not been nearly as dramatic as the growth of distributed Web-based search service indexes. Despite not having to deal with the storage of remote documents, keeping up with daily changes in the amount of indexable content remains challenging for most of these services. The growth of the indexes developed by these services is also driven by two factors. The indexing of multilingual content in distributed systems has enormous implications for the size and growth of term indexes. With a much larger population of potential term types to be indexed, new types are added more frequently than in a single language environment, thereby increasing the number of infrequently occurring terms, while the tokens of frequently occurring terms increase less rapidly due to the greater diversity in term types. Also, the inclusion of "artificial" terms such as URLs and e-mail addresses in indexes contributes to the higher number of infrequently occurring terms.

The occurrence of spelling errors within IR systems, in addition to preventing the retrieval of documents, can unduly increase file space requirements by adding new terms that really should represent additional postings of existing terms (Fedorowicz, 1982a). Misspellings will increase the number of infrequently occurring terms within an index while decreasing the frequency of occurrence of higher frequency terms. Bourne (1977) found a spelling error rate that ranged from less than 0.5 to over 20 percent in a survey of eleven bibliographic databases. In a study of low frequency terms indexed in the MEDLINE database, Fedorowicz (1982a) observed that over 30 percent of sampled terms, constituting approximately 0.5 percent of all postings from the sample, represented spelling errors. Since the time of these studies, automated spell checking has become more consistent, but it has not eliminated misspellings of terms based on similar words. With today's distributed systems indexing both formal, published content that has undergone editorial processing and personal content that has not, spelling errors are still of concern.

7.3.3 Database and Index Compression

From a space economy perspective, the efficient allocation of disk space for repetitive content makes sense. Space benefits may also be achieved through the application of data compression techniques. The time and space trade-offs associated with the process of data compression and decompression must be weighed. As Bookstein, Klein, and Raita (1997) point out, compression need only be performed once, making its computational cost less important. Decompression, however, takes place every time the compressed content is accessed, making efficiency a greater concern.

The use of a trie structure for IR systems goes back to the earliest days of automated IR. A trie is a tree with *N* nodes that provide access to subsequent tree levels based on digits or characters (Knuth, 1973, sect. 6.3). A trie is often not as efficient in providing fast access as other tree structures, particularly for lengthy terms that share word roots, requiring one node traversal per common letter. But its usage of character sequences to build words makes it well suited for text searching. Maly (1976) proposes the use of a compressed trie, where instead of complete characters for each node, the presence or absence of a character could be represented as bits.

Heaps (1978) devotes a chapter in his monograph on IR to the coding and compression of databases. Huffman coding (Huffman, 1952) has long been used to compress character codes so that the most frequent characters occupy the fewest bits. The same idea may be applied to index terms, where the most frequent terms are assigned the fewest bits. Or, similarly, terms may be compressed by assigning abbreviations. Schuegraf (1976) examined the use of run-length coding for the representation of inverted file content as binary vectors where the presence of an index term within a document was represented as a "1" in an ordered list of terms, with the absence of a term represented as a "0." With run-length coding, also used in image compression, lengthy strings of zeroes could be replaced with a set of bits representing the length of the zero run, thereby saving storage space. Bookstein, Klein, and Raita (1997) have looked at the modeling of word occurrences for the compression of concordances (postings) using bitmaps of documents, similar to Schuegraf. However, in this case the co-occurrence tendencies of terms are also incorporated. The authors used n-state Markov models to describe the clustering tendencies and were able to reduce the model to no more than four states and demonstrate, through the application to several databases of the improvement in space, savings by the methods used over models that assume independence of term co-occurrences. Wisniewski (1986) examined the compression of a term dictionary in an inverted file system using short fixed-length word codes. Storage space was reduced by almost 90 percent, but with some marginal degradation in precision performance as a result of some terms being assigned the same codes.

7.4 IR System Process Design and Implementation

File design and space planning considerations are useful for system developers but represent transparent processes to the user, who may only be aware of file design issues peripherally based on system responsiveness. On a more tangible level for the user, characteristics of system content and use can be incorporated into the query and document matching process. These can be implemented as system search or document presentation features. Examples of how informetric regularities may be applied to system design features include automatic indexing of documents, relevance ranking of documents based on occurrence characteristics of search terms, index term discriminative capacity and document spaces for identification of potentially relevant documents, document organization, and interface design for more effective and efficient navigation. The idea of applying informetrics to system design is not new (see, e.g., Yermish, 1975), but it has gained more attention over the past decade. Ding, Chowdhury, Foo, and Qian (2000) provide an overview of a number of recently developed systems that incorporate informetric analysis as a design and presentation tool.

7.4.1 Automatic Indexing and Query Expansion

By far the simplest application of term frequency distributions to IR system design is for the creation of stopword lists. The most frequently occurring term types within a database often represent those words that contain little semantic content or are so frequent that they occur in almost every document indexed, thus greatly limiting their utility in distinguishing documents. Definite and indefinite articles, the most frequently occurring nouns, and words of less than three characters serve as examples of words that are often included in stopword lists. The tail end of size-frequency (or the low end of rank-frequency) term distributions provides prime candidates for inclusion in stopword lists. A cutoff point on the distribution may serve as the demarcation between terms that are indexed or ignored by automatic indexing routines. However, relying on frequency alone can be too simplistic. Potential terms may occur with great frequency within a small number of documents, making them useful for retrieving those documents. Harter (1975a, 1975b) demonstrated that specialty words, or those useful for retrieval, are more accurately modeled by a 2-Poisson model (see Chapter 4, Section 4.4.3) and developed a method for identifying those terms.

The assignment of term weights will often be based on the term frequency within the document and/or the frequency of the term across documents. The higher the term frequency within the document, the higher the weight assigned to the term. Conversely, the higher the frequency of the term across documents, the lower the weight that will be assigned. For inverse document frequency assignment, the assumption made is that infrequently occurring terms are better at distinguishing one document from another (see Chapter 5, Section 5.2.3).

Co-occurrence of index terms can serve as a mechanism for supporting query expansion (Efthimiadis, 1996). Additional search terms for user queries may be added based on the frequency of co-occurrence of index terms, where the most frequently co-occurring terms could serve as additional query terms. Similarly, co-occurrence data may be used in the construction of search aids such as thesauri (Schütze & Pedersen, 1997), where the frequencies of co-occurrence and the patterns of co-occurrence across terms can help to determine the relatedness of terms. The inverse relationship for co-occurrence, where few term pairs occur with great frequency, means that only a few index terms would serve as candidates for query expansion (Peat & Willett, 1991). Care must be taken in assessing the level of co-occurrence. The most frequently occurring term in an index will likely appear close to the top of many co-occurrence lists but may add little value to the expanded query. Applying Salton's theory of indexing (Salton, 1975), the benefits of term co-occurrence would best be applied to individual terms of mid-frequency occurrence, leaving the majority of terms, which occur infrequently, less suitable for co-occurrence determinations.

7.4.2 Relevance Ranking of Retrieval Results

Document relevance ranking, which permits the presentation of document sets to users in decreasing order of calculated relevance, provides users with an assessment mechanism not found in systems where only binary determinations of relevance/nonrelevance are possible. Most relevance ranking mechanisms are fundamentally based on frequency counts of IPPs, where the most productive sources result in the highest rankings. Of course this is an oversimplification; other factors in addition to frequency will be used in the determination of relevance.

In systems with variable length documents, frequency counts of indexed terms alone do not serve as a good measuring stick of relevance. Longer documents may contain more occurrences of a given set of terms, but proportionately they may not be as frequent as in a shorter document where the density of the term's occurrence is higher. In this case it makes sense to factor in document length when determining relevance.

Term location within a document also can affect system relevance assessment. Terms occurring near the beginning of a document may be assigned a higher weight than those occurring later in a document. In structured database environments with defined fields, the occurrence of terms within selected fields such as titles or subject headings could carry more weight than terms occurring in the main textual body. The practice of Web site developers artificially inflating term frequencies to increase their site's relevance ranking has been counteracted by some search engines. Search engines look for frequently repeated words hidden in metatags or on backgrounds of Web pages. Sites employing these techniques are penalized for unfair indexing practices and are assigned a low relevance ranking.

The use of hyperlinks, particularly inlinks, serves as another measure of relevance assessment (Brin & Page, 1998). Just as with citation analysis, the greater the number of inlinks to a given page, the more it may be valued over documents possessing few inlinks. The effectiveness of using inlinks as a determining factor in assessing potential relevance is evident in the success of Google, which has been ranked in comparative studies as the most effective search system among several publicly accessible search engines (see, e.g., http://www.searchenginewatch.com). Hypertext linkages are also used as a means of determining document relevance in the BIRD (BIbliometric Retrieval of Documents) system formerly available on the Web. User judgments of interdocument relatedness are also incorporated into relevance calculations of documents. In contrast, for bibliographic databases containing references, interdocument relatedness can also be determined based on the use of co-citations, although this is rarely done (see Chapter 5, Section 5.5).

Document visitation data are used in relevance ranking within some Web-based IR services (e.g., Alexa at http://www.alexa.com). In circumstances where a set of documents may have similar relevance rankings based on term frequencies or inlinks, the popularity of documents measured in terms of hits the document receives provides an additional assessment criterion. To some degree, inlinks and particularly document visitations can enhance the Mathew Effect (see Chapter 3, Section 3.8.2), where a popular document becomes even more popular because it appears near the top of ranked lists, which makes it more likely that the document is selected again, further increasing its hit rate.

7.4.3 Term Discriminative Capacity and Document Spaces

Indexing characteristics will affect the document space of vector-based retrieval systems. Salton (1975) outlined how index terms can be good discriminators of documents by changing the properties of the document space. Good or positive discriminators are those terms that result in document spaces that are more "spread out," making it easier to distinguish between documents. Good discriminators, therefore, become desirable terms to be given preference for search and retrieval. Salton asserts that terms displaying good discrimination characteristics are those with skewed term weight distributions among documents, so that they appear with high weight in some documents and low weight in others.

Zhang and Wolfram (2001) demonstrate the ability to visualize changes in the document space using a visual vector-based retrieval system (DARE), noting that for the collection of documents used only a small number of terms exhibited positive or negative discriminative capacities, with most terms being indifferent discriminators. In a related study using simulated document sets based on system characteristics from a bibliographic data set, Wolfram and Zhang (2002) explored the impact of three indexing exhaustivity levels in combination with three term distributions on the size and density of the document space in the DARE visual information retrieval environment. By also using three term-weighting methods (term frequency, inverse document frequency, and combined term frequency and inverse document frequency), they are able to demonstrate through visualization the influence of indexing characteristics on each term weighting method. The term distribution more strongly influences the document space for the term frequency weighting mechanism, whereas the indexing exhaustivity more strongly influences the document space for the inverse document frequency and combined term weighting environment. In all cases, lower indexing exhaustivity and shallower term distributions result in denser document spaces, where distinctions between documents are smaller. With less dense document spaces, it becomes easier to distinguish one document from another, thereby making retrieval more robust. Wolfram and Zhang (2001) also examine the impact of terms of different frequencies on the document space, noting the impact of singly occurring terms on defining the characteristics of the overall document space. Removal of singly occurring terms results in document spaces that, again, are much more dense. However, in indexing environments where singly occurring terms are not indexed due to their infrequency, some of this influence can be overcome with higher indexing exhaustivity.

7.4.4 Interface Design

System processing features for more efficient and effective design are often transparent to users. Design applications of informetrics extend to the ways users may interact with IR systems. A number of systems have been developed in recent years that, through incorporation of informetric analysis, provide users with additional tools to visualize system content, or to help the user in decision making regarding the selection and retrieval of documents. For example, Harter (1993) has suggested the use of co-linked descriptors (i.e., descriptors that are linked to a third term through a thesaurus relationship) in a fashion similar to co-cited references, although in case of the descriptors, the relationship is symmetric, whereas for co-citations it is not. Users initially start with two candidate terms from the thesaurus. By allowing users to select a co-linked descriptor search option, users can become aware of additional descriptors potentially relevant to their information need. The application may be taken further to permit query expansion by including the resulting co-linked terms during the search process.

Hearst (1995) introduced the concept of TileBars to visualize term distribution characteristics in full-text environments. With TileBars, users are able to view document characteristics such as the relative document length, frequency of query terms, and their distribution properties across documents as rectangles. The TileBars use visual properties such as the use of shading to represent term density and their relative position within documents to allow users to make quick judgments about potential document relevance.

Quoniam, Balme, Rostaing, Giraud, and Dou (1998) have used Zipf's law to qualify all keywords of documents within a data set. By categorizing each keyword within a document into one of three categories (low frequency, medium frequency, and high frequency), cumulating the number of terms in each category, and calculating the proportional representation of each category, it is possible to represent a document graphically as a triangular plane in a three-dimensional space with each frequency category of terms representing a dimension. Eight zones were characterized based on combinations of relative term concentrations. Based on a data set of several thousand documents, the authors were able to categorize the documents into each of the zones, permitting documents to be isolated for further examination. Although this categorization operates independently of the semantics of terms, it is possible to focus on documents with specific indexing characteristics, such as those primarily indexed by low frequency terms or different combinations of term frequencies, by selecting documents from the different zones.

Ding, Chowdhury, Foo, and Qian (2000) have developed a Bibliometric Information Retrieval System (BIRS) that uses co-occurrence analysis based on author co-citations in addition to co-word (term) analysis to permit the development of multidimensional scaling maps to visualize relationships among these processes. A unified interface permits the construction of a list of search terms that may then be submitted to several Web-based search engines, library OPACs, and bibliographic databases. Results from a user study of the system indicate that the system is useful in helping users to better understand their search domain and to formulate and expand their queries.

7.4.5 System Planning for Efficient Resource Use

Cunha, Bestavros, and Crovella (1995) point to the need for accurate estimation of site usage in distributed document environments to estimate resource needs. In this case, the focus is on client software requests for files on Web servers. The authors demonstrate the applicability of power law (i.e., Pareto or Zipf) distributions to describe not only Web file usage but also document sizes and numbers of references to documents. They find that the majority of accessible files are small, with users accessing these files more frequently than larger sized files. By examining the impact of different sizes of caches, recommendations are made for caching strategies to reduce file transfer latency. Caching of many small, frequently requested files result in significant latency reduction.

Other techniques have been applied for the development of systems for efficient usage and system navigation. For a hypertext-based environment, Pirolli, Pitkow, and Rao (1996) relied on the traditionally used features in hypertext analysis of hyperlink structure and document text similarity, in conjunction with document meta information, page usage frequency, and hypertext usage paths for input into the arrangement of Web pages. Using several methods for model development, the authors were able to demonstrate new techniques for node typing in hypertext systems, the ability to extract groups of related pages, and the determination of document relevancy.

7.5 IR System Evaluation

The evaluation of existing systems provides valuable feedback to designers on systems design. It can also suggest room for improvement, where design features thought to be effective turn out not to help the retrieval process or to confuse the user. Evaluation data can be collected from analyses based on system content or usage, depending on the focus, whether interfacing issues or system indexing practices. For example, system usability would rely on explicit and implicit feedback from users. By examining user interactions with the system and usage of system features, and search outcomes, designers and evaluators may determine how well the system is meeting the users' needs. Similarly, evaluation studies may focus on system content, examining the efficacy of indexing policies. Ultimately, evaluation studies may be used to predict future system performance based on regularities observed in system interactions.

7.5.1 System Usability

Usability is a subjective concept. It may mean different things to different users of IR systems and to the researchers studying system usage. One often reads about system usability studies that measure objective user interactions with IR systems along with user affective response.

Assessing user response to the system provides investigators with an internalized perspective of system usability. But what users say about a system and what they do may not be the same. Information retrieval system usage characteristics can inform interface design and usability practice by providing additional objective data on which to base usability assessments. For example, Tague-Sutcliffe and Toms (1995) relied on transaction logs to develop measures that describe user search patterns in a Canadian patent database with hypertext linkages. Based on search characteristics, ways of improving user interfaces are suggested. The authors look at correlation distributions of system effectiveness and inefficiency measures with search patterns of different numbers of user actions. Based on the distributions of correlations, suggestions for presentation of indexes, browsing of records, and help design can be made.

7.5.2 System Indexing Practices

System indexing practices can be viewed from the perspective of the document inclusion in the index or the method for indexing within the documents themselves. Changes in document inclusion most often will result from the removal of a document so that it is no longer available and therefore should no longer be indexed. Bar-Ilan (2001) points to the significance of changes in document availability or content and their impact on informetric data sets collected using Web search engines.

Experiments with IR system contents have looked at the effects of system characteristics on retrieval effectiveness or system storage requirements. For example, Burnett, Cooper, Lynch, Willett, and Wycherley (1979) examined the effect of the size of controlled index term vocabularies on retrieval using the Cranfield test collections. The authors found that retrieval performance improved with an increase in the number of terms used to index documents, but the rate of improvement decreased as the number of index terms approached the complete set of terms from the original set. In a related study, Willett (1979) examined the use of fixed-length character strings for controlling the size of an indexing vocabulary on the same Cranfield data sets, using hashing, truncation, and n-gram encoding techniques, noting the performance of each approach.

The persistence of documents (see Chapter 5, Section 5.6.4) and their frequency of change affect the currency of indexes in dynamic environments. Bar-Ilan (1998) examined search result consistency from the six largest Web search engines in terms of indexed content over six search rounds. She noted how the results of all of the services vary not only across services but also within the services over time, with fluctuating precision performance. Because of the indexing practices of the search engines, they go through periods of "forgetting" and then "recovering" available sites, perhaps indicating that the service indexes need to be refreshed more frequently. Toward this end, Brewington and Cybenko (2000) studied over two million Web pages and their frequency of change to determine how frequently search engines would need to update their indexes. Basically, it is unfeasible for a search engine to re-index its holdings for every change that takes place in a document that is indexed. The rate of change observed across a document collection can provide an indication of how frequently indexing spiders or bots may need to revisit Web sites for re-indexing.

7.5.3 System Performance

In addition to modeling IR system contents for system efficiency studies (see Section 7.2), simulation may be used to study system effectiveness performance. A small number of studies to date have proposed that prediction of IR system performance may be inferred from characteristics of system usage, in addition to system characteristics. Gordon (1990) proposed a model for estimating recall by considering all documents and queries as a matrix, where document/query relationships may be indicated by the relevance/nonrelevance and retrieval/nonretrieval as a result of a given query. In this model, recall is treated as an indicator of the probability of retrieving a relevant document for a given query, or conversely as the likelihood of retrieving a given document for queries for which it is relevant.

Fallout, the proportion of nonrelevant items retrieved, as opposed to precision, is also used as a determination of probabilities for queries for which a given document is not relevant. Although not tested, the proposed model is argued to be useful for the comparison of different indexing methods and document matching functions. With knowledge of the frequency distributions of index terms and query terms, a more realistic assessment of performance may be made.

Sanderson and van Rijsbergen (1999) examine the impact of skewed term frequency distributions on retrieval effectiveness. It has long been known that term ambiguity can affect retrieval performance by retrieving documents that contain a given term that represents a different "sense" of the word (e.g., the term "set" has more than one meaning). The authors experimented with the use of pseudo-words, or terms that lump a common term with one or more additional terms to help disambiguate its sense, to determine the impact of the use of pseudo-words on retrieval performance. They demonstrate the importance of skewed frequency distributions of pseudo-senses on retrieval performance and that the resulting frequency skews provided good models for the frequency distributions of the actual senses of ambiguous words. Diminishing returns in improvement were observed with longer queries. The authors also briefly discuss potential implications for other areas of IR where skewed frequency distributions may play a role in retrieval effectiveness, including the use of document signatures (see Chapter 2, Section 2.3.3), stemming (see Chapter 2, Section 2.3.1), optical character recognition symbol usage, cross-language IR (see Chapter 2, Section 2.5.4), and query expansion (see Chapter 2, Section 2.3.2).

7.5.4 Predicting User and Usage Performance

Performance can also be estimated from the user perspective. Cooper (2001) analyzed transaction logs from a Web-based OPAC for variables that define the relevance of end user searches. Actions associated with documenting one or more retrieved items through printing, mailing, downloading, or saving to disk were used as determinations of relevance for a user search session. Thirty-two base variables collected directly from the transaction logs, along with a number of derived variables calculated from the base variables, were used in the statistical analysis. Using principal components analysis followed by logistic regression, the author was able to develop a statistical model that can predict the relevance of a search with a high degree of accuracy based solely on usage characteristics without having to collect any user demographic data. With this knowledge, one can gain a better understanding of best practices for training, where users may be better guided to a successful conclusion to their searches. These implications extend to electronic commerce, covered in the next section. Nielsen

(1997a) discusses the prospect of increasing returns with Web sites. He argues that large Web sites will guide a disproportionately larger amount of traffic to their sites, when compared to smaller Web sites with far fewer linkages.

7.6 Targeting of Services to IR System Users

Perhaps the most economically motivated application of user interactions with IR systems is for the marketing of products and services, or to provide recommendations to users for document visitation. Public search service developers, who make available search engines and commercial Web sites, collect copious amounts of information on user search and browsing habits to better meet the needs of their users or to make users aware of products that may interest them.

7.6.1 System Usage for Targeting and Recommendation of Resources

User profiling has been used for years in IR research to serve as a query surrogate (see Korfhage, 1997, ch. 6). Profiles are used to help modify a query to pre- or post-filter returned results to better anticipate user information needs.

User browsing regularities in public hyperlinked environments such as the Web, both in terms of paths taken and path lengths, can be informative for identifying preferred routes, which can affect system organization. The distribution of path lengths will provide an indication of how persistent users are in their browsing of a system. This in turn can be used to determine average maximum depth of browsable hierarchical environments so that resources are reachable before the average number of nodes visited per user is encountered. The range of paths generated by user site visitation will provide evidence of most popular paths taken. The adage of "location, location, location" in business also applies in the virtual environment, where products are strategically placed on system nodes with frequent visitation.

There has been much focus in recent years in business on the study of consumer Internet usage patterns to support online marketing for targeting of products. Online services such as DoubleClick (http://www.doubleclick.net) and Accipiter (http://www.accipiter.com) specialize in online marketing research by tracking user behaviors across Web sites to better understand browsing habits and user interests. Online marketing is beyond the scope of this work, but more detailed treatment of this area can be found in many works published in recent years (e.g., Silverstein, 2001; Zimmerman, 2001).

Regularities observed in the way users browse systems, and the specific documents/sites they visit during system usage, can provide additional options for subsequent users. Systems may provide recommendations for additional relevant sites for users to consider that may not have been retrieved as a result of the initial search. Web search aids such as Alexa (http://www.alexa.com) will inform users of additional Web sites they may wish to consider based on the browsing habits and explicit recommendations of previous users. The more users follow the sequence of sites, the stronger the connection between the adjacently visited sites becomes. The strength of the connection may be one way or two way, so that recommended sites may only appear if they were visited subsequently to the first site, or the relationship between sites may be treated as an undirected graph. Again, Mathew Effect (see Chapter 3, Section 3.8.2) issues may arise in this situation, unless the recommending system keeps track of site visitation paths that result from initial browsing or system recommendations.

7.6.2 Query Formulation

Many public commercial search services owe their continued existence to income generated from advertisers, whose products and services will appear as advertisements on a search page depending on terms and queries entered by users. Charges to advertisers may be levied based on a block number of impressions, or appearances, of their advertisements to users. The appearance of the advertisement will be determined by the term(s) requested by the advertiser. The more frequently an indexed term is used in a query, the more opportunities the advertiser will have for an advertisement to appear to a user. Economics ultimately dictates which terms are cost-effective. This is tied to the frequency distribution of query terms. If an advertiser is charged on a per impression basis, the most frequently appearing query terms will certainly provide the most exposure but may end up being cost-prohibitive. For example, among the most frequently occurring query terms in Table 6.1, the term “sex” occurs close to 5,000 times in less than one day. When tallied over the course of several months, the cost associated with the number of impressions may be too high for a single advertiser, despite the number of users who will see the advertisement. Conversely, terms that are entered infrequently will not gain as wide an audience. Again, a term occurring with mid-range frequency may provide a balance in terms of cost and exposure.

7.7 Summary

Whether to advance IR theory, to obtain a better understanding of IR system processes, or for applications to IR system design for more effective and efficient systems, informetric study of IR systems content and their use can provide insights that allow one to see the forest for the trees, or rather, the data sets for the regularities. The ability to model patterns of occurrence and use makes it possible to develop simulation models to test file design and plan for resource utilization. On the user side, observed patterns in user interactions with IR systems can inform system feature design and evaluation of system effectiveness.

Past research into IR system design, evaluation, and use in many cases have neglected the unique characteristics of the regularities in recorded discourse and their use by not factoring in the Zipfian distributions of system characteristics and usage. In other cases, researchers have recognized the need to incorporate these regularities, but without making the connection to the wealth of informetric research outside of IR system studies. Research studies incorporating applications of informetrics into IR studies have demonstrated many applications. By and large these studies have been rare and widely scattered over time and across publication sources. The majority of the available research has focused on systems-centered aspects of IR systems design, but more recently applications arising from user-centered studies have appeared, due in large part to the wider accessibility of IR systems and availability of user-based data sources.

Other applications of informetrics for IR system design, evaluation, and use are now just emerging. With the wider availability of data sets of system content and use, a better understanding of system and user dynamics is now possible, thereby improving IR systems. A number of areas remain to be explored. Directions for further research follow in Chapter 8.

8

Future Directions

As the grandest mill in the world will not extract wheat flour from peascods, so pages of formulas will not get a definite result out of loose data.

—T. H. Huxley, 1869

8.1 The Future of Informetric Study of IR Systems

Chapter 1 began with a quote that speaks to the importance of quantification and measurement as the basis for understanding natural phenomena. This final chapter begins with a more guarded perspective; one that recognizes that quantitative methods of observed phenomena alone must be tempered with the qualitative properties of the data used. This is particularly true of social phenomena. Just as citation counts alone cannot reflect the true merit of the source being referenced, one cannot always easily substitute a single measure as a representation of a social indicator. As noted by Paisley (1990), informetric data sets may have high reliability, but the validity of generalizations made can be questionable. Corroboratory evidence is often needed to confirm the validity of the conclusions drawn.

The cyclic growth spurts of informetrics literature, especially applications-oriented studies, reflect the ebb and flow of research fronts and the influence on them of ideological and technological developments. Currently we are experiencing a period of rapid growth in research contributions as a result of widescale interest in electronic information access and use facilitated by the Internet. This wider availability of electronic data has also influenced how informetric research is carried out in general. Electronic forums are an additional medium through which recorded discourse may be studied. Whether this medium represents simply a change in *type* or a more significant change in *kind* is debatable. However, the fluid and immediate nature of the electronic medium for document production, access, and use requires that we revisit how we define fundamental ideas in informetrics, whether in reference to a document/publication, source, reference/citation, or method of access/use. Also, the wider availability of documentary sources permitted in a networked environment will affect how one characterizes the user population, where previously this population was defined by more limited access channels.

At present, part of the popular interest in how users interact with IR systems stems from public curiosity about the Internet, its content, and how it is being used. Although this is of continuing interest for business market research, the general public may soon move on to the next wave of popular interest. Regardless, there remain areas of research investigation for informetricians and system developers to explore. The growth of IR systems for a broader range of resources and rise in levels of information literacy in using IR systems opens up a number of areas to stimulate research interest. Potential areas for further research are presented in this chapter, along with inherent challenges that remain.

8.2 The User Revolution and "Real-World" IR Studies

Information retrieval research has usually taken place in controlled settings, where investigators may study user interactions through direct observation and user feedback. The advantages of being able to control experimental parameters to reduce or eliminate influences by external factors are clear. But direct experimental research with subjects is costly, time-consuming, and arguably artificial due to the controlled environment. Participants may not be representative of the user population at large. With many systems now collecting logs of user sessions, it becomes possible to analyze large data collections. Combined with the wider availability of IR systems accessible over the Internet, in a period of less than a decade we have gone from IR technology being accessed primarily in libraries as OPACs, CD-ROM-based databases, or online vendor-based products, to free, Internet-accessible systems available to anyone worldwide with Internet connectivity. These growing audiences now allow IR user studies to take place on a much larger scale than was previously possible in lab-based settings.

The IR system interface and the content it indexes will ultimately determine how users interact with the system and for what purpose it is used. These influences define different contexts in which IR activities take place. The wider availability of IR technology has made it possible to index a broader range of content, whether traditional bibliographic and full-text published sources available through vendors, organizational documents available through intra- and extranets, or a combination of these and popular interest resources characterized by public Internet search engines. As an example, IR studies of traditional environments often reflect purposeful searching for topic areas promulgated by a defined information need. Searchers tend not to "surf" systems with subject-specific content. Therefore regularities in observed search behaviors are characteristic of the specialized populations these IR environments exist to serve. The recent studies of public search engine search characteristics focus on more general content and user population environments.

If one were to consider the population of Internet users as representative of the larger general population—as of yet not the case, but increasingly becoming so as levels of computer literacy and Internet connectivity increase—the study of user search topics, for example, could reflect the information interests of society at that time. Changes in the most popular search topics can provide a snapshot of public interest. As revealed in Spink, Jansen, Wolfram, and Saracevic (2002), these shifts in an electronic environment can be apparent over a period of several years. The shift away from entertainment and adult-oriented material toward business- and commerce-oriented requests may be indicative of changes in how the Internet is being used to access information. With additional data sets over a longer period of time, longitudinal studies that track short-term and long-term changes in user search behavior should be undertaken. Of particular interest is how general search behaviors evolve as users become more accustomed to IR concepts and systems. Do search behaviors become more sophisticated, as measured by the number of search terms entered, the search options used, and the types of browsing users engage in? With new users continuing to be introduced to IR concepts, will we just continue to see more of the same, where, as the user populations grow, there will be a relatively stable percentage of novice users whose behaviors balance those of more sophisticated users?

The more dynamic nature of what constitutes an IR system today points to the need for additional comparative studies of different environments and their implications for design and use. Traditional IR environments are more static, in the sense that documents, once present, do not change, although new content can be added. Conversely, systems indexing networked resources more closely resemble the dynamic environment of database management systems, where content is constantly changing. How does the difference in these environments affect user search sessions and the design of systems in terms of file organization? One difficulty that remains for the comparative study of IR system content and use is the lack of any uniform analytical and evaluative standards across the different types of IR systems. Different interfaces, search and presentation features, and content representation methods make it difficult to compare systems and environments. In this regard, informetric research can be helpful in the development of standardized metrics for IR system evaluation.

8.3 Informetric Study of Nontextual Documentary Content

Informetric studies of the content of documentary sources have relied almost exclusively on the textual components of documents such as word frequency, document length, references and citations, field lengths, and authorship. Historically, this has been due to the ready availability of textual documentary components for study, whether in print-based or electronic documents. Today's IR systems incorporate not only textual components but also other media formats that may be studied with equal scrutiny to determine if similar regularities exist in the production and use of nontextual containers of intellectual discourse. As image, music, sound, and video retrieval systems become more feasible, informetric study of these nontextual information systems becomes possible. An example of nontextual analysis is the work of Nelson and Downie (2001), who study the distribution of music n-grams (strings of *n* notes to represent words) using different representations of note intervals as characters. By converting musical notation to a form that is comparable to text, they are able to apply text-based informetric analysis methods to a music database of folk songs. The authors conclude that the frequency distributions of musical note sequences of certain n-gram lengths composed of defined intervals resembled those distributions found in text. Other aspects of musical document representation await investigation. These concepts present challenges using current informetric methodologies because musical concepts such as note duration and polyphony (i.e., multiple notes played simultaneously) have no equivalents in text-based information representation and add an extra dimension of complexity for analysis (Byrd & Crawford, 2002).

The informetric properties of multimedia documents, consisting of regularities in the appearance of image attributes and content, are only now being investigated. At least two approaches to the study of image attribute regularities are possible: their presence in documents and their properties. First, the frequency of occurrence of images within documents as an attribute of the documents themselves can be studied in the same way that outlinks in hypertext documents are studied. Extraction of image attribute data may be studied in document collections formatted with markup languages such as HTML, SGML, or XML. Toward this end, Woodruff, Aoki, Brewer, Hauthier, and Rowe (1996) investigated the average frequency of use of different markup language tags within Web documents but did not report on the frequency distributions of occurrence of these tags. As an initial foray into this area, Ajiferuke and Wolfram (submitted b) have investigated the frequency distribution of image tags within Web pages using data sampled from top-level Web pages across five high-level domains (.com, .edu, .gov, .net, .org) and from sample pages within individual Web sites. A GIGP, with its ability to represent a zero class, resulted in good fits for four of the five high-level domain image frequency distribution data sets. The authors also noted that top-level pages from the .com domain contained a significantly higher average number of images per page than the other four domains. Distributions within individual Web sites were much more variable, with bimodal and multimodal distributions observed that could not be adequately fitted to standard unimodal models. Additional studies are needed for corroboration of these initial findings.

Image intensive document collections require more disk space to store and more time to transfer across networks. A shallow frequency distribution of images per document, indicating a higher proportion of documents with a larger number of images, can point to a space and, hence, a bandwidth intensive collection. Conversely, a relatively steep distribution reveals a more conservative use of image attributes. A high degree of image references may present challenges for sight-impaired users, so the frequency distribution of images within the collection can provide an indication of accessibility for some users. Similarly, the distribution of specific image occurrences within or across documents is another avenue for investigation. Specific instances of image types within individual documents or across a document set could be investigated in the same way that text tokens and types are currently studied, where file names correspond to image types, and instances of a given image are treated as tokens. Such analyses would reveal patterns of duplication in image usage, such as in the repetitive use of iconic images. Identification of image types could be problematic, as images representing different types may share a common name. The use of image size information could be useful in distinguishing the different types with common names. The distribution of image type frequency across a document set would be useful for determining redundancy in image content across a Web site. Because images can be quite large, having multiple copies of images across a site can increase disk space requirements. Repetition could also have implications for image representation integrity. As an example, on academic or corporate Web sites there may be an expectation for every page to use the same banner image. With multiple copies of the image scattered throughout a server, if the image needs to be modified, changes would need to be reflected on every instance of the image. If the distribution of image occurrence reveals a lot of redundancy, images could be accessed from a centralized location.

Second, the properties of the images themselves may lend themselves to study in image retrieval systems, as outlined in Chapter 2, Section 2.5.2. Two types of image retrieval systems are currently used: those based on concepts contained within the image and those based on determination of the actual content. Concept-based image IR systems focus on the textual representations of the subject and image object content. With image content translated to a textual form, in essence representing subject headings for the topicality of the image and its properties, image indexing exhaustivity and concept frequency are open for investigation. It is unknown at this time whether these properties follow similar distributions as do text-based document systems. The varying complexity of images stored and level of indexing will no doubt influence the nature of the distributions. Content-based image retrieval systems rely on the properties of the images themselves as the basis of retrieval. Image characteristics such as color, texture, saturation level, and numbers and placement of identifiable objects within each image may produce empirical regularities that have implications for the storage and retrieval of images, equivalent to terms and postings in text-based retrieval systems. However, measurement of many of these attributes would be on a continuous scale, as opposed to the discrete nature of objects traditionally studied in informetrics. At present, concept-based IR is still challenging researchers, requiring sophisticated pattern recognition and matching algorithms. Similar challenges exist for digital video-based systems storage and retrieval systems, in which a temporal component and movement of objects within frames add extra dimensions of complexity.

8.4 Applications for Visualization Research

Information visualization has become an active area of research in human-computer interaction over the past decade. Research fronts and interests have extended into the IR domain (see Chapter 2, Section 2.5.1). With visualization, the ability to perceive system content and document interrelations becomes possible, something that is not supported in IR systems with linear textual displays of document sets that represent document relations in a single dimension. Informetric properties of IR system content provide additional vehicles through which visualization may be achieved. Using visualization, documents may be viewed in relation to one another, or characteristics of individual documents may be viewed as parts of subsets of document collections.

Hearst's introduction of the visual paradigm of TileBars (Hearst, 1995) demonstrates the potential of visualization of informetric characteristics of system content at the individual document level. The visualization of term frequencies within and across documents presents a new way to convey document content to the user, from which informed decisions may be made on document browsing. Indexing exhaustivity and term frequencies will affect how document TileBars are represented. Steeper term distributions, with many singly occurring and few frequently occurring terms, should result in more distinct outcomes.

Visualization of document sets in a low (usually two) dimensional space permits the browsing of document sets based on proximities and the clumping of documents. The artificial neural network technique of Kohonen's feature map algorithm (Kohonen, 2001, also referred to as a self-organizing map, has been applied to vector-based representations of document sets (Lin, 1997). Resulting maps display index term relationships using a two-dimensional grid in a manner similar to how a geographic map outlines political boundaries. Larger areas within a map indicate more frequent occurrence of terms. Proximities of terms to each other are indicative of the frequencies of co-occurrences of the terms, with neighboring terms defining higher co-occurrence frequencies. Thus, term frequency and co-occurrence characteristics make it possible to view term interrelationships when deciding which terms to use for system querying. The maps may also reveal larger conceptual categories evident from the clumping of groups of terms. Currently the process of creating these maps is computationally expensive, but for relatively static document collections they can be created beforehand as a search aid. Again, the nature of the term distributions and indexing exhaustivity will play a strong role in shaping the resulting map. Higher levels of exhaustivity will ensure a rich set of term co-occurrences. However, given the high proportion of singly occurring terms within most indexes and low weight assigned to the most frequently occurring terms, these terms are often removed to permit focus on mid-frequency terms. Future research could examine the impact of these indexing characteristics on map outcomes.

The high percentage of singly occurring indexed terms within a document set permits vector-based systems to distinguish between documents but does not provide significant benefits for users looking to retrieve more than a single document (Wolfram & Zhang, 2001). Singly occurring terms are valuable from a document representation perspective, but as the basis for searching for groups of documents they have limited utility.

Hypertext links within documents as "sitations" present another area for permitting visualization of interdocument relationships. With so many links to explore within hyperlinked environments, users can benefit from the ability to look ahead to which linked documents most closely resemble the current document or present the most likely avenues for exploration based on user search criteria, where potential relevance of linked documents to a user-specified query can be represented in a two-dimensional space (see, e.g., the WebStar system at http://www.uwm.edu/~jzhang/webstar). Co-sitations or the number of outlinks pointing to two documents, or the hypertext equivalent of bibliographic coupling/co-referencing (see Chapter 3, Section 3.3.2), could also be applied in the hypertext environment, where the number of common outlinks among hyperlinked documents could serve as an indication of document relatedness. Most research employing linkage content for relevance assessment to date has favored the use of inlinks for determining document ranks.

At present the majority of retrieval environments that make use of visualization techniques are fairly small document sets or subsets to keep computational and user cognitive burden manageable. With faster technologies and a focus on document subsets within a larger database, visualization techniques will become more feasible.

8.5 Final Thoughts

Both IR and informetrics have long-standing separate histories as areas of investigation. They share common intellectual foundations but arose from different traditions with different areas of emphasis. Technology has been an important factor in recognizing some of the common areas of investigation. Intellectual mechanisms for providing access to documentary sources have long been in place for organizing and accessing sources, but the technological advances to facilitate this intellectual access are of more recent origin. Similarly, recognition of the existence of patterns in recorded discourse largely became possible with the development of indexing services that brought together surrogate representations of documentary sources.

A main goal in writing this book has been to highlight the mutually beneficial nature of two key areas of investigation within the field of information science, particularly in how informetrics can serve as a tool in helping to design and evaluate information retrieval systems. For a field that is characterized by a comparatively small number of research literature outlets for both IR and informetrics, the interactions between these two areas historically has been nominal. The dearth of research that has appeared over the years addressing the utility of informetrics for IR research attests not to the lack of overlap between the two but to the undertapped potential that emerges from their synergy. Traditional methods for design and evaluation in IR may inherently employ quantitative analysis of system content and use, but without the full potential being realized. As this work has highlighted, there has been growing interest in recent years in how users interact with IR systems. The tools and methods informetrics brings to these research areas present many options for better understanding the human process of information seeking and retrieval, not so much at the individual level but at the level of users as a whole. With this understanding, future systems can more effectively be developed to accommodate the needs of IR system users.

References

Abramowitz, M., & Stegun, C. A. (Eds.). (1972). *Handbook of mathematical functions with formulas, graphs, and mathematical tables*. New York: Dover.

Adamic, L. A., & Huberman, B. A. (2001). The Web's hidden order. *Communications of the ACM, 44*(9), 55-59.

Adler, R. J., Feldman, R. E., & Taqqu, M. S. E. (1998). *A practical guide to heavy tails: Statistical techniques and applications*. Boston: Birkhäuser.

Ajiferuke, I. (1991). A probabilistic model for the distribution of authorships. *Journal of the American Society for Information Science, 42*(4), 279-289.

Ajiferuke, I. & Wolfram, D. (submitted a). Modeling Internet search and browsing characteristics.

Ajiferuke, I. & Wolfram, D. (submitted b). Analysis of image tag distribution characteristics in Web pages.

Ajiferuke, I. & Wolfram, D. (submitted c). Modeling the characteristics of Web page outlinks.

Ajiferuke, I., Wolfram, D., & Xie, H. (submitted). Modeling Web site visitation and resource usage data.

Albert, R., Jeong, H., & Barabasi, H.-L. (1999). Diameter of the World-Wide Web. *Nature, 401*(6749), 130.

Allen, B. L. (1996). *Information tasks: Toward a user-centered approach to information systems.* San Diego: Academic Press.

Almind, P., & Ingwersen, P. (1997). Informetric analyses on the World Wide Web: Methodological approaches to "Webometrics." *Journal of Documentation, 53*, 404-426.

Avramescu, A. (1979). Actuality and obsolescence of scientific literature. *Journal of the American Society for Information Science, 30*(5), 296-303.

Ayres, F. H., & Yannakoudakis, E. J. (1979). The bibliographic record: An analysis of the size of its constituent parts. *Program, 13*(3), 127-142.

Baayen, R. H. (2001). *Word frequency distributions*. Boston: Kluwer.

Baeza-Yates, R., & Ribeiro-Neto, B. (1999). *Modern information retrieval.* New York: ACM Press.

Bar-Ilan. (1998). Search engine results over time: A case study on search engine stability. *Cybermetrics, 2/3*. Available: http://www.cindoc.csic.es/cybermetrics/articles/v2i1p1.html. (Accessed April 19, 2003).

Bar-Ilan, J. (2001). Data collection methods on the Web for informetric purposes—A review and analysis. *Scientometrics, 50*(1), 7-32.

Bar-Ilan, J., & Peritz, B. C. (1999). The life span of a specific topic on the Web: The case of "informetrics" a quantitative analysis. *Scientometrics, 46*(3), 371-382.

Belew, R. K. (2000). *Finding out about: A cognitive perspective on search engine technology*. Cambridge, UK: Cambridge University Press.

Bennett, B. S. (1995). *Simulation fundamentals*. New York: Prentice Hall.

Bennett, J. M. (1975). Storage design for information retrieval: Scarrott's conjecture and Zipf's Law. In E. Gelenbe & D. Poitier (Eds.), *International computing symposium* (pp. 233-237). Amsterdam: North Holland.

Berkson, J. (1978). Minimum chi-square, not maximum likelihood! *The Annals of Statistics, 8*(3), 457-487.

Berson, A., Smith, S., & Thearling, K. (2000). *Building data mining applications for CRM*. New York: McGraw-Hill.

Bird, P. R. (1974). The distribution of indexing depth in documentation systems. *Journal of Documentation, 30*(4), 381-390.

Björneborn, L., & Ingwersen, P. (2001). Perspectives of webometrics. *Scientometrics, 50*(1), 65-82.

Bookstein, A. (1973). Statistical behaviour of search keys. *Journal of Library Automation, 6*(2), 109-116.

Bookstein, A. (1974). Hash coding with a non-unique search key. *Journal of the American Society for Information Science, 25*(4), 232-236.

Bookstein, A. (1977). Patterns of scientific productivity and social change: A discussion of Lotka's law and bibliometric symmetry. *Journal of the American Society for Information Science, 28*(4), 206-210.

Bookstein, A. (1990a). Informetric distributions—1: Unified overview. *Journal of the American Society for Information Science, 41*(5), 368-375.

Bookstein, A. (1990b). Informetric distributions—2: Resilience to ambiguity. *Journal of the American Society for Information Science, 41*(5), 376-386.

Bookstein, A. (1997). Informetric distributions 3: Ambiguity and randomness. *Journal of the American Society for Information Science, 48*(1), 2-10.

Bookstein, A., Klein, S. T., & Raita, T. (1997). Modeling word occurrences for the compression of concordances. *ACM Transactions on Information Systems, 15*(3), 254-290.

Bookstein, A., & Swanson, D. R. (1974). Probabilistic models for automatic indexing. *Journal of the American Society for Information Science, 25*(5), 312-318.

Borgman, C. L. E. (1990). *Scholarly communication and bibliometrics.* Newbury Park, CA: Sage.

Borko, H. (1968). Information science: What is it? *American Documentation, 19*(1), 3-5.

Bourne, C. P. (1977). Frequency and impact of spelling errors in bibliographic data bases. *Information Processing & Management, 13*(1), 1-12.

Boyce, B. R., Meadow, C. T., & Kraft, D. H. (1994). *Measurement in information science.* San Diego: Academic Press.

Bradford, S. C. (1934). Sources of information on specific subjects. *Engineering, 137*, 8-96.

Bradford, S. C. (1948). *Documentation.* London: Crosby Lockwood.

Brewington, A. E., & Cybenko, G. (2000). How dynamic is the Web? *Computer Networks and ISDN Systems, 30*, 107-117.

Brin, S., & Page, L. (1998). *The anatomy of a large-scale hypertextual Web search engine.* Available: http://www7.scu.edu.au/programme/fullpapers/1921/com1921.htm. (Accessed April 19, 2003).

Broglio, J., Callan, J., & Croft, W. B. (1994). *InQuery system overview.* Paper presented at the TIPSTER Text Program (Phase 1), San Francisco.

Brookes, B. C. (1977). Theory of the Bradford law. *Journal of Documentation, 33*(3), 180-209.

Brookes, B. C. (1984a). Ranking techniques and the empirical log law. *Information Processing & Management, 20*(1-2), 37-46.

Brookes, B. C. (1984b). Towards informetrics—Haitun, Laplace, Zipf, Bradford and the Alvey program. *Journal of Documentation, 40*(2), 120-143.

Brookes, B. C. (1988). *Comments on the scope of bibliometrics.* In L. Egghe & R. Rousseau (Eds.), *Informetrics 87/88: Select proceedings of the First International Conference on Bibliometrics and Theoretical Aspects of Information Retrieval* (pp. 29-40). Amsterdam: Elsevier.

Brooks, T. A. (1987). Bradford analysis of authorship dispersion for database design. *Proceedings of the ASIS Annual Meeting, 24*, 20-24.

Brooks, T. A. (1988). Repetitive bibliographical information in relational databases. *Journal of the American Society for Information Science, 39*(1), 2-7.

Brown, E. W., Callan, J. P., & Croft, W. B. (1994). *Fast incremental indexing for full-text information retrieval.* Paper presented at the 20th VLDB Conference, Santiago, Chile.

Buckland, M. K. (1991). *Information and information systems.* New York: Praeger.

Burnett, J. E., Cooper, D., Lynch, M. F., Willett, P., & Wycherley, M. (1979). Document retrieval experiments using indexing vocabularies of varying size: I. Variety generation symbols assigned to the fronts of index terms. *Journal of Documentation, 35*(3), 197-206.

Burrell, Q. (1988). Modelling the Bradford phenomenon. *Journal of Documentation, 44*(1), 1-18.

Burton, R. E., & Kebler, R. W. (1960). The "half-life" of some scientific and technical literature. *American Documentation, 11*(1), 18-22.

Bush, V. (1945). As we may think. *The Atlantic Monthly, 176*(1), 101-108.

Byrd, D., & Crawford, T. (2002). Problems of music information retrieval in the real world. *Information Processing & Management, 38*(2), 249-272.

Catledge, L. D., & Pitkow, J. E. (1995). Characterizing browsing strategies in the World Wide Web. In *The Third International World Wide Web Conference.* Darmstadt, Germany. Available: http://www.igd.fhg.de/www/www95/proceedings/papers/80/userpatterns/UserPatterns.Paper4.form.atted.html. (Accessed April 19, 2003).

Chen, H.-M., & Cooper, M. D. (2001). Using clustering techniques to detect usage patterns in a Web-based information system. *Journal of the American Society for Information Science and Technology, 52*(11), 888-904.

Chen, H.-S., & Leimkuhler, F. S. (1986). A relationship between Lotka's law, Bradford's law, and Zipf's law. *Journal of the American Society for Information Science, 37*(5), 307-314.

Chen, Y.-S. (1989). Analysis of Lotka's law: The Simon-Yule approach. *Information Processing & Management, 25*(5), 527-544.

Christodoulakis, S. (1984). Implications of certain assumptions in database performance evaluation. *ACM Transactions on Database Systems, 9*(2), 163-186.

Cleverdon, C. W. (1984). Optimizing convenient on-line access to bibliographic data bases. *Information Services and Use, 4*(1), 37-47.

Coile, R. C. (1977). Lotka's frequency distribution of scientific productivity. *Journal of the American Society for Information Science, 28*(6), 366-370.

Conover, W. J. (1999). *Practical nonparametric statistics* (3rd ed.). New York: Wiley.

Cooper, M. D. (1973). A simulation model of an information retrieval system. *Information Storage and Retrieval, 9*, 13-32.

Cooper, M. D. (1998). Design considerations in instrumenting and monitoring Web-based information retrieval systems. *Journal of the American Society for Information Science, 49*(10), 903-919.

Cooper, M. D. (2001). Usage patterns of a Web-based library catalog. *Journal of the American Society for Information Science and Technology, 52*(2), 137-148.

Cooper, R. A., & Weekes, A. J. (1983). *Data, models and statistical analysis.* Totowa, NJ: Barnes & Noble.

Courtial, J.-P., Callon, M., & Sigogneau, A. (1993). The use of patent titles for identifying the topics of invention and forecasting trends. *Scientometrics, 26*(2), 231-242.

Cowan, G. (1998). *Statistical data analysis.* Oxford: Clarendon Press.

Croft, W. B., & Thompson, R. H. (1987). I^3R: A new approach to the design of document retrieval systems. *Journal of the American Society for Information Science*, *38*(6), 389-404.

Cronin, B., & Atkins, H. B. (Eds.). (2000). *The web of knowledge: A festschrift in honor of Eugene Garfield.* Medford, NJ: Information Today.

Crovella, M. E., Taqqu, M. S., & Bestavros, A. (1998). Heavy-tailed probability distributions in the World Wide Web. In R. J. Adler, R. E. Feldman, & M. S. Taqqu (Eds.), *A practical guide to heavy tails: statistical techniques and applications* (pp. 3-25). Boston: Birkhäuser.

Cunha, C. R., Bestavros, A., & Crovella, M. E. (1995). *Characteristics of WWW client-based traces.* Available: http://cs-pub.bu.edu/faculty/crovella/paper-archive/TR-95-010/paper.html. (Accessed April 19, 2003).

Deerwester, S., Dumais, S., Furnas, G., Landauer, T., & Harshman, R. (1990). Indexing by latent semantic analysis. *Journal of the American Society for Information Science, 41*(6), 391-407.

Devroye, L. (1986). *Non-uniform random variate generation.* New York: Springer-Verlag.

Ding, Y., Chowdhury, G. G., Foo, S., & Qian, W. (2000). Bibliometric Information Retrieval System (BIRS): A Web search interface using bibliometric research results. *Journal of the American Society for Information Science, 51*(13), 1190-1204.

Diodato, V. (1994). *Dictionary of bibliometrics.* New York: Haworth.

Downie, J. S., & Nelson, M. (2000). Evaluating a simple and effective music information retrieval method. In N. J. Belkin, P. Ingwersen, & M-K. Leong (Eds.), *Proceedings of the 23rd annual international ACM SIGIR Conference on Research and Development in Information Retrieval* (pp. 73-80). New York: ACM Press. .

Efthimiadis, E. (1990). The growth of the OPAC literature. *Journal of the American Society for Information Science, 41*(5), 342-347.

Efthimiadis, E. (1996). Query expansion. In M. Williams (Ed.), *Annual review of information science and technology* (Vol. 31, pp. 121-187).

Egghe, L. (1988). On the classification of the classical bibliometric laws. *Journal of Documentation, 44*(1), 53-62.

Egghe, L. (1990). The duality of informetric systems with applications to empirical laws. *Journal of Information Science, 16*, 17-27.

Egghe, L. (1997). Fractal and informetric aspects of hypertext systems. *Scientometrics, 40*(3), 455-464.

Egghe, L. (2000). New informetric aspects of the Internet: Some reflections—many problems. *Journal of Information Science, 26*(5), 329-335.

Egghe, L., & Rao, I. K. R. (1992). Classification of growth models based on growth rates and its applications. *Scientometrics, 25*(1), 5-46.

Egghe, L., & Rousseau, R. (1990). *Introduction to informetrics: Quantitative methods in library, documentation and information science.* Amsterdam: Elsevier.

Egghe, L., & Rousseau, R. (1995). Generalized success-breeds-success principle leading to time-dependent informetric distributions. *Journal of the American Society for Information Science, 46*(6), 426-445.

Faloutsos, C. (1990). Signature-based text retrieval methods: A survey. *Data Engineering, 13*(1), 25-32.

Faloutsos, C., & Christodoulakis, S. (1987). Description and performance analysis of signature file methods. *ACM Transactions on Office Information Systems, 5*(3), 237-257.

Fedorowicz, J. (1981a). *Modeling an automatic bibliographic system: A Zipfian approach.* Pittsburgh: Carnegie-Mellon University.

Fedorowicz, J. (1981b). *A Zipfian model of inverted file storage requirements.* Paper presented at the Proceedings of the Twelfth Annual Pittsburgh Conference on Modeling and Simulation, Research Triangle Park, NC.

Fedorowicz, J. (1982a). A Zipfian model of an automatic bibliographic system: An application to Medline. *Journal of the American Society for Information Science, 33*(4), 223-232.

Fedorowicz, J. (1982b). The theoretical foundation of Zipf's law and its applications to the blibliographic database environment. *Journal of the American Society for Information Science, 33*(5), 285-293.

Fedorowicz, J. (1987). Database performance evaluation in an indexed file environment. *ACM Transactions on Database Systems, 12*(1), 85-110.

Fernández, M. T., Cabrero, A., Zulueta, M. A., & Gómez, I. (1993). Constructing a relational database for bibliometric analysis. *Research Evaluation, 3*(1), 55-62.

Frakes, W. B., & Baeza-Yates, R. (Eds.). (1992). *Information retrieval: Data structures and algorithms*. Englewood Cliffs, NJ: Prentice Hall.

Fuhr, N. (1992). Probabilistic models in information retrieval. *The Computer Journal, 35*(3), 243-255.

Garfield, E. (1998). From citation indexes to informetrics: Is the tail now wagging the dog? *Libri, 48*(2), 67-80.

Garfield, E., & Sher, I. H. (1963). New factors in the evaluation of scientific literature through citation indexing. *American Documentation, 14*(3), 195-201.

Geisler, E. (2000). *The metrics of science and technology*. Westport, CT: Quorum Books.

Gordon, M. D. (1990). Evaluating the effectiveness of information retrieval systems. *Journal of the American Society for Information Science, 41*(5), 313-323.

Griffiths, J. M. (1975). Index term input to IR systems. *Journal of Documentation, 31*(3), 185-190.

Griffiths, J. M. (1978). *The computer simulation of information retrieval systems.* Unpublished doctoral thesis, University College, London.

Groos, O. V. (1967). Bradford's Law and the Keenen-Atherton data. *American Documentation, 18*(1), 46.

Grossman, D. A., & Frieder, O. (1998). *Information retrieval: Algorithms and heuristics*. Boston: Kluwer Academic.

Haitun, S. D. (1982a). Stationary scientometric distributions: Part I. Different approximations. *Scientometrics, 4*(1), 5-25.

Haitun, S. D. (1982b). Stationary scientometric distributions: Part II. Non-Gaussian nature of scientific activities. *Scientometrics, 4*(2), 89-104.

Haitun, S. D. (1982c). Stationary scientometric distributions: Part III. The role of the Zipf distribution. *Scientometrics, 4*(3), 181-194.

Harter, S. P. (1975a). A probabilistic approach to automatic keyword indexing: Part I. On the distribution of specialty words in a technical literature. *Journal of the American Society for Information Science*, *25*(4), 197-206.

Harter, S. P. (1975b). A probabilistic approach to automatic keyword indexing: Part II. An algorithm for probabilistic indexing. *Journal of the American Society for Information Science*, *25*(5), 280-289.

Harter, S. P. (1993). Colinked descriptors: An application of bibliometrics to interface design. In S. Bonzi (Ed.), *ASIS '93 Proceedings of the 56th ASIS Annual Meeting* (pp.131-134). Medford, NJ: Learned Information.

Heaps, H. S. (1978). *Information retrieval: Computational and theoretical aspects*. New York: Academic Press.

Hearst, M. A. (1995). TileBars: Visualization of term distribution information in full text information access. In *Proceedings of the ACM SIGCHI Conference on Human Factors in Computing Systems* (pp. 59-66). New York: ACM. Available: http://www.acm.org/sigchi/chi95/Electronic/documnts/papers/mah_bdy.htm. (Accessed April 19, 2003).

Heine, M. (1998). Bradford ranking conventions and their application to a growing literature. *Journal of Documentation, 54*(3), 303-331.

Heine, M. D. (1981). Simulation, and simulation experiments. In K. Sparck Jones (Ed.), *Information retrieval experiment* (pp. 179-198). London: Butterworths.

Henry, G., & Diodato, V. (1991). The rates of assignment of thesaurus terms in the ERIC information retrieval system: An analysis of hierarchies and levels. *Journal of Documentation, 47*(3), 276-283.

Henzinger, M. R., Heydon, A., Mitzenmacher, M., & Najork, M. (2000). On near-uniform URL sampling. In *Proceedings of the Ninth International World Wide Web Conference, Amsterdam, Netherlands, May 15-19, 2000.* Available: http://www9.org/w9cdrom/88/88.html. (Accessed April 19, 2003).

Hill, E. (1978). Analysis of an inverted data base structure. *SIGIR Forum, 13*(1), 37-64.

Hoelscher, C. (1998). How Internet experts search for information on the Web. In H. Maurer & R.G. Olson (Eds.), *Proceedings of WebNet98—World Conference of the WWW, Internet & Intranet*. Charlottesville, VA: Association for Advancement of Computing in Education.

Houston, N., & Wall, E. (1964). The distribution of term usage in manipulative indexes. *American Documentation, 15*(2), 105-114.

Huberman, B. A. (2001). *The laws of the Web: Patterns in the ecology of information*. Cambridge, MA: MIT Press.

Huberman, B. A., & Adamic, L. A. (1999). Growth dynamics of the World Wide Web. *Nature, 401*, 131-133.

Huberman, B. A., Pirolli, P., Pitkow, J. E., & Lukose, R. M. (1998). Strong regularities in World Wide Web surfing. *Science, 280*(April 3), 95-97.

Hubert, J. J. (1978). Relationship between two forms of Bradford's law. *Journal of the American Society for Information Science, 29*(3), 159-161.

Hubert, J. J. (1981). General bibliometric models. *Library Trends, 30*(1), 65-82.

Huffman, D. A. (1952). A method for the construction of minimum redundancy codes. *Proceedings of the Institute of Radio Engineers, 40*, 1098-1101.

Ingwersen, P. (1998). The calculation of Web impact factors. *Journal of Documentation, 54*(2), 236-243.

Ingwersen, P., & Christensen, F. H. (1997). Data set isolation for bibliometric online analyses of research publications: Fundamental methodological issues. *Journal of the American Society for Information Science, 48*(3), 205-217.

Irwin, J. O. (1975). The generalized Waring distribution: Part 1, part 2, part 3. *Journal of the Royal Statistical Society, Series A, 138*, 18-31, 204-227, 374-384.

Jacquesson, A., & Schieber, W. D. (1973, February). Term association analysis on a large file of bibliographic data using a highly-controlled indexing vocabulary. *Information Storage and Retrieval, 9*, 85-94.

Jansen, B. J., & Pooch, U. (2001). A review of Web searching studies and a framework for future research. *Journal of the American Society for Information Science and Technology, 52*(3), 235-246.

Jansen, M. B. J., Spink, A., Bateman, J., & Saracevic, T. (1998). Real life information retrieval: A study of user queries on the Web. *SIGIR Forum, 32*(1), 5-17.

Jansen, B. J., Spink, A., & Saracevic, T. (2000). Real life, real users, and real needs: A study of user queries on the Web. *Information Processing & Management, 36*(2), 207-227.

Järvelin, K., Ingwersen, P., & Niemi, T. (2000). A user-oriented interface for generalised informetric analysis based on applying advanced data modelling techniques. *Journal of Documentation, 56*(3), 250-278.

Johnson, N. L., & Kotz, S. (1969). *Discrete distributions*. New York: Wiley.

Johnson, N. L., Kemp, A. W., & Kotz, S. I. (1993). *Univariate discrete distributions* (2nd ed.). New York: Wiley.

Johnson, N. L., Kotz, S., & Balakrishnan, N. (1997). *Discrete multivariate distributions*. New York: Wiley.

Jones, S., Cunningham, S. J., & McNab, R. (1998). Usage analysis of a digital library. In *Proceedings of the Third ACM Conference on Digital Libraries* (pp. 293-294). New York: Association for Computing Machinery.

Keen, E. M. (1971). Evaluation parameters. In G. Salton (Ed.), *The SMART retreival system—Experiments in automatic document processing* (pp. 74-111). Englewood Cliffs, NJ: Prentice-Hall.

Kessler, M. M. (1963). Bibliographic coupling between scientific papers. *American Documentation, 14*(1), 10-25.

Kinnucan, M., & Wolfram, D. (1990). Direct comparison of bibliometric models. *Information Processing & Management, 26*(6), 777-790.

Knuth, D. E. (1973). *The art of computer programming* (Vol. 3). Reading, MA: Addison-Wesley.

Koehler, W. (1999) An analysis of Web page and Web site constancy and permanence. *Journal of the American Society for Information Science, 50*(2), 162-180.

Kohonen, T. (2001). *Self-organizing maps* (3rd ed.). New York: Springer.

Korfhage, R. R. (1997). *Information storage and retrieval*. New York: Wiley.

Kostoff, R. N., del Río, J. A., Humenik, J. A., Garcia, E. O., & Ramírez, A. M. (2001). Citation mining: Integrating text mining and bibliometrics for research user profiling. *Journal of the American Society for Information Science and Technology, 52*(13), 1148-1156.

Kowalski, G. (1997). *Information retrieval systems: Theory and implementation*. Boston: Kluwer Academic.

Kraft, D. H., & Boyce, B. R. (1991). *Operations research for libraries and information agencies*. San Diego: Academic Press.

Kramer, G. E. (1994). *Auditory display : Sonification, audification, and auditory interfaces*. Reading, MA: Addison-Wesley.

Kučera, H., & Francis, W. N. (1967). *Computational analysis of present-day American English*. Providence, RI: Brown University Press.

Larson, R. R. (1991). The decline of subject searching: Long-term trends and patterns of index use in an online catalog. *Journal of the American Society for Information Science, 42*(3), 197-215.

Larson, R. R. (1996). *Bibliometrics of the World Wide Web: An exploratory analysis of the intellectual structure of cyberspace*, Available: http://sherlock.berkeley.edu/asis96/asis96.html. (Accessed April 19, 2003).

Lawrence, S., & Giles, C. L. (1998a). Searching the World Wide Web. *Science, 280*(April 3), 98-100.

Lawrence, S., & Giles, C. L. (1998b). *How big is the Web? How much of the Web do the search engines index? How up to date are the search engines?* Available: http://www.neci.nec.com/~lawrence/websize.html. (Accessed April 19, 2003).

Lawrence, S., & Giles, L. (1999). Accessibility of information on the Web. *Nature, 400*(July 8), 107-109.

Leydesdorff, L. (1997). Why words and co-words cannot map the development of the sciences. *Journal of the American Society for Information Science, 48*(5), 418-427.

Leydesdorff, L. (2001). *The challenge of scientometrics: The development, measurement, and self-organization of scientific communications* (2nd ed.). Leiden, Netherlands: DSWO Press/Leiden University.

Lin, X. (1997). Map displays for information retrieval. *Journal of the American Society for Information Science, 48*(1), 40-54.

Line, M. B. (1993). Changes in the use of literature with time—Obsolescence revisited. *Library Trends, 41*(4), 665-683.

Linhart, H., & Zucchini, W. (1986). *Model selection*. New York: Wiley.

Little, A. E., Harris, R. M., & Nicholls, P. T. (1990). Text to reference ratios in scientific journals. In L. Egghe & R. Rousseau (Eds.), *Informetrics 89/90: Selection of papers submitted for the second international Conference on Bibliometrics, Scientometrics and Informetrics* (pp. 211-216). Amsterdam: Elsevier.

Long, J. M., Barnhard, H. J., & Levy, G. C. (1967). Dictionary buildup and stability of word frequency in a specialized medical area. *American Documentation, 18*(1), 21-25.

Losee, R. M. (1994). Term dependence: Truncating the Bahadur Lazarsfeld Expansion. *Information Processing & Management, 30*(2), 293-303.

Losee, R. M. (1998). *Text retrieval and filtering: Analytic models of performance*. Boston: Kluwer.

Lotka, A. J. (1926). The frequency distribution of scientific productivity. *Journal of the Washington Academy of Science, 16*(12), 317-323.

Luk, R. W. P., Leong, H. V., Dillon, T. S., Chan, A. T. S., Croft, W. B., & Allan, J. (2002). A survey in indexing and searching XML documents. *Journal of the American Society for Information Science and Technology, 53*(6), 415-437.

Maly, K. (1976). Compressed tries. *Communications of the ACM, 19*(7), 409-415.

Mandelbrot, B. (1953). An information theory of the statistical structure of language. In W. Jackson (Ed.), *Communication theory* (pp. 486-502). London: Butterworths.

Mandelbrot, B. (1954). Structure formelle des textes et communication: Deux etudes. *Word, 10*, 1-27.

Marchionini, G. (1995). *Information seeking in electronic environments*. Cambridge, UK: Cambridge University Press.

Marshakova, I. V. (1973). System of document connections based on references (in Russian). *Nauchno-Tekhnicheskaya Informatsiya, ser. 2, 6*, 3-8.

McCain, K. W. (1990). Mapping authors in intellectual space: Population genetics in the 1980s. In C. L. Borgman (Ed.), *Scholarly communication and bibliometrics* (pp. 194-216). Newbury Park, CA: Sage.

McCormick, B., DeFanti, T., & Brown, R. E. (Eds.). (1987). Visualization in scientific computing and computer graphics [Special issue]. *Computer Graphics, 21*(6).

McFadden, F. R., Hoffer, J. A., & Prescott, M. B. (1999). *Modern database management* (5th ed.). Reading, MA: Addison-Wesley.

McHaney, R. (1991). *Computer simulation: A practical perspective*. San Diego: Academic Press.

Meadow, C. T., Boyce, B. R., & Kraft, D. H. (2000). *Text information retrieval systems* (2nd ed.). San Diego: Academic Press.

Meadows, J. (2000). The growth of journal literature: A historical perspective. In B. Cronin & H. B. Atkins (Eds.), *The web of knowledge: A festschrift in honor of Eugene Garfield* (pp. 87-107). Medford, NJ: Information Today.

Mena, J. (1999). *Data mining your Website*. Boston: Digital Press.

Merton, R. K. (1968). The Mathew Effect in science. *Science, 159*, 56-63.

Millsap, L., & Ferl, T. (1993). Search patterns of remote users: An analysis of OPAC transaction logs. *Information Technology and Libraries, 11*(3), 321-343.

Montgomery, A., & Faloutsos, C. (2001). Identifying Web browsing trends and patterns. *Computer, 34*(July), 94-95.

Mooers, C. N. (1951). Zatocoding applied to mechanical organization of knowledge. *American Documentation, 2*, 20-32.

Morgan, B. J. T. (2000). *Applied stochastic modelling*. New York: Oxford University Press.

Nacke, O. (1979). Informetrie: Ein neuer name für eine neue disziplin. *Nachrichten für Dokumentation, 30*(6), 212-226.

Nalimov, V. V., & Mul'chenko, Z. M. (1969). *Naukometriya. Izuchenie razvitiya nauki kak informatsionnogo protsessa*. Moscow: Nauka.

Nelson, M., & Downie, J. S. (2001). Informetric analysis of a music database: Distribution of intervals. In M. Davis & C. S. Wilson (Eds.), *Proceedings of the 8th International Conference on Scientometrics and Informetrics* (pp. 477-484). Sydney: Bibliometric & Informetric Research Group, University of New South Wales.

Nelson, M. J. (1982). *Probabilistic models for the simulation of bibliographic retrieval systems.* London, ON: University of Western Ontario.

Nelson, M. J. (1983). The use of term co-occurrence information in information retrieval. *Canadian Journal of Information Science, 8*, 67-73.

Nelson, M. J. (1988). Correlation of term usage and term indexing frequencies. *Information Processing & Management, 24*(5), 541-547.

Nelson, M. J. (1989). Stochastic models for the distribution of index terms. *Journal of Documentation, 45*(3), 227-237.

Nelson, M. J., & Tague, J. M. (1985). Split size-rank models for the distribution of index terms. *Journal of the American Society for Information Science, 36*, 283-296.

Nicholls, P. T. (1986). Empirical validation of Lotka's Law. *Information Processing & Management, 22*(5), 417-419.

Nicholls, P. T. (1988). Price's square root law: Empirical validity and relation to Lotka's law. *Information Processing & Management, 24*(4), 469-477.

Nicholls, P. T. (1989). Bibliometric modeling processes and the empirical validity of Lotka's Law. *Journal of the American Society for Information Science, 40*(6), 379-385.

Nielsen, J. (1997a). *Do websites have increasing returns?* Available: http://www.useit.com/alertbox/9704b.html. (Accessed April 19, 2003).

Nielsen, J. (1997b). *Zipf Curves and Website popularity*. Available: http://www.useit.com/alertbox/zipf.html. (Accessed April 19, 2003).

Oard, D. W., & Diekema, A. R. (1998). Cross-language information retrieval. In M. Williams (Ed.), *Annual review of information science and technology* (Vol. 34, pp. 223-256). Medford, NJ: Information Today.

Olsen, K. A., Korfhage, R. R., Sochats, K. M., Spring, M. B., & Williams, J. G. (1993). Visualization of a document collection: The VIBE system. *Information Processing & Management, 29*(1), 69-81.

Ozmutlu, H. C., Spink, A., & Ozmutlu, S. (2002). Analysis of large data logs: An application of Poisson sampling on Excite Web queries. *Information Processing & Management, 38*(4), 473-490.

Paisley, W. (1990). The future of bibliometrics. In C. L. Borgman (Ed.), *Scholarly communication and bibliometrics* (pp. 281-299). Newbury Park, CA: Sage.

Pao, M. L. (1985). Lotka's Law: A testing procedure. *Information Processing & Management, 21*(4), 305-320.

Pao, M. L. (1986). An empirical exmination of Lotka's Law. *Journal of the American Society for Information Science, 37*(1), 26-33.

Pareto, V. (1897). *Cours d'economie politique* (Vol. 2). Lausanne: Université de Lausanne.

Peat, H. J., & Willett, P. (1991). The limitations of term co-occurrence data for query expansion in document retrieval systems. *Journal of the American Society for Information Science, 42*(5), 378-383.

Peters, C. (Ed.). (2000). *Cross-language information retrieval and evaluation*. New York: Springer.

Pirolli, P., & Card, S. (1995). Information foraging in information access environments. In *Proceedings of the ACM Conference on Human Factors in Computing Systems (CHI '95)* (pp. 51-58). New York: ACM Press.

Pirolli, P., Pitkow, J., & Rao, R. (1996). Silk from a sow's ear: Extracting usable structures from the Web. In R. Bilger, S. Guest, & M. J. Tauber (Eds.) *CHI*

96—Electronic Proceedings. Available: http://www.acm.org/sigchi/chi96/proceedings/papers/Pirolli_2/pp2.html (Accessed April 19, 2003).

Press, W. H. (1989). *Numerical recipes: The art of scientific computing*. Cambridge, UK: Cambridge University Press.

Price, D. J. d. S. (1963). *Little science, big science*. New York: Columbia University.

Price, D. J. d. S. (1970). Citation measures of hard science, soft science, technology, and nonscience. In C. E. Nelson & D. K. Pollock (Eds.), *Communication among scientists and engineers* (pp. 3-22). Lexington, MA: Heath.

Price, D. J. d. S. (1976). A general theory of bibliometric and other cumulative advantage processes. *Journal of the American Society for Information Science, 27*, 292-306.

Pritchard, A. (1969). Statistical bibliography or bibliometrics? *Journal of Documentation, 25*(4), 348-349.

Pu, H. T., Chuang, S. L., & Yang, C. (2002). Subject categorization of query terms for exploring Web users' search interests. *Journal of the American Society for Information Science and Technology*, 53(8), 617-630.

Qiu, L. (1990). An empirical investigation of the existing models for Bradford's Law. *Information Processing & Management, 26*(5), 655-672.

Qiu, L. (1993). Markov models of search state patterns in a hypertext information retrieval system. *Journal of the American Society for Information Science, 44*(7) , 413-427.

Qiu, L. (1994). Frequency distributions of hypertext path patterns: A pragmatic approach. *Information Processing & Management, 30*(1), 131-140.

Qiu, L., & Tague, J. M. (1990). Complete or incomplete data sets: The Groos droop investigated. *Scientometrics, 19*(3-4), 223-237.

Quoniam, L., Balme, F., Rostaing, H., Giraud, E., & Dou, J. M. (1998). Bibliometric law used for information retrieval. *Scientometrics, 41*(1-2), 83-91.

Rosenberg, A. L., & Snyder, L. (1981). Time- and space-optimality in B-trees. *ACM Transactions on Database Systems*, *6*(1), 174-183.

Ross, N. C. M., & Wolfram, D. (2000). End user searching on the Internet: An analysis of term pair topics submitted to the Excite search engine. *Journal of the American Society for Information Science, 51*(10), 949-958.

Ross, S. M. (1997). *Simulation* (2nd ed.). San Diego: Academic Press.

Rousseau, R. (1990). Relations between continuous versions of bibliometric laws. *Journal of the American Society for Information Science, 41*(3), 197-203.

Rousseau, R. (1997). Sitations: An exploratory study. *Cybermetrics, 1*(1). Available: http://www.cindoc.csic.es/cybermetrics/articles/v1i1p1.html. (Accessed April 19, 2003).

Salton, G. (1975). *A theory of indexing*. Philadelphia: Society for Industrial and Applied Mathematics.

Salton, G. (1989). *Automatic text processing: The transformation, analysis and retrieval of information by computer*. Reading, MA: Addison-Wesley.

Salton, G., Buckley, C., & Yu, C. T. (1983). An evaluation of term dependence models in information retrieval. In G. Salton & H.-J. Schneider (Eds.), *Research and development in information retrieval* (Vol. 146, pp. 151-165). Berlin: Springer-Verlag.

Salton, G., Fox, E. A., & Wu, H. (1983). Extended Boolean information retrieval. *Communications of the ACM, 26*(11), 1022-1036.

Salton, G., & McGill, M. J. (1983). *Introduction to modern information retrieval.* New York: McGraw-Hill.

Sampath, S. (2001). *Sampling theory and methods*. Boca Raton, FL: CRC Press.

Sampson, W. B., & Bendell, A. (1985). Rank order distributions and secondary key indexing. *Computer Journal, 28*(3), 309-312.

Sanderson, M., & van Rijsbergen, C. J. (1999). The impact on retrieval effectiveness of skewed frequency distributions. *ACM Transactions on Information Systems, 17*(4), 440-465.

Saracevic, T. (1975). Relevance: A review of and a framework for the thinking on the notion in information science. *Journal of the American Society for Information Science, 26*(6), 321-343.

Saracevic, T. (1995). Evaluation of evaluation in information retrieval. In E. A. Fox, P. Ingwersen, & R. Fidel (Eds.), *SIGIR '95: Proceedings of the 18th annual international ACM SIGIR Conference on Research and Development in Information Retrieval* (pp. 138-146). New York: ACM.

Saracevic, T. (1997). Users lost: Reflection on the past, future, and limits of information science. *SIGIR Forum, 31*(2), 16-27.

Saxena, A., Gupta, B. M., & Jauhari, M. (2001). Forecasting growth of literature: All models are wrong, some are useful! In M. Davis & C. S. Wilson (Eds.), *Proceedings of the 8th international Conference on Scientometrics and Informetrics* (pp. 647-656). Sydney: Bibliometric & Informetric Research Group, University of New South Wales.

Schuegraf, E. J. (1976). Compression of large inverted files with hyperbolic term distribution. *Information Processing & Management, 12*, 177-184.

Schultz, C. K., Schwartz, P. D., & Steinburg, L. (1961). A comparison of dictionary use within to information retrieval systems. *American Documentation, 12*, 247-253.

Schütze, H., & Pedersen, J. O. (1997). A cooccurrence-based thesaurus and two applications to information retrieval. *Information Processing & Management, 33*(3), 307-318.

Schwartz, E. S. (1963). Dictionary for minimum redundancy encoding. *Journal of the Association for Computing Machinery, 10*, 413-439.

Shannon, C. E., & Weaver, W. (1959). *The mathematical theory of communication*. Urbana: University of Illinois Press.

Shneiderman, B. (1998). *Designing the user interface: Strategies for effective human-computer interaction* (3rd ed.). Reading, MA: Addison-Wesley.

Sichel, H. S. (1985). A bibliometric distribution which really works. *Journal of the American Society for Information Science, 3*(5), 314-321.

Sichel, H. S. (1992). Anatomy of the generalized inverse Gaussian-Poisson distribution with special applications to bibliometric studies. *Information Processing & Management, 28*(1), 5-17.

Siler, K. F. (1976). A stochastic evaluation model for database organizations in data retrieval systems. *Communications of the ACM, 19*(2), 84-95.

Silverstein, B. (2001). *Business-to-business Internet marketing: Seven proven strategies for increasing profits through Internet direct marketing* (3rd ed.). Gulf Breeze, FL: Maximum Press.

Silverstein, C., Henzinger, M., Marais, H., & Moricz, M. (1999). Analysis of a very large web search engine query log. *SIGIR Forum, 33*(1). Available: http://www.acm.org/sigir/forum/F99/Silverstein.pdf. (Accessed April 19, 2003).

Small, H. (1973). Co-citation in the scientific literature: A new measure of the relationship between two documents. *Journal of the American Society for Information Science, 24*(4), 265-269.

Small, H. (1995). Relational bibliometrics. In M.E. D. Koenig & A. Bookstein (Eds.), *Proceedings of the fifth biennial Conference of the International Society for Scientometrics and Informetrics* (pp. 525-532). Medford, NJ: Learned Information.

Snyder, H., & Bonzi, S. (1998). Patterns of self-citation across disciplines (1980–1989). *Journal of the American Society for Information Science, 24*(6), 431-435.

Sornil, O., & Fox, E. A. (2001). Hybrid partitioned inverted indices for large-scale digital libraries. In S. R. Urs, T. B. Rajashekar, & K. S. Raghavan (Eds.), *The 4th international Conference of Asian Digital Libraries* (pp. 192-207). Bangalore, India: ICADL, 2001.

Sotolongo-Aguilar, G. R., Suárez-Balseiro, C. A., & Guzmán-Sánchez, M. V. (2000). Modular bibliometric information system with proprietary software (MOBIS-ProSoft: A versatile approach to bibliometric research tools. *LIBRES: Library and Information Science Research, 10*(2). Available: http://libres.curtin.edu.au/libres10n2/modular.htm. (Accessed April 19, 2003).

Sparck Jones, K., & Willett, P. E. (1997). *Readings in information retrieval.* San Francisco: Morgan Kaufmann.

Spink, A., Jansen, B. J., Wolfram, D., & Saracevic, T. (2002). From e-sex to e-commerce: Web search changes. *Computer Magazine, 35*(3), 107-109.

Spink, A., Wolfram, D., Jansen, B. J., & Saracevic, T. (2001). Searching the web: The public and their queries. *Journal of the American Society for Information Science and Technology*, *52*(3), 226-234.

Stein, G. Z., Zucchini, W., & Juritz, J. M. (1987). Parameter estimation for the Sichel distribution and its multivariate extension. *Journal of the American Statistical Association*, *82*, 938-944.

Su, L. (1992). The relevance of recall and precision in user evaluation. *Journal of the American Society for Information Science, 45*(3), 207-217.

Swanson, D. R. (1986). Undiscovered public knowledge. *Library Quarterly, 56*(2), 103-118.

Swanson, D. R. (1990). The absence of co-citation as a clue to undiscovered causal connections. In C. L. Borgman (Ed.), *Scholarly communication and bibliometrics* (pp. 129-137). Newbury Park, CA: Sage.

Swets, J. A. (1969). Effectiveness of information retrieval methods. *American Documentation, 20*(1), 72-89.

Switzer, P. (1965). Vector images in document retrieval. In M. E. Stevens, V. E. Giuliano, & L. B. Heilprin (Eds.), *Statistical Association methods for mechanized documentation* (pp. 163-171). Washington, DC: National Bureau of Standards.

Tabah, A. N. (1992). Nonlinear dynamics and the growth of literature. *Information Processing & Management*, *28*(1), 61-73.

Tague, J. (1988). What's the use of bibliometrics? In L. Egghe & R. Rousseau (Eds.), *Informetrics 87/88: Select proceedings of the first international Conference on Bibliometrics and Theoretical Aspects of Information Retrieval* (pp. 271-278). Amsterdam: Elsevier.

Tague, J. (1990). Ranks and sizes: Some complementaries and contrasts. *Journal of Documentation, 36*, 314-321.

Tague, J., & Nelson, M. (1983). Simulation of bibliographic retrieval databases using hyperterms. In G. Salton & H.-S. Schneider (Eds.), *Research and development in information retrieval* (Vol. 146, pp. 194-208). Berlin: Springer-Verlag.

Tague, J., Nelson, M., & Wu, H. (1981). Problems in the simulation of bibliographic retrieval systems. In S. E. Robertson, C. J. van Rijsbergen, & P. W. Williams (Eds.), *Information retrieval research* (pp. 236-255). London: Butterworths.

Tague, J., & Nicholls, P. (1987). The maximal value of a Zipf size variable: Sampling properties and relation to other parameters. *Information Processing & Management, 23*(3), 155-170.

Tague-Sutcliffe, J. (1992). The pragmatics of information retrieval experimentation, revisited. *Information Processing & Management, 28*(4), 467-490.

Tague-Sutcliffe, J. M. (1995). *Measuring information*. San Diego: Academic Press.

Tague-Sutcliffe, J. M., & Toms, E. G. (1995, June 1995). *Information system design via the quantitative analysis of user transaction logs.* Paper presented at the Fifth International Conference on Scientometrics and Informetrics, River Forest, IL.

Tahai, A., & Ribsby, J. T. (1998). Information processing using citations to investigate journal influence in accounting. *Information Processing & Management, 34*(2), 341-359.

Tomasic, A., & Garcia-Molina, H. (1993). Query processing and inverted indices in shared-nothing document information retrieval systems. *VLDB Journal*, *2*(3), 243-275.

Trueswell, R. W. (1969). Some behavioral patterns of library users: The 80/20 rule. *Wilson Library Bulletin, 43*, 458-459.

Trybula, W. J. (1999). Text mining. In M. Williams (Ed.), *Annual review of information science and technology* (Vol. 34, pp. 385-419). Medford, NJ: Information Today.

van Rijsbergen, C. J. (1977). A theoretical basis for the use of co-occurrence data in information retrieval. *Journal of Documentation, 33*(2), 106-119.

van Rijsbergen, C. J. (1979). *Information retrieval* (2nd ed.). London: Butterworths.

van Rijsbergen, C. J. (1981). Retrieval effectiveness. In K. Sparck Jones (Ed.), *Information retrieval experiment* (pp. 32-42.). London: Butterworths.

Willett, P. (1979). Document retrieval experiments using indexing vocabularies of varying size: II. Hashing, truncation, digram and trigram encoding of index terms. *Journal of Documentation, 35*(4), 296-305.

Williams, M. E., & Shefner, J. (1976). Data element statistics for the MARC II data base. *Journal of Library Automation, 9*(2), 89-100.

Wilson, C. S. (1999). Informetrics. In M. Williams (Ed.), *Annual review of information science and technology* (Vol. 34, pp. 107-247). Medford, NJ: Information Today.

Wilson, P. (1973). Situational relevance. *Information storage and retrieval, 9*, 457-469.

Wisniewski, J. L. (1986). Compression of index term dictionary in an inverted file oriented database: Some efficient algorithms. *Information Processing & Management, 22*, 493-501.

Wolfram, D. (1992a). Applying informetric characteristics of databases to IR system file design, Part I: Informetric models. *Information Processing & Management, 28*(1), 121-133.

Wolfram, D. (1992b). Applying informetric characteristics of databases to IR system design, Part II: Simulation comparisons. *Information Processing & Management, 28*(1), 135-151.

Wolfram, D. (1996). Inter-record linkage structure in a hypertext bibliographic retrieval system. *Journal of the American Society for Information Science, 47*(10), 765-776.

Wolfram, D. (1999). Term co-occurrence in Internet search engine queries: An analysis of the Excite data set. *The Canadian Journal of Information and Library Science, 24*(2/3), 12-33.

Wolfram, D. (2000a). Applications of informetrics to information retrieval research. *Informing Science, 3*(2), 77-82. Available: http://inform.nu/Articles/Vol3/indexv3n2.htm. (Accessed April 19, 2003).

Wolfram, D. (2000b). A query-level examination of end user searching behaviour on the Excite search engine. In H. Olson (Ed.), *Proceedings of the 28th annual Conference of the Canadian Association for Information Science*. Available: http://www.slis.ualberta.ca/cais2000/wolfram.htm. (Accessed April 19, 2003).

Wolfram, D., Chu, C. M., & Lu, X. (1990). Growth of knowledge: Bibliometric analysis using online database data. In L.Egghe and R. Rousseau (Eds.), *Informetrcs 89/90: Selection of papers submitted for the second international*

Conference on Bibliometrics, Scientometrics and Informetrics (pp. 355-372). Amsterdam: Elsevier.

Wolfram, D., & Xie, H. (2000). End user database searching over the Internet: An analysis of the state of Wisconsin's BadgerLink service. In M. E. Williams (Ed.), *Proceedings of the 21st National Online Meeting* (pp. 503-512). Medford, NJ: Information Today.

Wolfram, D. & Xie, H. (2002). Traditional IR for Web users: A context for general audience digital libraries. *Information Processing & Management, 38*(5), 627-648.

Wolfram, D., & Zhang, J. (2001). The impact of term indexing characteristics on a document space. *Canadian Journal of Information and Library Science, 26*(4), 21-35.

Wolfram, D., & Zhang, J. (2002). An investigation of the influence of indexing exhaustivity and term distributions on a document space. *Journal of the American Society for Information Science and Technology, 53*(11), 943-952.

Woodruff, A., Aoki, P. M., Brewer, E., Hauthier, P., & Rowe, L. A.(1996). An investigation of documents from the World Wide Web. In *Proceedings of the fifth international World Wide Web Conference*, Paris, France, May 6-10, 1996. Available: http://www5conf.inria.fr/fich_html/papers/P7/Overview.html. (Accessed April 19, 2003).

Wormell, I. (1998). Informetrics: Exploring databases as analytical tools. *Database, 21*(5), 25-30.

Yermish, I. R. A. (1975). *A citation based interactive associative information retrieval system.* Unpublished doctoral dissertation, University of Pennsylvania, Philadelphia.

Yitzhaki, M., & Ben-Tamar, D. (1991). Number of references in biochemistry and other fields: A case study of the *Journal of Biological Chemistry* through 1910–1985. *Scientometrics, 41*(1-2), 243-254.

Yoon, Y. (2000). Discovering knowledge in corporate databases. In S. Purba (Ed.), *Data management handbook* (3rd ed., pp. 783-794). Boca Raton, FL: Auerbach.

Zadeh, L. A. (1965). Fuzzy sets. *Information and Control, 8*, 338-353.

Zhang, J., & Korfhage, R. (1999). DARE: Distance and angle retrieval environment: A tale of the two measures. *Journal of the American Society for Information Science, 50*(9), 779-787.

Zhang, J., & Wolfram, D. (2001). Visualization of term discrimination analysis. *Journal of the American Society for Information Science and Technology, 52*(8), 615-627.

Zimmerman, J. (2001). *Marketing on the Internet* (5th ed.). Gulf Breeze, FL: Maximum Press.

Zipf, G. K. (1935). *The psycho-biology of language*. Cambridge, MA: MIT Press.

Zipf, G. K. (1949). *Human behavior and the principle of least effort*. Cambridge, MA: Addison-Wesley.

Zunde, P., & Slamecka, V. (1967). Distribution of indexing terms for maximum efficiency of information transmission. *American Documentation, 18*, 104-108.

Index